ALLEN SUSSER'S NEW WORLD CUISINE AND COOKERY

BY ALLEN SUSSER

TEXT BY KATHLEEN GORDON

DOUBLEDAY

NEW YORK

LONDON

TORONTO

SYDNEY

AUCKLAND

ALLEN
SUSSER'S
NEW
WORLD
CUISINE
AND
COOKERY

PUBLISHED BY DOUBLEDAY
a division of Bantam Doubleday Dell Publishing Group, Inc.
1540 Broadway, New York, New York 10036

DOUBLEDAY and the portrayal of an anchor with a dolphin are
trademarks of Doubleday, a division of Bantam Doubleday Dell
Publishing Group, Inc.

Book design by Marysarah Quinn
Illustrations by Kate Brennan Hall

Library of Congress Cataloging-in-Publication Data
Susser, Allen.
[New world cuisine and cookery]
Allen Susser's New world cuisine and cookery / text by Kathleen
Gordon.—1st ed.
p.   cm.
Includes index.
1. Cookery, American.   2. Cookery, Latin American.   3. Cookery,
Caribbean.   4. Chef Allen's (Restaurant).   I. Gordon, Kathleen.
II. Title.   III. Title: New world cuisine and cookery.
TX715.S9535   1995
641.5973—dc20   94-19411
                                                                        CIP

ISBN 0-385-47111-4
Copyright © 1995 by Allen Susser
Illustrations copyright © 1995 by Kate Brennan Hall
All Rights Reserved
Printed in the United States of America
March 1995
First Edition

10   9   8   7   6   5   4   3   2   1

*This book is dedicated
to the women who influenced me—
my grandmother Rose, my mother Molly,
my wife Judi, and my daughter Deanna*

ACKNOWLEDGMENTS

There are many people I want to thank:

I must begin by thanking Judi, my wife, whose love and love of food and life will always be the motivation that piques me.

To Deanna, whose youth inspires me to look at our future's food choices.

To my parents, Molly and Paul, my sister, Susie, and my brothers Howie and Theo, for shaping my early food culture.

To Janet and Maury, who are always supportive of me and their daughter.

To Henry and Bruce, who were my earliest culinary fans and who savored my wood-burning techniques.

To Jay, my first cooking partner.

To Dr. Ahrens, who arranged for my culinary experience at the Bristol Hotel in Paris.

To my original culinary team in Florida—Nick, Norman, Laleau, and Seth.

To Kathy, who knew this book was within reach.

To my current culinary and service staff at Chef Allen's; with a special thanks to Michele, my pastry chef.

To the Mango Gang—Robbin, Norman, Doug, Mark, and Suki.

To all the unassuming cooks and great cooks from whom I've learned about food.

To all the fabulous people who have been part of our Chef Allen's family.

CONTENTS

I remember, as a child, making honey cakes baked in brown-paper-bag liners in my grandmother's kitchen, and using a hand grinder for grinding up meats for the vegetable-meat stuffing for intestines—what we called *kishka*. The birth of my cooking desires came during the days when Americans still loved the convenience of cans, when only quaint old ethnic ladies grew and used their own fresh herbs. No one envisioned the future that is now, when people have access to a whole new range of fresh fruits, fresh vegetables, and fresh fish, which are the components to New World Cuisine.

Even then, while making the kishka with Rose Rosenkranz, I understood that cooking expressed love. That it could be, and should be—as in the New World Cuisine—an adventure. But it wasn't until my first job at a hot dog stand amid the crowds and carney music at a Rockaway amusement park that I decided to go to school to learn the restaurant business, to learn the art of cooking. At New York City Tech, Professor Panzerino, formerly of the Four Seasons restaurant, schooled us in the classics of French cuisine, in the grand style of haute cooking from Carême to Escoffier. Up until that time I had eaten in many ethnic restaurants, but now I began discovering the grand French restaurants in New York: Lutèce, Le Cirque, La Côte Basque, and La Grenouille.

My first hotel job was at an American plan hotel in the mountains of upstate New York. I worked six days a week, split shift, preparing breakfast, lunch, and dinner for between six and eight hundred hotel and country club guests. We had to cook in such large quantities, and work so quickly, that creativity went down the kitchen sink (so to speak). But I discovered a radically different universe the summer after my graduation from New York City Tech, when I landed in Paris, in the hotel kitchen at Le Bristol on the rue du Faubourg St. Honore.

One of my first lessons as an innocent *américain* in a

serious French kitchen came when I watched the delivery of the day's chickens. The poultry arrived the way God made them, still equipped with heads, beaks, and feathers, which meant someone had to clean them. Since I was that someone, I started by pulling off the feathers one by one. Next I cut off the necks and pulled out the insides. "Dear Mom," I wrote, in one of my early letters home, "I now realize that chickens don't come with their insides in a plastic pouch."

Cuisines develop by give and trade. The Caribe Indians invented barbecue—grilling on green branches they called "barbou"—five or six hundred years ago. Following Columbus's landing in the New World, subsequent European colonizers brought with them their own cultures, their know-how, their cuisines, and their cooking techniques. Twenty years back, while working at Le Bristol, I could accept the familiar European cooking techniques such as poaching or braising, but not the use of the Caribe-inspired wood grill. That seemed to me to be a cumbersome and antiquated contraption, especially as I had the job of cleaning out the coals and the ash.

The head chef at Le Bristol was an imposing dark-haired man who worked composing menus in a glassed-in office overlooking the kitchen. According to the strict decorum observed in this classic kitchen, anyone wishing to communicate with this formidable gentleman was supposed to do so through one of the sous chefs. I, being on a mission of enlightenment, being young, brash, and also looking to escape my dirty work, straightened my small white toque and knocked on his door.

"At home in the United States, we don't use wood anymore," I told the chef. "We now have gas. It works a lot easier, and you don't have to worry about cleaning out the coals and building the fire."

The head chef never even looked up from the work on his desk as he commanded me back where I belonged. "Do it," was what he said to me. It wasn't long before I understood the advantages of wood-burning grills, and appreciated the flavor and the burnish they give to food. Many years later and years wiser, when I opened my own restaurant, Chef Allen's in North Miami Beach, Florida, I installed a wood-burning grill, imported from the same company in France that has manufactured the Lyonnaise grills used at the Le Bristol Hotel since the turn of the century.

Fresh herbs such as basil, thyme, tarragon, and savory arrived daily at Le Bristol, and the difference these herbs made to the flavors of the food was another epiphany. Equally eye-opening were the street markets, the cafés, the *boulangeries* and *charcuteries* beyond the hotel, along the side streets, in the working-class districts of Paris. The French are said to spend more money, more time, and more love on their meals than any other people in the world. Every day I watched as Parisians scouted the vendors' stalls for that which was the freshest and the best. All over the city, shop windows displayed pâtés, terrines, glazed ducks, pastries, and chocolates, all arranged to compose a feast for the eyes.

In contrast to New York, where people were always in a hurry trying to keep appointments, fighting the clock, bolting down something from a box for breakfast and from a brown bag for lunch, people in Paris found time for leisure, and leisure included an appreciation of food and wine. The Parisians began their mornings with coffee and fresh croissants. They would stop at a local café on their way to work much the same way the people in Miami's Little Havana now stop in neighborhood *cafecitas*.

Just as the pleasure the French took in their food deeply impressed me, so did the fabulous meals I ate in the three-, two-, and one-star Michelin restaurants in Paris and its environs. The skilled balance between taste and texture that these marvelous chefs brought to their dishes is the balance I aim for in my New World Cuisine.

New World Cuisine, with its global village references, is a cuisine of contrasts—between hot and cold, crisp and soft, crusty and smooth, bitter and lush, the familiar and the exotic.

Traveling through the various regions of France, through Champagne, Bordeaux, and Provence, I became aware of how much more food was influenced by geography there than it was in the United States. Land contours, elevation, weather, and proximity to the sea were all factors in what foods were used and in what ways. I discovered that same respect for the relationship between land and produce, between geography and cuisine, when I traveled through Italy, sampling the incomparable Italian olive oils, *proscuittos, parmesanos,* and white truffles.

After my return to the United States, when I was working at Le Cirque with Alain Sailhac, I watched the purveyors coming to the back door with chanterelles from upstate New York, fresh basil from their backyards, and a wonderful colorful variety of fresh seafood such as sea urchin, turbot, and scallops with their roe. Even then, in the seventies, Le Cirque was ahead of its time, anticipating the desires of the American public for light, fresh, exciting foods.

The American marketplace is being transformed. Over the next few years the population will become more than 20 percent Latin. Even now supermarkets in many parts of the country carry quite a few of the fruits and vegetables traditional in the Latin American markets and cuisine—fruits like the mamey, black sapote (sapodilla), canistels, carambola, jaboticaba, and lychees. Many of these can be eaten raw, and many can be eaten with a cooked dish. These Latin fruits may be cooked for a long time to blend and harmonize the flavors, say for a savory sauce, or may be used raw in fresh sharp sauces or salsas. Unripe papaya makes delicious papaya pickles or green papaya chutney. My ripe papaya becomes red papaya salsa, or a papaya and rum sauce, or even a papaya–red wine and wild mushroom sauce.

Seasons play a great role in New World Cuisine. Some of the tropical fruits don't grow year-round, as many people think. In May, June, and July, we find mamey, black sapote, white sapote, canistels, jaboticaba, mango, and lychees. Carambola comes into season in August through winter, as do avocados. New World Cuisine is a current cuisine, one of the marketplace. Every day I'm inspired by what's available in the market, by what's fresh, ripe, what looks good, and what came in today. It is a cuisine, however, that isn't limited to regional produce, since now we can get fresh foods from all over the world. If truffles or porcinis from Italy come in, I'm not going to ignore them. I'm going to do fresh pompano with porcini with a New World twist, using a local method or local cooking style, and adding some local flavors.

The tremendous variety of starch vegetables, such as boniato, malanga (taro), yuca (cassava), and breadfruit is also an integral part of New World Cuisine. Like the tropical fruits, they have different textures and demand different preparations depending on their stage of ripeness. Take plantain, a starchy vegetable. When green, it's used very much as a traditional starch. When ripe, it is very sweet and often whole-roasted in the shell or husk. I love to use these starches in place of the more conventional ingredients in familiar recipes—such as yuca fries with a mango ketchup.

Yuca is a starch well-suited to making fries, but for variety, we use mango instead of tomatoes to make the ketchup. It is a simple preparation, and the mangos have the full robust flavor you'd want from a ketchup.

At Chef Allen's, purveyors arrive daily with some of the most exciting raw materials for cooking anywhere in the world, including the game fish and shellfish that form the basis of such dishes as roasted mangrove snapper with a ragout of lobster, fennel, and fire-roasted peppers; or grilled tuna with mango salsa. Fish is light, and its variety of colors and textures heightens the adventure that is New World Cuisine. There are short-flake fish and wide-flake fish; red- and white-fleshed fish; fish that are cooked all the way through, such as fish on the bone (a yellowtail snapper, for example); and fish that tastes better cooked medium rare, such as tuna.

Wahoo, one of our local fresh fishes, is a firm-fleshed circular-flaked fish very much like a swordfish. But this mackerel cousin is better a little undercooked, which keeps it very moist and flavorful. I serve wahoo grilled with a fricassee of lobster, mango, and ginger. This produces a colorful great-textured, great-looking, full-flavored dish of the tropics. It's easy to prepare, easy to approach, and wonderful to eat.

Some of my other favorite fish are cobia, strawberry grouper, and pompano. The local seafood I like to use are rock shrimp, spiny lobster, and Indian River soft-shell crabs. Why do I use these unusual fish ingredients when common ones are available? I use them simply for variety, for interest, for excitement, and for sun-drenched tropical pleasures.

What else creates that New World experience, that New World excitement? In herbs, it's ginger; turmeric; cilantro; oregano; vanilla; and those tiny, lovely, potent Scotch bonnet or *habanero* peppers. It's wild mushrooms such as chanterelles, king boletus, or porcini; and the matsutakes, which are the great white mushrooms from the Oregon pines.

The Caribe Indians and their colonizers never had it so good. Shipwreck me on a tropical island and I'd dream about red snapper with chayote and plantains in a cool orange sauce. Or barbecued leg of lamb with a Creole crust, fresh red beets, and a boniato cake. Or grilled quail breasts with fresh lychees, shiitakes, ginger, and rum. Incorporated into each recipe is a little of that tropical Caribbean and Latin American flavor, a little of that spice, that heat, that flourish, that exotic excitement.

New World Cuisine is a cuisine for modern appetites, a sensible, healthy cuisine with backbone and soul, composed of fresh unadulterated fruits, vegetables, nuts, and fish. Especially in south Florida, but in most other parts of the world as well, we need foods that make sense to a body in heat. This is a warm-weather cuisine designed to satisfy the growing population in the sunbelt, but one that will also make sense in Boston, Chicago, Minneapolis, Dallas, San Diego, or New York—wherever people appreciate what is fresh, flexible, and stimulating.

GLOSSARY

A cuisine inspired by sea and sun should encourage freedom and flexibility, and so the following glossary on the fruits, vegetables, herbs, and seafoods that define New World Cuisine is meant to guide you, not confine you. Many of these ingredients will be familiar to you, some will not, but you should be able to find all of these items either in your local supermarket or your nearest Latin or Oriental market.

The substitutions I've given for many of the items listed below are suggestions, not laws. When you can't find the exact item listed for a recipe in its freshest and most beautiful stage, do what the great chefs do—substitute. If you already have a drawerful of root vegetables and fresh herbs that aren't the roots and herbs listed in a specific recipe, or if you're snowed-in or rained-in or feeling too fine and lazy out by the pool to venture into the stores, substitute—roots for roots, herbs for herbs, fruits for fruits, and starches for starches. The dish you produce may not taste exactly like the recipe that's guiding you, but it will be splendid nonetheless—and your own unique creation reflecting your mood, the season, and the geography of the place where you live.

SPICES

Allspice: The best allspice comes from Jamaica. It is the dark brown berry of an evergreen tree from the myrtle family. It has a pleasant fragrant aroma and is available both whole and ground. Whole, it resembles small peppercorns. Allspice was one of the original spices brought back to Europe by Columbus.

Annatto Seed: Grown throughout the American tropics, the annatto tree provides the seeds that yield this natural food color and flavoring. Its extract is a brilliant yellow color. Also known as bixin.

Annatto Oil: An oil infused with annatto seed (see page 8).

Coriander: Indigenous to the Mediterranean, where the seeds are used primarily for cooking. The leaves of the plant are light green, resemble flat-leaf parsley, and are completely different in taste and character from the seeds. Coriander is thought to be a member of the carrot family. It is used in many ethnic cuisines and is also known as cilantro or Chinese parsley. Use perky-fresh leaves.

Cumin: Is available as both seed and ground. It has a flowery aroma and imparts a slight yellow color to food. This is one of the essential spices of Caribbean cuisine. It is also one of the characteristic flavors of curry.

Edible Flowers: Include the petals of nasturtiums, pansies, roses, violets, hibiscus. Find these organically grown flowers in specialty produce markets and gourmet food stores.

Nutmeg: Is grown in Jamaica and Grenada and is a powerful, sweetly aromatic spice. Use a small grater to obtain the spice from the nut.

Peppercorns, black: My favorites are grown in the Tolamanca rain forest of Costa Rica. Buy only whole peppercorns and grind them fresh as needed. I would suggest investing in a good pepper mill with an adjustable grinder.

Peppercorns, white: These are shelled black seeds and do not impart color to the food. They are not as flavorful or aromatic as black peppercorns.

VEGETABLES

Boniato: Is a white- or yellow-fleshed sweet potato. It has a thin reddish skin; a slightly irregular shape; and a dry, sweet, chestnutlike flavor. Boniato originated in Central America and is very popular in Latin America. It is much less sweet than our unrelated orange sweet potato. The sweet potato is not related to the potato family, but is in the same family as the boniato. It is often known as the Louisiana yam. Both have a moist orange-colored flesh with brown skin.

Substitution—Sweet potato or yam

Breadfruit: Of *Mutiny on the Bounty* fame, was brought to the Caribbean from the South Seas and quickly became a starchy vegetable staple of that region. When breadfruit is green it is similar to a potato. When cooked slightly ripe, its taste is extremely starchy and almost yeast flavored, reminiscent of partially cooked bread.

Substitution—Acorn squash or turnip

Calabaza: Also known as the West Indian or green pumpkin, it is really a squash. Many are large ovals or round with outer green and yellow splotches. The flesh should be firm, with a yellow-reddish color. Sold whole or in large chunks, calabaza can be cooked in many pumpkin recipes—often more successfully because of its fine grain, sweetness, and moisture.

Substitution—Pumpkin, acorn squash, or Hubbard squash

Chayote: A pear-shaped gourd about five to six inches long. It is usually available in a pale green skin, though the white is just as tasty. Its flavor is somewhat like a cross between zucchini and cucumber.

Substitution—Zucchini or crookneck squash

Hearts of Palm: Commonly the heart of the sable palm, which is farmed for this purpose. Hearts of palm are found in several forms in the marketplace. The fresh two-foot logs need to be trimmed to the soft flesh of the heart. Currently, they are most often found canned.

Malanga: Is derived from a tropical plant that bears edible tubers. The skin is usually deep brown, its flesh white to yellow. The tubers are cooked much like the potato but require a little less cooking time.

    Substitution—Red- or brown-skin potato, or rutabaga

Mezuna: A Japanese green with sharp-edged leaves and narrow white ribs. Its flavor is mild and slightly peppery.

PEPPERS

Sweet and hot, fresh and dried chilies all belong to the genus Capsicum annum. Though peppers are native to the New World, they spread rapidly in the trade for roots around the world, handled mainly by the Portuguese spice traders. Chili peppers have become popular in most tropical countries. *Scolville heat units* are used to measure the heat intensity of a chili pepper. This scale, a subjective rating devised by professional tasters, measures the heat in your mouth. The range can vary from 0 to 5 units for sweet peppers; 1,500 to 2,000 for jalapeños; 60,000 to 80,000 for Tabasco; to 100,000 to 250,000 for Scotch bonnets. Peppers also range individually in heat, so taste a little from the small end before deciding how much you'll need for a dish. Much of the extreme heat is in the seeds and ribs.

FRESH CHILIES:

Anaheim: Four inches long, this is a narrow, slightly twisted chili, pleasantly bittersweet in taste.

Jalapeño: Two and a half inches long and dark green, this type of pepper has a smooth, thick flesh and is probably the most popular chili. Many hybrid jalapeños exist in the market, so their heat can vary tremendously.

Poblano: Three inches long with shiny green skin, it is similar in shape to a flattened green bell pepper. The poblano tends to be unusually mild.

Scotch bonnet: Small and lantern shaped, this extremely hot citrus-flavored pepper ranges, in its three stages of ripening, from green to yellow to red.

Serrano: This is tiny and thin, with a dark green skin, but it packs an immediate heat that is intense with a lasting bite.

DRIED CHILIES:

Ancho: Three to four inches long, with wrinkled skin, this pepper has a rich, full, mild flavor.

Chipotle: Has a brick-red color, smoked flavor, and is mildly hot.

Quinoa: Is a South American grain with a semifine texture and a mild nutty flavor.

Tatsoi: Is a round-leafed medium green lettuce with an herbivorous, summery taste. Its leaves occur on individual stalks rather than in heads. Tatsoi may be purchased year-round at your local greengrocer.

Yam: Comes from a vine that grows everywhere in the tropics, and is a large edible root. Yams (or *ñame)* come in many sizes. The skin is usually brown with a white-yellow flesh. The texture is slightly mealy with a nutlike flavor. What we are used to calling a yam here in the United States is actually a sweet potato.

Substitution—Celery root or rutabaga

Yuca, or Cassava, or Manioc: Is a tuber widely used in Latin American and Caribbean kitchens and a native root of Brazil. This spindle-shaped root is usually sold waxed and has a shiny barklike skin. The flesh is white, crisp, and hard. During cooking it tends to split apart into wedges, perfect for yuca steak fries. Tapioca is made from processing the starch of the yuca plant roots.

Substitution—Idaho potato, lotus root, or Jerusalem artichoke

FRUITS

Bananas: Many newly available varieties are in the marketplace. For a change in taste, try red bananas, finger bananas, or citrus bananas.

Florida Oranges: The most common is the Valencia. It is usually thin-skinned with slight wind-burn markings. Its thin skin makes this orange the juiciest, with very sweet juice. The Temple is considered Florida's best eating orange.

Guava: A small, round, thin-skinned, pulpy fruit, usually with many seeds. It is astringent when green but very aromatic when ripe. The acidic, ripe flesh has a pleasant gritty texture. It is also available in the form of a paste or jelly.

Key Limes: These limes are much smaller and rounder than other limes and their color is yellow-green. This lime variety is not as readily available, but its citrus characteristic is tart-sour with just a hint of sweetness.

Substitution—Fresh-squeezed lime juice

Kumquats: A small golden or orange fruit about 1½ inches long and oval. The rind of this fruit is often sweeter than its flesh, which is usually very sour. Technically this is not a citrus.

Substitution—Oranges with the pith

Limes: Are almost indispensable in New World Cuisine and the most acidic of all fruits. Look for bright green fruit. Ninety percent of the world's lime production comes from south Florida.

Lychees: Available fresh in late spring, the lychee is a small, red, rough-skinned cluster fruit. Peel away the skin and you'll discover its creamy white flesh, which tastes like a wonderful tropical grape. Florida has probably the only commercial crop of lychees on the U.S. mainland.

Substitution—Canned or frozen

Mamey: Is probably the most favored and esteemed fruit in the Cuban community. Its matte brown skin gives way to a rosy-colored, lush, custardlike pulp. The flavor is a cross between peach, apricot, and almond. Most fruits are the size of an oversized grapefruit though somewhat oblong.

Substitution—Ripe peaches

Mangos: As many as 120 varieties are grown around the world. The exterior skin color ranges from green when unripe, to a yellow-orange and a rich orange-red when ripe. When a mango is ripe, it will give a little to finger pressure and will have a wonderful, sweet, perfumed aroma. Readily available varieties of mango are the Haden, Keitt, Kent, and Tommy Atkins. A Dominican cook told me a story about mangos back home. He described mango or *mango bajito* as an "attitude." He said it was the lazy man's fruit since the mango tree offers shade and sustenance. When mangos become ripe they fall off the tree to the ground. A man at ease, resting from the hot sun, need only sit under the tree to receive his delight and refreshment. Another common Latin mango expression is *Le zumba el mango!* ("That takes the cake!")

Papayas: Unripened, these are usually found oversized, with firm, deep green skin and light green to pink flesh, and are used as a vegetable. Ripe papaya is available from the Caribbean, Mexico, and Hawaii. The pulp is sweet and can be eaten uncooked. The flavor is somewhat tropical-floral.

Passion Fruit: Comes in two varieties, yellow, and the more common purple. Its interior consists of a yellow pulp with soft-shelled, edible seeds. Its flavor is reminiscent of pineapple, peaches, and grape juice.

Plantains: Are members of the same family as bananas and bird-of-paradise. They are much larger but not palatable raw. They can be used in many stages of ripeness from green, which have a firm texture and are eaten as a potatolike starch or fried as a chip, to yellow or yellow-brown, which are eaten more as a vegetable. Plantains ripen all the way to the almost black *plantanos maduros,* which can be cooked as a fruit.

Substitution—Potato for green plantains, banana for ripe plantains

Sour Orange or Bitter Orange: If this rough skinned, reddish-orange fruit is not readily available, you can substitute a combination of orange and lime juices. Bitter or

Seville orange is too sour to eat raw, but that tartness is wonderful for marinades and marmalades.

Starfruit or Carambola: Now being grown extensively in south Florida. Look for yellow-orange, ripe fruit. The fruit is four to five inches long with a glossy yellow skin and sharply angled ribs that form a star shape when cut crosswise. They are very juicy and have a crisp, sweet flesh. New, sweeter varieties, such as the Arkin and the beautiful full-flavored Fwang Tung, are currently being developed.

Tamarind: Grows on big, beautiful trees in the Caribbean, Central America, and Florida. (I have several growing where I live.) Their velvety-gray bean pods are filled with brown, gooey pulp surrounding large, shiny brown seeds. Tamarind has a wonderful sweet-tart tropical flavor with a unique quenching finish.

FISH

Caviar: The key to caviar is freshness. The eggs should have the pleasant aroma of a sea-water breeze. Beluga, Ossetra, and Sevruga caviar are from three different sturgeons, all originating in the Caspian Sea in eastern Europe; each of these caviars has its own distinctive nuance. "Malossal" printed on a label refers to the small amount of salt used in preserving the fish eggs. Other kinds of caviar or fish roe come from all around the world. American varieties range from salmon, trout, spoonbill and hackleback sturgeon, to paddlefish.

Cobia: A warm-water game fish excellent for eating. No other known species of fish is related to cobia; it is in a family by itself. Sometimes it is mistaken for shark in the water. This fish has snowy white, sweet flesh best cooked in steak form and is available year-round.

Substitution—Grouper, ocean perch, or mahimahi

Conch: Until recently, fresh conch had not been readily available. Thanks to some conch farming in the Caribbean, this situation is changing. It is usually best to tenderize the meat with a mallet, which results in cracked conch, or by grinding it. If you are using frozen conch, keep it covered while you defrost it slowly, to retain its flavor.

Substitution—Langoustine, abalone, or shrimp

Grouper: These are members of the sea bass family. The flesh is snowy white and can be cooked cut thin as fillets or cut thick as steaks. Grouper is most often available in fillets because the fish grows to be very large—between fifteen and twenty-five pounds. Black grouper or Nassau grouper are among the most desirable varieties. Red grouper and Warsaw grouper are usually the largest of the grouper family.

Substitution—Sea bass, black sea bass, scamp, or brill

Mahimahi: Are also known as dolphin, but bear no relation to the mammal. They are large-flaked and sweetly moist fish. Their skin is a brilliant blue-green-silver-gold. Mahimahi is available throughout the world from tropical and subtropical seas. Their sizes vary greatly but they are good eating as either steaks or fillets.

Substitution—Gray sole, lemon sole, or Atlantic halibut

Parrot Fish: A beautiful, colorful, tropical fish familiar to divers. Historically, this was a popular eating fish of the Old World. The parrot fish has a sweet, soft, white flesh, usually cooked as fillets, and is available year-round.

Substitution—Snapper, grouper, tilefish, or flounder

Pompano: Average between one and a half to two pounds and are usually sold whole. Silvery skinned, this is possibly one of the tastiest fish in the sea, and, usually, one of the most expensive. The pompano has small or short flake, a firm texture, and a moderate amount of "good oils," which give its flesh a rich taste. It is found fresh in the market from October to May.

   Substitution—Amberjack, kingfish, bluefish, or salmon

Prawns: A term often misused to refer to larger shrimp. Prawns are different in shape and flavor from shrimp; their meat is deliciously sweet, and their texture a little softer than shrimp. Through successful aqua-culture farming, prawns are much more available now than they have been in the past.

   Substitution—Shrimp

Rock Shrimp: These are small, hard-shelled shrimp. Because they are difficult to clean, they have not been in abundant supply in the market until recently. Now, however, they are widely available shelled and cleaned, mostly during the winter months. Rock shrimp meat tastes a bit more like lobster than shrimp.

   Substitution—Lobster meat or small shrimp

Shark: Mako, blue, and blacktip, are among the many varieties of shark available on the market. I prefer mako for its firm texture and swordfishlike flavor. Shark is a lean meat with firm circular-flaked flesh. It is available year-round.

Snapper: The flesh is white, small-flaked, and sweet tasting. Snapper is available in both round (whole, cleaned) $1\frac{1}{2}$- to $2\frac{1}{2}$-pound fish, and in the form of fillets coming from larger, 3- to 5-pound fish. Among the numerous snapper varieties available are red snapper, yellowtail, mutton, gray, schoolmaster, and mangrove.

Substitution—Sole, striped bass, rockfish

Soft-shell Crabs: These are blue crabs in the molting stage that have shed their outer shells completely. The entire soft body, legs, and shell, is rendered edible and delicious. Look for them fresh from May 20 to September 20.

Spiny Lobster: This lobster is abundant in Florida and the Caribbean, and is available in warm waters throughout the world. In simplest terms, this lobster has no claws. Most of the meat is in the tail. Also known as Florida lobster, Bahamian lobster, rock lobster, langoustine, and langosta. It is available all year round.

Substitution—Maine or Canadian lobsters

Stone Crabs: Stone crabs are truly the pride of Florida's gourmet natural resources. The meat is rich, sweet, and firm in texture. Floridians have long been zealously passionate about—and protective of—their stone-crab resources. The claw meat is available in jumbo, extra-large, large, and medium. Jumbos weigh two to a pound, extra-large four or five per pound, large six to eight per pound, and medium nine to ten per pound. While jumbos are often the most prized for their grandeur and convenient eating, they are also the most costly; large or medium claws are great for cocktail parties or as finger food. Stone crabs are available fresh from October 15 to May 15. They are always cooked by the crab trappers immediately after they are caught, so they are available only cooked.

Substitution—Blue crab meat, Dungeness crab meat, or Jonah crab meat

Tuna: Tuna has become one of the most important fish in the market. Fresh tuna is bright red to rosy pink, depending on its variety and fat content. The Japanese revere *toro,* which is the fatty meat from the bluefin tuna. Two other excellent varieties are yellowfin and bigeye tuna.

Wahoo: Is the gourmet's mackerel, though much leaner than any mackerel. It has a white, fine, circular flake with a delicate texture. This is a favorite of game fisherman who yell Wahoo! when they hook one. You may see this listed on the menu at Japanese sushi bars as *ono.*

Substitution—Mackerel, pompano, swordfish

CHICKEN STOCK

5   *pounds chicken backs, necks, and wings*

2   *large onions, chopped*

2   *large carrots, chopped*

3   *large celery stalks, chopped*

1   *large turnip, chopped*

4   *cloves whole garlic*

15   *black peppercorns*

1   *teaspoon chopped fresh thyme*

1   *bay leaf*

4   *quarts cold water*

MAKES 3 QUARTS

To begin the stock: In a large stockpot combine all the ingredients. Bring the mixture to a simmer. Simmer gradually for 2 hours, skimming and removing any scum and fat that comes to the surface.

To finish the stock: Remove from the heat and let the stock rest for 30 minutes. Complete a final skim. Strain the stock through a fine sieve lined with cheesecloth. Set aside to allow it to cool to room temperature. Cover and refrigerate. Before use, remove any fat that congeals on top.

FISH STOCK

3 *pounds fish heads and bones*
2 *tablespoons olive oil*
2 *large onions, chopped*
2 *large celery stalks, chopped*
1 *large leek white, chopped*
2 *cups dry white wine*
10 *white peppercorns*
1 *teaspoon chopped fresh thyme*
1 *bay leaf*
2 *quarts cold water*

MAKES 2 QUARTS

To prepare the fish parts: Chop the fish heads and bones into 2- to 3-inch pieces. Place in a colander and rinse well under cold running water.

To start the stock: Warm the olive oil in a large stockpot. Add the onions and cook until translucent. Add the other vegetables and the fish parts then stir well. After a minute, add the remaining ingredients. Bring the stock to a slow simmer. Skim off any scum or fat that rises to the surface. Simmer for about 30 minutes.

To finish the stock: Remove from the heat and let the stock rest for 10 minutes. Complete a final skim. Strain the stock through a fine sieve lined with cheesecloth. Set aside to allow the stock to come to room temperature. Cover and refrigerate. Before use, remove any fat that congeals on top.

Green Apple Pancakes with Caviar

Rock Shrimp Beggar's Purses

Coconut Curry Shrimp *served with*
Guava Barbecue Sauce

Allumette Vegetables with Beef Carpaccio

Spicy Crab and Corn Tostones

Plantain Chips/Tostones

Tuna Tartare on Toasted Orange Brioche

Yuca Chips, Goat Cheese, and Shiitakes

Smoked Salmon Bundles with Lime Couscous

Creole Won Tons *served with* Annatto-Citrus Vinaigrette

Rock Shrimp Star Fritters

Crisp Lobster Truffles

Cracked Conch Fritters *served with* Papaya Chutney

Tea-Smoked Scallops *served with* Pistachio Pesto

Mango Tarte Tatin with Foie Gras

Root Vegetable Chips

Boniato Chips with Smoked Tomato Salsa

Yam Chips with Caramelized Tuna Loin

Plantain Chips with Black Bean Dip

CHAPTER 1

HORS D'OEUVRES, TAPAS, AND FINGER FOODS

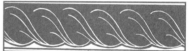

My grandmother Rose used to call hors d'oeuvre *forshpeitz.* These were what she put on the table on family birthdays or anniversaries and at Chanukah and Passover, to welcome guests as they came into the house. I remember her roasted chick-peas steamed in a kettle with olive oil and lots of black pepper; eggplant roasted over an open flame, then chopped up with onion and a touch of olive oil; carp roe with onion and lemon juice; and fruits and nuts. As a kid going to Jewish weddings and bar mitzvahs, I thought of hors d'oeuvres as stuffed cabbages, meatballs, pigs in blankets, chicken liver, steak tidbits with pineapple, mini corn beef sandwiches.

In Escoffier's time hors d'oeuvres such as caviar and oysters, sea-spanking fresh, were served as a prelude to supper and influenced by Russian flavors. For lunch at the Bristol Hotel, we served a variety of small salads as hors d'oeuvres: poached eggs or smoked salmon coated in gelatin, braised mushrooms, cauliflower à la grecque, beet salad, pâtés and terrines, and smoked mussels, all arranged on a cart that was rolled over to the table at the diner's request. At dinnertime in Paris, hors d'oeuvres were customary only at banquets, and then we served puff pastries filled with crab, vol-au-vents, puffs with cheese, sweetbreads, brains, lamb, miniature pâtés, and sausages wrapped in puff pastry.

There are many different ways to look at hors d'oeuvres: as that first extension of hospitality as guests arrive, as a way to excite people before the start of a serious dinner, or as a way to punctuate the cozy festivities of a Sunday afternoon with family or the special conviviality of holidays. At Chef Allen's I like to serve a number of small tastes of hors d'oeuvres before the main course: I prepare a seafood or Caribbean antipasto, or a mushroom sampler that gives the guest a full variety of tastes all within the same theme. That way the diner can enjoy small portions, say, of tamarind chili barbecue shrimp;

jerk calamari; smoked scallops; green papaya slaw; mango salsa; black bean salsa; fresh fruit such as mango, papaya, and citrus, and stone crabs; a variety of smoked fish such as swordfish, kingfish, redfish—all within the Caribbean framework.

My only rule when it comes to serving hors d'oeuvres is that they should be fun for the cook as well as for the guests. Look into your refrigerator and see what you can do with leftovers and small amounts of food. If you don't have enough shrimp for a main course (or are feeding so many people that the cost becomes prohibitive), use the shellfish in an hors d'oeuvre. Serve these on odd-shaped colorful plates, such as those in the shapes of fruits, birds, fish, and vegetables. They will enhance the festivities and have everyone anticipating the marvels to come.

Hors d'oeuvres are as much about promise as a first kiss.

GREEN APPLE PANCAKES WITH CAVIAR

SERVES 6

1   large Granny Smith apple

3   small red potatoes

3   tablespoons chopped sweet onion

1   large egg

2   tablespoons bread crumbs

½   teaspoon kosher salt

¼   teaspoon fresh ground black pepper

2   tablespoons olive oil

1   ounce Ossetra caviar

I suggest using Granny Smith apples here because they're both tart and sweet, a combination that provides a great foil for the caviar. Ossetra caviar gives this hors d'oeuvre a nice nutty flavor.

To prepare the apple: Peel the Granny Smith apple. On a box grater, hand grate the apple in the largest holes. Do the same for the potatoes. Combine the apple, potatoes, onion, egg, bread crumbs, salt, and pepper.

To cook the pancakes: Warm the olive oil in a skillet on a slow flame. Using a small round soup spoon, portion small pancakes into the pan. Flatten out the pancakes with the back of the spoon and cook for a minute before turning them to brown on the other side for about 30 seconds. When the pancakes are crisp, remove them from the pan and drain on paper towels.

Garnish with the caviar and serve immediately.

The rock shrimp combine with the phyllo to become crisp, small bundles of flavor. If rock shrimp are unavailable, regular shrimp or scallops can be substituted.

To prepare the rock shrimp: Combine the rock shrimp, diced chives, Dijon mustard, tarragon, cumin, and salt.

To prepare the purses: Make sure to cover the phyllo sheets not in use with a damp towel, or else they will dry out. One by one, brush 3 sheets with clarified butter, then layer them. Cut the sheets into 12 squares. Fill each square of phyllo with some of the rock shrimp mixture, then gather the corners to meet in the center, crimping the phyllo just below the top. Repeat with the other 3 sheets and the remainder of the rock shrimp. Bake the beggar's purses in a 375° oven for 5 minutes, or until golden brown.

To serve: Remove the purses from the oven and tie each with an individual strand of wilted chive, made by plunging the chives into boiling water and removing them immediately.

ROCK SHRIMP BEGGAR'S PURSES

SERVES 6

½   cup peeled, chopped, uncooked rock shrimp

1   teaspoon diced fresh chives, plus 12 chives, wilted

1   teaspoon Dijon mustard

½   teaspoon minced fresh tarragon

¼   teaspoon ground cumin

½   teaspoon kosher salt

6   sheets phyllo dough

1   tablespoon clarified butter

COCONUT CURRY SHRIMP

SERVES 6

12 jumbo uncooked shrimp

1 teaspoon kosher salt

½ teaspoon fresh ground black pepper

1 cup flaked coconut

3 tablespoons curry powder

1 tablespoon ground turmeric

½ teaspoon ground cinnamon

1 tablespoon ground cumin

4 large egg whites

4 cups peanut oil for deep frying

GUAVA BARBECUE SAUCE

MAKES 2 CUPS

2 tablespoons peanut oil

¼ cup diced shallots

1 cup guava paste

2 tablespoons Dijon mustard

¼ cup apple cider vinegar

¼ cup brown sugar

½ cup diced tomato

¼ teaspoon ground cinnamon

¼ teaspoon ground allspice

2 cups red Zinfandel

When people think of the Caribbean and the tropics they think of coconuts and exotic spices. This hors d'oeuvre practically sings calypso.

To prepare the shrimp: Peel and clean the shrimp. Split the shrimp completely in half, seasoning them with half the salt and pepper. Set them aside in a stainless-steel bowl.

To season the coconut: In a bowl, combine the coconut, curry, turmeric, cinnamon, cumin, salt, and pepper.

To coat the shrimp: Add the egg whites to the shrimp. Then individually dredge each half-shrimp in the seasoned coconut.

To cook: Preheat the oil to 350° and deep-fry the coconut shrimp for about 2 minutes, until golden brown.

Serve with the Guava Barbecue Sauce.

ACCOMPANIMENT:
GUAVA BARBECUE SAUCE

In a small saucepot warm the peanut oil. Add the shallots and cook until they become translucent. Add the remaining ingredients and cook for approximately 30 minutes, or until thickened to well coat the back of a spoon. Strain the sauce and let cool.

Several cuts of beef will work for carpaccio. I prefer to use filet mignon for its superior texture and flavor.

To prepare the allumette vegetables: Cutting vegetables into allumette or matchstick-size julienne strips takes just a little patience and a sharp French knife. Cut each of the vegetables into strips $1/8$ inch wide by $1\frac{1}{2}$ inches long. Keep the vegetable strips stacked separately until assembling.

To prepare the carpaccio: Cut the filet into 6 thin slices. Using plastic wrap to sandwich the beef, pound it with a mallet until almost translucent. Cut each piece into small strips approximately 2 inches long and $1/2$ inch wide.

To assemble: Thinly spread the Dijon mustard on the beef carpaccio strips, then season with salt. Stack one of each of the vegetable strips and roll the bundle in the beef strip. Continue until all the vegetables and beef strips are used up. There should be about 20 bundles. Serve on a 10-inch glazed ceramic plate.

ALLUMETTE VEGETABLES WITH BEEF CARPACCIO

SERVES 10

$1/2$	large red bell pepper
$1/2$	large yellow bell pepper
5	snow peas
1	large Anaheim chili
1	medium carrot
4	ounces filet mignon
1	tablespoon Dijon mustard
1	teaspoon kosher salt

SPICY CRAB AND CORN TOSTONES

SERVES 6

3/4 cup sweet corn kernels

2 tablespoons olive oil

3 tablespoons diced red onion

2 tablespoons diced Anaheim chilies

1/2 teaspoon chopped garlic

2 teaspoons lime juice

1/2 teaspoon ground cumin

1 tablespoon chopped fresh cilantro

1/4 teaspoon minced Scotch bonnet chili

3/4 cup cleaned, cooked crab meat

Dash kosher salt

12 crisp Tostones (recipe follows)

In a hot pan start to caramelize the corn kernels by tossing constantly over medium heat until the corn is well browned. Remove the corn, add the olive oil, and begin to sauté the onion. After a few minutes, return the corn to the pan and add the chilies, garlic, lime juice, and cumin and sauté for about 10 seconds each. Finish the mixture by adding the cilantro, Scotch bonnet, and crab meat. Sauté for 30 seconds and remove from the heat. Adjust the seasoning with a dash of salt.

Serve on the hot Tostones, about 2 per person.

Plantains can be used in all stages of ripeness, from green to overripe. Ripe plantains are good for grilling; riper still, in the brown-skin stage, they make wonderful plantanos maduros. *But in the green stage, the way we use them in this recipe, plantains are very starchy, and perfect for making chips or tostones, a twice-cooked plantain and a Puerto Rican favorite.*

To make plantain chips: First peel the green skin from the fruit. These chips can be sliced either crosswise into coins or lengthwise into long strips, and as thin as possible. You should get about 45 chips. Soak them in cold salted water until ready to fry. Preheat the oil to 375°. Fry until crisp and golden brown, about 1 minute.

To make tostones: Peel the skin from the fruit. Cut each plantain on the bias about 1/2 inch thick. You should end up with 12 to 15 slices. Soak in salted water for 20 minutes. Preheat the oil to 350°. Fry the plantains for several minutes, until they start to turn golden. Remove from the oil and let cool for a moment. With a mallet, smash each tostone once, being careful not to break it but to flatten it. (To make a cuplike hors d'oeuvre, I like to use my tostone press, which I found while on holiday in Puerto Rico.) Refry the tostones now in 375° oil, until they're golden brown.

PLANTAIN CHIPS/ TOSTONES

SERVES 6

3   *large plantains*
2   *tablespoons kosher salt*
2   *quarts peanut oil for frying*

TUNA TARTARE ON TOASTED ORANGE BRIOCHE

SERVES 6

12 ounces fresh, raw yellowfin, big eye, or bluefin tuna

2 teaspoons capers

2 tablespoons finely diced red onion

2 anchovy fillets, minced

1/2 teaspoon wasabi powder

1 teaspoon vodka

1 teaspoon chopped fresh cilantro

1/2 teaspoon Tabasco sauce

1 tablespoon unsalted or sweet butter

1 small orange brioche, sliced into 12 small rounds

Raw tuna is one of my favorite first courses.

To prepare the tuna tartare: Dice the tuna with a sharp French knife, then continue to chop it together. In a bowl, combine the capers, onion, and anchovy, and mix these together well with a wood spoon. Moisten the wasabi with the vodka and add to the caper mixture. Now add all of this to the diced tuna at the same time, finishing with the cilantro and Tabasco.

To serve: Brush a little butter on each brioche round and toast them, then top each with a mound of tuna tartare.

The contrasting textures of crisp yuca chips, soft goat cheese, and silky sautéed shiitakes in this recipe prove that a simple dish can offer complex pleasures.

To prepare the shiitakes: Trim the bottoms of the shiitakes and then slice them. Sauté the slices in the olive oil for about 1 minute, until they're cooked through but not brown, then season them with the salt and pepper. Set them aside to cool.

To serve: Combine the goat cheese and chives. Put the mixture in a small pastry bag fitted with a small fluted tip. Pipe a dollop of goat cheese on a yuca chip and top with a few slices of the shiitakes. Continue until all the ingredients are used up.

NOTE: If the goat cheese is not softened, it will not go through a pastry bag easily.

YUCA CHIPS, GOAT CHEESE, AND SHIITAKES

SERVES 10

10	large shiitake mushrooms
1	tablespoon olive oil
1	teaspoon kosher salt
1/2	teaspoon coarse ground black pepper
1/2	cup softened goat cheese (see Note)
1	tablespoon minced fresh chive
24	crisp yuca chips (page 42)

SMOKED SALMON BUNDLES WITH LIME COUSCOUS

SERVES 6

2	cups instant couscous
1	quart hot chicken stock
1/4	cup seeded and diced cucumber
1/4	cup peeled, seeded, and diced tomato
3	tablespoons chopped scallions
2	tablespoons chopped fresh flat-leaf parsley
3	tablespoons lime juice
2	tablespoons olive oil
1	tablespoon kosher salt
1 1/2	teaspoons coarse ground black pepper
12	slices smoked salmon
12	chives, wilted

This dish, with smoked salmon and lime couscous, is especially lovely in summer—and fantastic in multiple first-course meals.

To make the couscous: Put the couscous in a large bowl. Pour the hot chicken stock over the couscous. Cover with plastic wrap and set aside for 5 minutes. Fluff the couscous and re-cover for another 5 minutes, then add the diced cucumber, tomato, scallions, and parsley, and toss well. Season with the lime juice, olive oil, salt, and pepper, then cover for another few minutes. Fluff the whole mixture before you fill the salmon with it.

To form the bundles: Cut each piece of salmon in half. Place a tablespoon of couscous in the center of one half-slice. Wrap the salmon around the filling. Wrap the other half of the slice around in the other direction. Finish by tying the bundle with a piece of chive that has been dipped into boiling water for 3 seconds to wilt. Continue making bundles with the remaining ingredients.

When most people think of won tons they think of Oriental or Pacific flavors. This New World won ton is part Caribbean, part New Orleans, and totally delicious.

To prepare the filling for the won tons: Begin by boiling the green bananas in a pot of lightly salted water until they are soft throughout, approximately 20 minutes. Drain the bananas and mash them. Add the diced red onion, capers, green olives, and garlic. Season with the cumin, salt, oregano, and dried red pepper flakes. Blend this all together with the annatto oil. Add the cilantro and crab meat and combine.

To fill the won tons: Arrange the won ton skins separately on the work surface. Place a teaspoon of filling in the center of each of the won tons. Brush water on the edges of each won ton and close them by folding in half and pressing the edges together to seal them.

To cook: Boil the won tons in a pot of lightly salted water for about 5 minutes, then drain well.

Serve with the Annatto-Citrus Vinaigrette drizzled over them.

ACCOMPANIMENT:
ANNATTO-CITRUS VINAIGRETTE

Remove the zest from the fruits and reserve it for garnish. Squeeze the citrus juice into a stainless-steel bowl. Add the sherry vinegar, garlic, salt, and red pepper. Whisk in the annatto oil, then add the zest garnish.

CREOLE WON TONS

SERVES 12

2	large green bananas
3	tablespoons chopped red onion
1	tablespoon chopped capers
2	tablespoons chopped green olives
1/2	teaspoon chopped garlic
1	teaspoon ground cumin
1	teaspoon kosher salt
1	teaspoon minced fresh oregano
1/2	teaspoon dried red pepper flakes
1/4	cup annatto oil (page 9)
2	tablespoons chopped fresh cilantro
1/2	cup crab meat
12	medium won ton skins

ANNATTO-CITRUS VINAIGRETTE

MAKES 1 CUP

1	large lemon
1	large lime
1	medium orange
3	tablespoons sherry vinegar
1/2	teaspoon minced garlic
1/4	teaspoon kosher salt
1/4	teaspoon dried red pepper flakes
1/2	cup annatto oil (page 9)

ROCK SHRIMP STAR FRITTERS

SERVES 10

- 4   tablespoons olive oil
- 3   tablespoons diced sweet onion
- 1   medium tomato, peeled, seeded, and diced
- 2   tablespoons chopped scallion
- 1   cup diced uncooked rock shrimp
- 1   teaspoon minced garlic
- 1   teaspoon chopped fresh basil
- 1   teaspoon kosher salt
- 1/2 teaspoon fresh ground black pepper
- 2   large eggs
- 3   tablespoons untoasted bread crumbs
- 4   large starfruit

The occasion for which I created this hors d'oeuvre was the SOS Taste of the NFL, a benefit dinner for 1,500 people to raise money for the hungry. The location was in Minnesota, on January 30, in the dead of winter, and I wanted to provide a touch of Florida heat and sunshine along with my cooking.

To make the shrimp filling: In a skillet warm 2 tablespoons of the olive oil with the onion. When the onion becomes translucent, add the tomato and scallion. Sauté together for a moment, then add the rock shrimp. Add the garlic and basil, then season with salt and pepper. Remove the mixture from the heat and let cool. Add the eggs and finally the bread crumbs to bind the whole mix.

To prepare the starfruit: Cut the starfruit into 1-inch-thick stars. Using a very small round cookie cutter or a paring knife, carefully cut out the center of each of the starfruit slices. Fill the center with as much rock shrimp mix as you can fit in the hole. When they are all filled, sauté the stars in the remaining olive oil, turning once carefully with a spatula, until golden brown, about 2 minutes on each side.

I use local Bahamian lobster for these truffles, though Maine lobster will be just as delicious. You can also make this dish with potato, but the boniato's unique flavor is well worth the trip to a specialty market.

To prepare the lobster: Cut the lobster meat into small ¹/₂-inch cubes. Combine the vanilla, saffron, sherry, salt, and pepper in a bowl and marinate the lobster cubes in the mixture for 25 minutes. Add the egg whites and mix well. Let the lobster mixture rest 5 more minutes.

To make the truffles: Remove each lobster cube and roll it in the grated boniato. Continue to pack the boniato onto the lobster cubes until it completely encases the meat. Set the truffles aside.

To cook the truffles: Heat the peanut oil to 350° and deep-fry the truffles until crisp and golden brown, about 2 minutes.

CRISP LOBSTER TRUFFLES

SERVES 6

2	12-ounce lobster tails
¹/₂	medium vanilla bean, split
¹/₈	teaspoon crushed saffron threads
¹/₄	cup dry sherry
1	teaspoon kosher salt
¹/₂	teaspoon cayenne pepper
3	large egg whites
2	large boniato, peeled and grated
2	quarts peanut oil for frying

CRACKED CONCH FRITTERS

SERVES 10

1 1-pound conch
1 tablespoon plus 1 teaspoon kosher salt
1 large red bell pepper, diced
1 medium onion, diced
1 medium jalapeño
½ cup all-purpose flour
½ teaspoon baking powder
2 large eggs
2 tablespoons dark Jamaican rum
2 quarts peanut oil for frying

Caribbean conch has a unique texture and flavor. Its meat is sweet, with something of a gumlike texture until it's tenderized or ground. Fresh conch is always preferable, but frozen grade 1 is a good substitution.

To prepare the conch: Rinse the conch under cold running water. Trim any of the thick, dense muscle—mostly in the end cylindrical part—with a small paring knife. Crack the conch several times with a mallet. Season with a tablespoon of kosher salt and continue to crack and beat the conch. Grind the conch in a meat grinder using a medium blade.

To make the fritter mix: Combine the ground conch, bell pepper, onion, jalapeño, flour, and baking powder. Fold in the eggs and the rum and season with 1 teaspoon of salt.

To cook the fritters: The trick here is to use very hot— 375°—peanut oil. Using a large tablespoon, drop the fritters into the deep fryer or large skillet of oil, being careful not to overcrowd the cooking space. Fry until golden brown, about 1 minute, then drain on paper towels or newspaper.

Serve the fritters with Papaya Chutney or a cup of Mango Ketchup (page 301) on a colorful platter or in a hollowed-out watermelon.

ACCOMPANIMENT:
PAPAYA CHUTNEY

To prepare the fruits: Clean the papaya, remove the seeds, and dice the flesh into large chunks. Clean the guava and reserve the pulp.

To cook the chutney: In a pan melt the butter and add the onion. Brown well. Add the brown sugar, pepper, cider vinegar, salt, ginger, and turmeric. Cook for 5 minutes, then add the fruits. Bring to a boil and simmer for 45 minutes. Remove the chutney from the heat and let cool.

PAPAYA CHUTNEY

MAKES 2 CUPS

4	medium ripe papayas
2	medium ripe guava
1	tablespoon sweet butter
1	medium red onion, diced
4	tablespoons brown sugar
1/2	teaspoon dried red pepper flakes
3	tablespoons cider vinegar
1	teaspoon kosher salt
1	tablespoon minced fresh ginger
1	teaspoon ground turmeric

TEA-SMOKED SCALLOPS

SERVES 6

6   jumbo uncooked scallops

3   tablespoons Japanese green tea leaves

1   tablespoon minced fresh thyme

2   tablespoons soy sauce

1/2   teaspoon minced fresh ginger

1/2   teaspoon chopped garlic

1/4   teaspoon coarse ground black pepper

2   tablespoons peanut oil

12   1-inch baguette toast circles

PISTACHIO PESTO

MAKES 1/4 CUP

3   tablespoons unsalted pistachio nuts

2   tablespoons grated Parmesan cheese

2   tablespoons sun-dried tomatoes

2   tablespoons olive oil

1   tablespoon garlic

1   teaspoon tarragon vinegar

4   tablespoons fresh basil

Like fresh herbs, teas will wilt and lose their flavor and aroma, so it's important that you buy fresh, loose green tea leaves for this recipe. The scallops are smoked in a cold smoker—a small readily available unit that allows you to smoke indirectly, without cooking, as opposed to hot barbecue–type smokers.

To smoke the scallops: Remove the small side muscle from the scallops. Combine the tea, thyme, soy, ginger, garlic, and pepper. Marinate the scallops for 1 hour. Remove from the marinade and smoke for 15 minutes in a cold smoker.

To finish: Slice the scallops in half crosswise. Put each of the scallop halves on a toast circle and top with a small dollop of Pistachio Pesto.

ACCOMPANIMENT:
PISTACHIO PESTO

In a food processor using a metal blade, puree all the pesto ingredients. Store refrigerated in a covered jar for up to 3 weeks.

One of the things I love most about New World Cuisine is the freedom it gives the cook to combine flavors that are local and indigenous with flavors that belong to the grand haute cuisine of France. In this recipe the lush tropical flavors of the mango marry with the rich creaminess of foie gras in a crisp, savory, upside-down mango tart. After one bite you're liable to be seeing cancan dancers kicking up their heels on a Caribbean beach.

To prepare the mangos: Peel, clean, and cut the mangos into thick slices. Season with a pinch of salt and a good twist of fresh ground pepper. Combine the butter and sugar in a saucepan and cook over low heat for approximately 2 minutes, until the sugar just begins to caramelize. Divide the caramelized sugar evenly among 6 small ovenproof 4-ounce ramekins. Line the ramekins with the mango slices.

To prepare the tarte tatin: Roll out the puff pastry to approximately 1/4-inch thickness. Cut 6 circles from the pastry with a 3-inch-round cookie cutter. Place the puff pastry circles on top of the mango and pull them to the edges of the ramekin.

To bake and finish: Preheat the oven to 375°. Bake the tarts for about 15 minutes or until golden brown. Remove from the oven and cool for a few minutes, then turn the tarts out of the molds. Serve upside down.

To cook the foie gras: Slice the foie gras into six 1/2-inch-thick medallions. Season them well with salt and fresh ground pepper. In a very hot, non-stick pan sear the foie gras quickly on both sides for no more than 30 seconds. Remove the rounds and deglaze the pan with the balsamic vinegar and red wine.

To finish: Place one foie gras medallion on each of the mango tarte tatins and drizzle with wine glaze.

MANGO TARTE TATIN WITH FOIE GRAS

SERVES 6

3	medium ripe mangos
2	teaspoons kosher salt
1	teaspoon fresh ground black pepper
2	tablespoons sweet butter, melted
2	tablespoons sugar
1	sheet puff pastry
12	ounces foie gras
3	tablespoons balsamic vinegar
2	tablespoons dry red wine

ROOT VEGETABLE CHIPS

SERVES 6 TO 10

1	large potato
1	large sweet potato
1	large yuca, peeled
1	large beet, peeled
1	large boniato, peeled
2	quarts peanut oil
5	tablespoons kosher salt

Almost all root vegetables make good chips. One of the most important points to remember when making chips is to select fresh, unblemished vegetables. Also, try to use vegetables that are almost the same size.

Most vegetables don't require peeling, but they do need to be washed and dried well. Several exceptions to this are what I call the Latin root vegetables: yuca, malanga, boniato, taro, and yam. These Latin roots have a hard skin or protective shell that really is inedible and needs to be peeled or pared away before slicing.

To prepare the chips free form: Don't try to make all the slices uniform. I suggest cutting them in irregular sizes for an interesting mix of chips. Using a slicer or a mandolin, slice each of the vegetables as thin as possible. (The mandolin will yield even thickness but various dimensions in size.) Keep each vegetable in a separate container of cold water with about a tablespoon of salt until you're ready to cook.

To prepare the chips for hors d'oeuvres: Peel the vegetables. Using a paring knife, cut each of the vegetables into an even circumference around. The result should be vegetables that are pretty much the same size. Let these soak in cold salted water until you're ready to cook.

To fry the chips: Heat a deep fryer to 375°, or until just before smoking. Drain and pat dry each of the chips and fry them in small batches so they don't stick together, until golden and crisp, usually less than 1 minute for each batch. Drain well, then blot on paper towels.

Boniato are like white sweet potatoes. The smoked tomato makes for a very interesting combination with the crisp chips.

To smoke the tomatoes: Several ways may seem practical to you to smoke tomatoes, depending on the equipment in your kitchen:

* *If you have a smoker, you're one of the lucky few. Smoke the tomatoes whole, directly on the grill, for about 15 minutes.*

* *Use a barbecue or a gas grill with a lid. If you're using a charcoal barbecue, wait until most of the coals have died down to smoldering red or preheat a gas grill for 5 minutes. At this point, add some small wood chips that have been wrapped in aluminum foil with air holes punched out. Cut the tomatoes in half and smoke them directly on the grill for about 10 minutes.*

* *Charring the tomato skin on a direct flame will also impart a wonderful smoked flavor—and it's easy. Use a propane torch and slowly char the skin until it's blistered all over. You can also use a long fork over a gas burner.*

To make the salsa: Whichever method for smoking you use, proceed by halving the tomatoes and gently squeezing them to remove the seeds. Carefully dice the flesh and skin of the tomato. Add the red onion, cilantro, lime juice, jalapeño, and olive oil, and season with salt. Toss together and let the flavors develop for about 30 minutes at room temperature before serving.

Serve the crisp boniato chips on the side.

BONIATO CHIPS WITH SMOKED TOMATO SALSA

SERVES 6

3	medium ripe tomatoes
1	small red onion, chopped
2	tablespoons chopped fresh cilantro
3	tablespoons lime juice
1	large jalapeño, chopped
2	tablespoons extra-virgin olive oil
1	teaspoon kosher salt
24	crisp boniato chips (page 42)

YAM CHIPS WITH CARAMELIZED TUNA LOIN

SERVES 6

1	pound tuna loin
3	tablespoons Dijon mustard
1	tablespoon Thai garlic chili sauce
½	teaspoon minced fresh ginger
2	tablespoons honey
1	tablespoon olive oil
24	yam chips (page 42)

The idea here is to caramelize the tuna very quickly, leaving it rare on the inside and crisp outside. I got this idea on a recent cruise to St. Barts in the Caribbean, after seeing the products available in the marketplace there.

To prepare the tuna loin: Take a chunk of first-quality sushi tuna and cut it lengthwise to make small loin cuts about 2 inches wide and anywhere from 4 to 6 inches long. (You should get about 24 cuts.) Combine the Dijon mustard, garlic sauce, ginger, and honey. Roll the mini-loins in the mixture and let them set for about 20 minutes.

To cook: Using a very hot cast-iron pan, char the tuna loins with a drizzle of olive oil, turning them quickly to sear them on all sides. This should take no longer than 40 seconds. Cut each loin into small thin slices.

Serve each loin slice on a crisp yam chip.

I like to use the long green plantain chips that I talk about in the Plantain/Tostone recipe. It's easy to make a sofrito of ingredients cooked together to blend their flavors.

To prepare the sofrito: In a sauté pan warm the olive oil with the white onion and green pepper. Cook until both are translucent. Add the garlic, then the vinegar, turmeric, oregano, cilantro, cayenne, and salt. Remove the mixture from the heat.

To prepare the black bean dip: Drain the black beans. In a food processor, combine the beans and the olives on pulse. Add the sofritto while it's still warm and continue to puree.

To serve: Serve the black bean dip in a hollowed-out half-pineapple with crisp plantain chips on the side.

PLANTAIN CHIPS WITH BLACK BEAN DIP

SERVES 10

2   tablespoons olive oil

2   tablespoons diced white onion

3   tablespoons diced green bell pepper

2   teaspoons chopped garlic

2   tablespoons white vinegar

1   teaspoon ground turmeric

1   teaspoon minced fresh oregano

2   tablespoons minced fresh cilantro

1/2   teaspoon cayenne pepper

1   tablespoon kosher salt

2   cups cooked black beans

1/2   cup pitted black olives

2   large plantains made into chips (page 31)

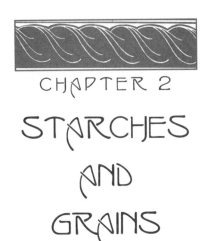

CHAPTER 2

STARCHES AND GRAINS

Saffron, Tangerine, and Gold Risotto

Calabaza and Toasted Almond Risotto

Boniato and Wild Mushroom Gratin

Quinoa Tart with Cherry Tomatoes *served with*
Lemon-Vanilla Vinaigrette

Jerk Foie Gras *served with*
Green Lentils in Balsamic Vinegar

Stewed Malanga with Cinnamon, Cloves, and Cream

Wild Rice Pancakes with
Chanterelle Mushrooms and Asparagus

Caviar Sundae

Plantain Confit and Polenta

Chef Allen's Breadsticks

When I was a child, starches meant the comfort of a billowy pile of mashed potatoes prepared simply with salt, pepper, and melted butter, or of egg noodles prepared in savory and sweet kugels for the holidays, or my mother's early-sixties' version of Fettuccine Alfredo—noodles plus cottage cheese. Like most kids, I was mad for macaroni and cheese, especially on winter days, especially during spring, summer, and fall.

As for grains, what I knew about them was limited to kasha varnishkas and Chinese fried rice. Kasha varnishkas, a dish that consists of kasha, fried onions, and bow-tie noodles, was a slowly developed taste on my part, but now I think it's a terrific flavor. At Chef Allen's, I prepare a dish with barley, egg noodles, and roast corn, and it's a big hit. Chinese rice was, for me, as a child in the early sixties, a source of wonder, suspicion, and sometimes—depending on where we were eating—a delight.

I didn't discover wild rice with all its subtle nutty nuances and texture until I began dining out in the mid-seventies, and I didn't discover couscous until my first trip to France, when I was an apprentice at the Bristol Hotel and one of my colleagues, a French–North African chef, introduced me to it. We, the help, all ate together and so took turns cooking for each other: people from the pantry made the salad, people from the hot line made hot foods, and the pastry chefs made the pastries. The North African chef served his couscous on a hot midsummer's day. The couscous, like the Paris sidewalks outside, was very hot, by which I mean it burned the tongue from tip to end, and was served in a steamy broth. We all sat in the kitchen eating and sweating, sweating and eating, and giggling. I loved couscous at first taste and was soon visiting the couscous restaurants in Paris every chance I got.

One pleasant adventure encourages another, in food as in love as in daring. In Amsterdam I sat down to a mere medium rijsttafel—a rice table consisting of twelve to fifteen tastes of dishes served with rice—and was transported. Large rijsttafels, when one can eat upward of thirty dishes, are for the heroic in spirit and body.

These are some of the experiences that led me to embrace other beautiful ingredients of the New World Cuisine—such as lentils (which have recently gained haute stature while maintaining their earthy satisfactions) and quinoa, a South American grain grown by the Aztec Indians. Experience plus knowledge—we've all been affected by the nutritional revelations of the past decade—have made me want to realign the proportions of a plate, to shift the focus away from gargantuan hunks of protein to a more healthful and graceful balance.

My New World sees the plate this way: starches and grains, 50 percent. Vegetables plus meat, the other 50 percent. Happy, healthful, joyful eating.

You can make this dish without the gold-plated chives, but they're a fabulous bit of whimsy for festive occasions—and completely edible. Gold sheets are available by mail order from many specialty shops.

To prepare the tangerines: In a small pot combine the tangerine juice and zest, ¹/₂ cup of the broth, and the saffron. Warm together.

To cook the risotto: In a heavy-sided saucepan melt 3 tablespoons of the butter and the olive oil together. Add the onion and cook for 1 minute. Add the arborio rice and cook for another minute, stirring well. Meanwhile, warm the rest of the broth to a slow simmer. Add ¹/₂ cup of the broth to the rice mixture, stirring constantly. As this liquid is absorbed, add another ¹/₂ cup. Continue to cook and add warm broth in this manner for 20 minutes. When most of the broth has been added to the rice, add the tangerine-saffron mix and remove from the heat. Finish the risotto with the remaining butter and the Parmesan cheese. Stir this in rapidly. Check the seasoning and add salt and pepper if necessary.

To assemble and serve: Carefully roll each chive in a pounded gold-leaf strip. Place the gold-plated chives in an **X** shape on top of the risotto. Serve immediately.

SAFFRON, TANGERINE, AND GOLD RISOTTO

SERVES 6

2	medium tangerines, zest and juice
5¹/₂	cups chicken or vegetable broth
¹/₄	teaspoon saffron threads, crushed
6	tablespoons sweet butter
3	tablespoons extra-virgin olive oil
1	medium onion, chopped
1¹/₂	cups arborio rice
¹/₄	cup grated Parmesan cheese
	Kosher salt and fresh ground black pepper, to taste
12	fresh chives
4	sheets 23K gold, each cut into thirds

CALABAZA AND TOASTED ALMOND RISOTTO

SERVES 6

1	cup diced calabaza
1/2	teaspoon minced fresh ginger
1/4	teaspoon saffron
5 1/2	cups chicken or vegetable broth
6	tablespoons sweet butter
3	tablespoons olive oil
1	medium onion, chopped
1 1/2	cups arborio rice
4	tablespoons grated Parmesan cheese

Kosher salt and fresh ground black pepper, to taste

6	tablespoons toasted almonds

Just when you thought you knew risotto, New World Cuisine brings you this one, flavored with calabaza, a sweet pumpkin whose combination with toasted almonds is epiphany.

To prepare the calabaza: In a small pot simmer the calabaza with the ginger and saffron in 2 cups of the chicken broth. Cook for 10 minutes, until the calabaza is firm yet cooked through. Drain the liquid back into the rest of the chicken broth. Hold the cooked calabaza aside.

To cook the risotto: In a heavy-sided saucepan melt 3 tablespoons of the butter and the olive oil together, then add the onion and cook for 1 minute until translucent. Add the arborio rice and cook for another minute, stirring well. Meanwhile, warm the rest of the broth to a slow simmer. Add 1/2 cup of the broth to the rice mixture, constantly stirring. As this liquid is absorbed, add another 1/2 cup. Continue to cook and add warm broth in this manner for 20 minutes. When most of the broth has been added to the rice, add the calabaza. Finish the risotto with the remaining butter and the Parmesan cheese. Stir this rapidly to incorporate. Add half of the almonds. Check the seasoning and add salt and pepper if necessary.

Serve with the remaining toasted almonds on top.

I love the combination of white sweet potatoes and wild mushrooms enhanced with the mild bite of goat cheese.

To prepare the boniatos: Peel and trim the boniatos. Boil them whole in salted water for approximately 20 minutes, until they are cooked yet firm. Remove them from the water and let cool. Cut the boniatos into $\frac{1}{3}$-inch-thick slices.

To prepare the mushrooms: Warm 2 tablespoons of the olive oil in a sauté pan. Add the shallots and cook until translucent. Then add the garlic and mushrooms. Sauté for another minute, then deglaze the pan with white wine and season with salt and pepper.

To finish the gratin: Preheat the oven to 350°. Lightly brush an 8-inch ovenproof dish with the remaining olive oil. Stack alternate layers of boniato and mushrooms by layering half of the boniato into the dish and topping it with a third of the cheese. Then add half of the mushrooms and top off with a third of the cheese. Finish with a layer of boniato, then the remaining mushrooms and finally the remaining goat cheese. Bake the gratin for 15 minutes, until nicely browned and bubbling.

BONIATO AND WILD MUSHROOM GRATIN

SERVES 6

1   pound boniatos

3   tablespoons extra-virgin olive oil

2   tablespoons diced shallots

1   teaspoon diced garlic

2   cups thinly sliced wild mushrooms (crimini, shiitake, oyster, chanterelle)

$\frac{1}{4}$ cup dry white wine

1   teaspoon kosher salt

1   teaspoon coarse ground black pepper

$\frac{1}{2}$ cup grated dry aged goat cheese

QUINOA TART WITH CHERRY TOMATOES

SERVES 6

2 cups quinoa

2 tablespoons olive oil

1/2 cup chopped sweet onion

3 cups chicken or vegetable broth

1 tablespoon kosher salt

1 tablespoon coarse ground black pepper

1/2 cup halved cherry tomatoes

Quinoa is a unique South American grain. Its mild nutty flavor may be an acquired taste, but it's an acquisition well worth your while.

To cook the quinoa: Rinse the quinoa under running cold water. In a small saucepot warm the olive oil. Add the onion and cook over medium heat until translucent. Add the quinoa and mix well. Add the broth, salt, and pepper and bring to a simmer. Lower the heat and cook, covered, for 20 minutes. When the quinoa is cooked, it will look like little tails have sprouted on each grain. Remove from the heat and cool.

To assemble the tart: Pack a sixth of the quinoa mixture into a 4-inch round cookie cutter, carefully turn it out onto a serving plate and remove the mold. Set up 6 plates with tart molds in this fashion. Garnish each with cherry tomato halves, then drizzle 1 1/2 to 2 tablespoons of Lemon-Vanilla Vinaigrette around each quinoa tart.

ACCOMPANIMENT:
LEMON-VANILLA VINAIGRETTE

This lively dressing starts off with a vanilla-infused oil made by splitting open 2 vanilla beans and immersing them in a small bottle of virgin olive oil. In about 2 or 3 days the oil will be flavored with the sweet essence of vanilla.

Combine the lemon juice and Dijon mustard in a large stainless-steel bowl. Whisk in the vanilla bean oil in an even drizzle until incorporated completely. Season the vinaigrette with salt and pepper, then stir in the chives.

LEMON-VANILLA VINAIGRETTE

MAKES 1 CUP

- 1/3   cup fresh squeezed lemon juice
- 2   tablespoons Dijon mustard
- 2/3   cup vanilla bean oil (see recipe head)
- 1   teaspoon sea salt
- 1   teaspoon fresh ground black pepper
- 2   tablespoons snipped fresh chives

JERK FOIE GRAS

SERVES 8

¼ cup ground allspice

1 teaspoon ground cinnamon

½ teaspoon grated nutmeg

1 tablespoon minced fresh cilantro

4 whole scallions, chopped

2 tablespoons chopped garlic

1 teaspoon tamarind pulp

1 cup dry red wine

4 tablespoons olive oil

1 teaspoon kosher salt

1 teaspoon minced Scotch bonnet

1 pound fresh foie gras

Rich, flavorful foie gras is usually accompanied by only the most subtle flavors, and jerk, or course, is anything but. What makes this combination work so beautifully is the counterpoint provided by the tartness of the tamarind. The fiery Scotch bonnet brings everything into startling harmony.

To prepare the foie gras: Combine the spices, cilantro, scallions, garlic, tamarind, red wine, 2 tablespoons of the olive oil, the salt, and Scotch bonnet. Separate the 2 lobes of the liver. Clean and remove the veins from the foie gras. Cut each lobe into 1½-inch-thick medallions. Marinate with the "jerk" seasoning in a ceramic bowl for 2 hours.

To cook: Preheat the grill, then grill each piece of foie gras for only 30 seconds on each side, charring the outside yet leaving the inside medium rare.

To serve: Put the Green Lentils on a bright ceramic plate and place the medallions of foie gras on top.

ACCOMPANIMENT:
GREEN LENTILS IN BALSAMIC VINEGAR

I prefer the small elegant green lentils from DePuy for their superior flavor as well as for their texture, which remains firm after cooking.

Cooking the lentils: Wash the lentils thoroughly. Warm the oil, add the onion, and cook them until they are translucent. Add the garlic and cook for another minute. Add the carrots and celery. Continue cooking these for 2 minutes. Add the lentils, water, and bay leaves. Simmer for 20 minutes, or until the lentils are slightly firm. Remove the bay leaves.

To serve: Combine the lentils with the lime zest and balsamic vinegar.

GREEN LENTILS IN BALSAMIC VINEGAR

SERVES 8

2½ cups green lentils
¼ cup olive oil
½ cup diced onions
2 teaspoons diced garlic
½ cup diced carrots
½ cup diced celery
6 cups water
2 bay leaves
2 tablespoons lime zest
¼ cup balsamic vinegar

STEWED MALANGA WITH CINNAMON, CLOVES, AND CREAM

SERVES 6

1   pound malangas

3   cups whole milk

2   teaspoons kosher salt

1   teaspoon coarse ground black pepper

1   cinnamon stick

2   whole cloves

1   bay leaf

3   tablespoons heavy cream

I think of this as a dish that has its roots in some-one's Caribbean home, in a kitchen where it's served in Grandma's bowl. Paired with a salad or one of the smaller fish dishes, this would make a fine meal.

To prepare the stew: Peel and cut the malangas into fairly large chunks, about 2 inches by 2 inches. Place the malanga in a small saucepot and add the milk to cover. Next add the salt, pepper, cinnamon, cloves, and bay leaf, then simmer the stew for approximately 25 minutes, or until the malanga is soft and cooked through.

To serve: Carefully remove the malanga to a serving dish. Add the cream to the cooking liquid, and reduce until thick enough to run off the back of a spoon, then strain through a fine sieve back onto the malanga and serve.

Annatto oil gives this satisfying dish a wonderfully unique flavor.

To cook the wild rice: In a pan heat 1 tablespoon of the annatto oil. Sauté half of the shallots until they're transparent. Add the rice and bay leaves. Stir the rice until it's well-coated with the oil, then add the stock and bring the mixture to a boil. Simmer the rice for approximately 15 minutes, then remove it from the heat and set aside.

To prepare the asparagus: Peel, then tie the asparagus together into a bundle. Place the bundle, points up, into a pot of boiling water for 2 minutes, or until the water returns to a boil—no longer. Next plunge the blanched asparagus into an ice-water bath.

To prepare the pancakes: Whisk together the flour, egg, milk, and remaining tablespoon of annatto oil. Add the rice and chopped chives. The mixture should be the texture of a crepe batter. Cook the pancakes in a 6-inch Teflon sauté pan. Prepare one pancake per serving.

To prepare the chanterelles: In a pan heat the butter and sauté the chanterelles with the rest of the shallots. Deglaze with the white wine and reduce until no liquid remains.

To assemble and serve: Roll 3 asparagus into each pancake with the tips sticking out. Brush lightly with clarified butter and heat in the oven. When the wild rice pancakes are hot, top them with the chanterelles and serve.

NOTE: To prepare the annatto oil, warm 2 tablespoons annatto seeds with 1 cup olive oil to approximately 100°. Remove from the heat and let it sit to cool for an hour before straining the seeds out.

WILD RICE PANCAKES WITH CHANTERELLE MUSHROOMS AND ASPARAGUS

SERVES 6

2	tablespoons annatto oil (see Note)
3	tablespoons diced shallots
½	cup wild rice, washed
2	bay leaves
¾	cup chicken stock
12	stalks asparagus
½	cup all-purpose flour
1	large egg
½	cup whole milk
½	bunch chives, chopped
2	tablespoons sweet butter
1	cup chanterelle mushrooms
2	tablespoons dry white wine
2	tablespoons clarified butter

CAVIAR SUNDAE

SERVES 6

2   cups water

1   cup polenta

½   tablespoon kosher salt

½   teaspoon white pepper

1   tablespoon sweet butter

6   tablespoons sour cream

1   tablespoon Hungarian paprika

3   large hard-boiled egg whites, chopped

3   tablespoons chopped fresh chives

1   ounce Ossetra or Sevruga caviar

Somehow, if the rich goodness and temperate hot and cold opposites of a hot fudge sundae can make you happy, then I think this will be right up your alley. I made it for Julia Child on one of her recent visits to my restaurant. She thought it was wonderful.

To prepare the polenta: In a large saucepot, boil the water. Add the polenta and stir well, then lower the heat to a simmer. Continue mixing and add the salt, pepper, and butter. Stir until the polenta begins to thicken. Continue cooking for another 2 minutes, and remove it from the heat. Mix in 3 tablespoons of the sour cream.

To set up the sundae: Using 6 small parfait glasses (3 or 4 inches high) or cup sundae glasses, dip the rims in paprika (like you would to salt a margarita glass). Then layer the bottom of each with about 1 inch of the egg whites. Next sprinkle with chives. Then add the warm polenta, layering about 2½ inches into the glass.

To finish the sundae: Dollop a teaspoon of sour cream onto each sundae and finish with a teaspoon of caviar.

A sensuous first course that also makes a great side dish for simple roasted chicken.

To prepare the plantains: Preheat the oven to 325°. Place the ripe plantains with their skins in a shallow baking dish. Bake for 35 minutes, or until the fruit is soft. Remove from the oven and cool slightly. Remove the skin from the plantains, and slice the fruit into 1/2-inch-thick coins. Return the plantains to the baking dish and season with the ginger and turmeric. Dot with the butter. Return to the oven for 10 more minutes to caramelize them well.

To prepare the polenta: In a heavy, deep saucepot bring the chicken broth to a simmer. Season with the garlic and oregano. Add the polenta and mix well. Continue to stir regularly to prevent lumping. After about 5 minutes, remove from the heat.

To finish: Divide the polenta into 6 individual ramekins, filling three quarters of the dish. Top the polenta with plantain confit and bake for 5 minutes in a 350° oven.

PLANTAIN CONFIT AND POLENTA

SERVES 6

4	medium ripe plantains
1	teaspoon minced fresh ginger
1/4	teaspoon ground turmeric
2	tablespoons sweet butter
2 1/2	cups chicken broth
1/2	teaspoon minced garlic
1/2	teaspoon minced fresh oregano
1 1/2	cups polenta

CHEF ALLEN'S BREADSTICKS

MAKES 36 BREADSTICKS

 1 envelope dry yeast

 1 tablespoon sugar

1½ cups warm water

3¼ cups all-purpose flour

 ½ teaspoon fine sea salt

 6 tablespoons olive oil

 1 tablespoon kosher salt

To prepare the dough: In a large mixing bowl equipped with a dough hook combine the yeast, sugar, and warm water. Mix on low speed to incorporate. Turn the mixer off. Add the flour, sea salt, and 4 tablespoons of the olive oil and turn the mixer on low to incorporate the ingredients. Then increase the speed to knead the dough for 5 minutes. Turn the dough out into a stainless-steel bowl coated with 1 tablespoon of the remaining olive oil. Cover with plastic wrap and set in a warm area in your kitchen.

To develop the dough: After approximately 45 minutes, when the dough has doubled in size, punch it down and let it rise again to double its size, this time for approximately 30 minutes.

To cut the dough: Turn the dough out onto a floured work surface and knead it for 1 minute. Roll out the dough with a rolling pin to about 1 inch thick. Cut the dough into 1-inch-thick strips about 6 inches long, and set these aside. Taking one strip at a time, roll the dough with your palm into a long thin breadstick. Place each breadstick carefully on a large sheet pan that will fit into your oven. When all the breadsticks are rolled and neatly placed side by side, brush them with the remaining olive oil and dust them with the kosher salt.

To bake: Preheat the oven to 350° and bake for 15 minutes, until the breadsticks are crisp and golden brown. Remove from the oven and let them cool.

Grilled Fruit and Vegetable Salad *served with*
Hot Citrus Vinaigrette

Ragout of Latin Root Vegetables and Chanterelles

Fresh Hearts of Palm with Citrus Juice and Caviar

Hearts of Palm Ceviche

Grilled Plantains with Black Bean
and Dried Fruit Salsa

Vegetable Strudel *served with*
Black Peppered Chick-peas

Black Beans and White Truffles
on Roasted Pimento Coulis

Grilled Portobello Mushroom, Avocado,
and Goat Cheese Club Sandwich

Purple Eggplant Timbale *served with* Tomato Coulis

Radicchio Rellenos with Spicy Couscous

Sweet Potato Soup with Fire-Roasted Corn

Cold Red Banana Bisque with Cinnamon Croutons

Boniato Vichyssoise Spiked with Horseradish

Spicy Gazpacho with Baked Brie Wrapped in Phyllo

CHAPTER 3
FRUITS AND VEGETABLES

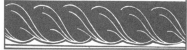

When I first arrived in south Florida from New York, I thought a plantain was just some funky banana. The first time I tried a sweet fried plantain, or *plantanos maduros,* was in a little Cuban restaurant down on South Beach, and I thought the texture and caramelized sweetness were delicious. Tomas, my former sous chef, was heavy into plantains and turned me on to Puerto Rican tostones. This is a dish that uses green plantains, cooked with olive oil and garlic, then smacked down and compressed and cooked again for results and uses that are entirely different from *plantanos maduros.*

I came to south Florida somewhat prepared for an introduction to the fruits and vegetables of the New World because my parents had nurtured me on those that were fresh and available in the fifties and sixties. At home in Brooklyn, Thursday meant shopping day. We used to go down to Thirteenth Avenue, which was an old-fashioned market area with a mix of individual stores. Near the fish store, the butcher shop, and the bakery, was an open-market fruit stand. Beneath the rolled-up awnings, behind big piles of the freshest and most seasonal produce available, four or five men practically sang about their wares to the twenty or thirty people, mostly Jews and Italians, vying to buy the fresh grapes or cantaloupes or strawberries.

The action was quick, intense, colorful. When it was our turn to buy they'd call to us, "Okay, what are you gonna have?" And we'd tell them, two pounds of peaches, or plums, or nectarines, or tomatoes. While my choice of fruits and vegetables is a good deal more varied today, availability and freshness are still what count when I'm composing a dish or menu.

New and Old World produce merge in these recipes. Fresh hearts of palm are united with tangerine ceviche and pink peppercorns; my vichyssoise is prepared with boniato and horseradish. Purple eggplant timbale is one of the great hits at Chef Allen's, and my ragout of Latin root vegetables and chanterelles would make a fine vegetarian meal.

Not too long ago, Americans were a meat-and-potatoes people, relegating vegetables other than spuds to a necessary but unexciting part of the plate that was to be endured—for health reasons—rather than enjoyed. In the New World, vegetables are enjoyed rather than endured, and for a reason more compelling than health. Who can argue, after all, with delectability?

GRILLED FRUIT AND VEGETABLE SALAD

SERVES 6

1	large tomato, sliced thick
1	large Spanish onion, sliced thick
1	large chayote, sliced thick
1	small green papaya, sliced thin
12	large asparagus, peeled
6	large figs, halved
2	tablespoons fresh ground black pepper
2	tablespoons kosher salt
¼	cup olive oil

This is a wonderful hearty salad that works equally well as a main dish for lunch or as a prelude to a larger evening meal. Serve it with crusty rustic bread.

To prepare the fruits and vegetables: Season them all with fresh ground black pepper and kosher salt. Drizzle with olive oil.

To grill the salad: Preheat a barbecue grill using charcoal and oak chips. (Though you could broil or roast the vegetables, you would lose the flavor.) Carefully grill each item separately to control the individual grilling times. Start with the tomato, then the onion, then the chayote and green papaya. Arrange the slices alternately on a large oval platter. Finally, grill the asparagus, then the figs. Arrange these in the center of the plate.

Serve with the Hot Citrus Vinaigrette.

ACCOMPANIMENT:
HOT CITRUS VINAIGRETTE

Florida oranges and grapefruits are the juiciest in the world. I like their flavor more than the desert-grown varieties.

To prepare the citrus: Peel each of the citrus fruits and cut the flesh into segments. Carefully dice the segments, cutting them but not crushing them. Save the liquids together.

To prepare the vinaigrette: In a stainless-steel bowl, whisk together the olive oil, vinegar, soy sauce, Scotch bonnet, and the collected fruit juices. Add the pink peppercorns, ginger, cilantro, diced fruit, and salt. Mix together carefully.

HOT CITRUS VINAIGRETTE

MAKES 1 CUP

1	large Florida orange
1/4	medium grapefruit
1/2	medium lime
1/2	medium lemon
1/2	cup extra-virgin olive oil
1/4	cup champagne vinegar
1 1/2	tablespoons soy sauce
1/2	teaspoon minced Scotch bonnet
2	teaspoons pink peppercorns
1	teaspoon julienned fresh ginger
1/4	cup fresh cilantro leaves
1	teaspoon sea salt

RAGOUT OF LATIN ROOT VEGETABLES AND CHANTERELLES

SERVES 6

1   *cup yuca, cut into large dice*

1   *cup boniato, cut into large dice*

4   *tablespoons olive oil*

2   *teaspoons kosher salt*

1   *teaspoon fresh ground black pepper*

1   *cup calabaza, cut into large dice*

1   *cup green plantain, cut into large dice*

1   *cup peeled and blanched pearl onions*

1   *cup trimmed chanterelle mushrooms*

1   *tablespoon chopped garlic*

1/2   *cup warm chicken stock*

2   *tablespoons chopped fresh cilantro*

To prepare the vegetables: Preheat the oven to 350°. Season the yuca and boniato with 3 tablespoons of the olive oil, 1 teaspoon salt, and ½ teaspoon pepper.

To cook the ragout: Roast the roots for 15 minutes, turning 2 or 3 times, browning them nicely. Then add the calabaza and green plantains with another tablespoon of olive oil. Season lightly with salt and pepper, and continue to roast, turning, for another 5 minutes. Then add the pearl onions, chanterelles, and garlic. After 5 minutes, add the chicken stock, mixing the ragout carefully to avoid breaking the roots and vegetables. Continue to cook for a final 5 minutes, and remove from the oven.

Garnish with the chopped cilantro.

From time to time I see fresh hearts of palm in the marketplace, but I know it will be a few years before they are generally available. If you can't find the fresh product in your area, you can use canned—though you might miss some of the crunch.

To marinate the hearts of palm: Slice the hearts of palm across the grain—very thin. The fresh palm may look a little splintered but that is normal. Place in a large bowl and cover with the combination of orange juice, grapefruit juice, salt, peppercorns, and olive oil. Let this marinate for 2 hours.

To finish the hearts of palm: Drain the marinade through a sieve. Place the palms back in the bowl, toss with the onion and caviar, and serve on a bed of butter lettuces.

FRESH HEARTS OF PALM WITH CITRUS JUICE AND CAVIAR

SERVES 6

1	pound hearts of palm
1	cup orange juice
1	cup grapefruit juice
1	tablespoon kosher salt
1	tablespoon pink peppercorns, ground
2	tablespoons olive oil
1	small onion, julienned
2	ounces salmon roe caviar

Butter lettuce leaves, washed

HEARTS OF PALM CEVICHE

SERVES 6

½ large fresh heart of palm (see Note)

6 large limes, juiced

1 large serrano chili, julienned

1 large red onion, shaved thin

2 large tomatoes, skinned, pulp removed, and julienned

1 tablespoon snipped fresh chives

1 tablespoon fresh chervil leaves

2 tablespoons fresh cilantro leaves

Kosher salt

To prepare the hearts of palm: Peel the bark from the heart of palm log, removing about half of its bulk until the flesh is soft and pliable. Slice the heart very thin on a short bias. Marinate this in the fresh squeezed lime juice for 1 hour.

To flavor the marinade: Add to the lime juice the serrano chili, red onion, tomatoes, chives, chervil, cilantro, and salt. Toss well and marinate the hearts of palm for about 30 minutes before serving.

NOTE: The process of ceviche is for fresh hearts of palm. If you must use canned, skip marinating the hearts in lime.

I prefer to use half-ripened fruit for this plantain preparation, which makes an excellent first course or side dish with roasted fish. The plantains should be just past the yellow stage, with only a few brown blemishes on the skin. If the plantains you buy are green, ripen them in a warm corner of your kitchen.

To prepare the black bean and dried fruit salsa: In a stainless-steel bowl combine all the ingredients except for 1 tablespoon of annatto oil and the plantains. Toss the mixture well and let it sit for 1 hour.

To grill the plantains: Peel the plantains, slice them lengthwise, and brush with the remaining tablespoon of annatto oil. Grill or broil on medium heat for 2 minutes on the first side, then turn and finish grilling another minute or so. Serve them with the black bean fruit salsa poured over them.

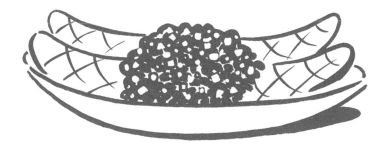

GRILLED PLANTAINS WITH BLACK BEAN AND DRIED FRUIT SALSA

SERVES 6

2   cups cooked black beans

1/2   cup diced sun-dried tomatoes

1/4   cup diced sun-dried apricot

1/4   cup diced sun-dried mango

1/4   cup minced jalapeño

1/4   cup diced red bell pepper

1/4   cup chopped scallion

1/4   cup minced fresh cilantro

1/4   cup lime juice

1   tablespoon kosher salt

4   tablespoons annatto oil (page 9)

3   large half-ripened plantains

VEGETABLE STRUDEL

SERVES 6

3 tablespoons olive oil

½ cup julienned onion

½ cup julienned shiitake mushrooms

¼ cup julienned carrot

½ tablespoon chopped garlic

½ cup peeled, seeded, and diced tomato

¼ cup chopped green olives

2 teaspoons kosher salt

1 teaspoon fresh ground black pepper

9 sheets phyllo dough

At home, when I was growing up, we used to eat sweet strudels on holidays, so they remind me of happy, festive occasions. This is a savory strudel, perfect for a first course, a holiday lunch, or cut into smaller portions for an appetizer.

To prepare the filling for the strudel: Warm 2 tablespoons of the olive oil and sauté the onion until translucent. Add the shiitakes and carrot, and continue to sauté. Add the garlic, then the tomato and olives. Sauté for a minute. Season with salt and black pepper. The mixture should be finished after another minute of cooking. Remove from the heat and cool.

To make the strudel: Preheat the oven to 400°. Layer 3 sheets of phyllo, brushing olive oil between each layer and making sure to keep the rest of the phyllo sheets covered with a damp towel. Cut the stacked sheets in half crosswise. Spread about 3 tablespoons of filling in each half sheet, then roll it up like a wide cigar and cover with a damp towel. When all the strudels are finished, bake them on a cookie sheet for 10 minutes, until golden brown.

To serve: Split each strudel in half on a bias. Serve with the hot Black Peppered Chick-peas.

ACCOMPANIMENT:
BLACK PEPPERED CHICK-PEAS

This is a dish my grandmother, Rose Rosenkranz, used to prepare in a pressure cooker. At family get-togethers we would go through bowls of it.

To cook the chick-peas: Rinse the chick-peas under cold running water. Place them in a pot with the cold water. Add the bay leaf and 1 teaspoon of kosher salt. Simmer for 45 minutes, until the chick-peas are cooked but still with firm centers. Strain the chick-peas.

To season: Place the chick-peas in a large glass bowl and season with the extra-virgin olive oil, remaining salt, pepper, and parsley. Mix well. Cover the bowl with plastic film. After 5 minutes uncover the bowl, toss gently with a squeeze of fresh lime juice, and serve.

BLACK PEPPERED CHICK-PEAS

SERVES 6 (2 CUPS)

2   *cups raw chick-peas*

4   *cups cold water*

1   *bay leaf*

2   *teaspoons kosher salt*

2   *tablespoons extra-virgin olive oil*

1   *tablespoon fresh ground black pepper*

2   *tablespoons chopped fresh flat-leaf parsley*

1   *medium lime, juiced*

BLACK BEANS AND WHITE TRUFFLES ON ROASTED PIMENTO COULIS

SERVES 6

2 cups black beans

8 cups cold water

¹/₂ cup diced onion

1 bay leaf

¹/₂ head garlic, whole

2 tablespoons kosher salt, plus extra, to taste

3 large red bell peppers

¹/₂ cup white wine

1 teaspoon white pepper

2 tablespoons white truffle oil (available in many gourmet specialty shops)

4 tablespoons aged sherry vinegar

2 tablespoons extra-virgin olive oil

12 sprigs chives, 6 chopped and 6 cut in 2-inch lengths

1 large white truffle, shaved

Fresh white truffles are available in late fall, so that's when I'd serve this dish, either as a first course or as an accompaniment to quail. Truffles and black beans may seem to be at opposite ends of the food spectrum (with fresh white truffles costing $1,200 a pound and black beans costing 12 cents per pound) but their combined flavors prove that opposites really do attract.

To prepare the black beans: Place the black beans in a tall stockpot. Cover the beans with the cold water. Add the onion, bay leaf, and garlic head, with 2 tablespoons of salt and let simmer for 1 hour 45 minutes, until the beans are tender but still hold their shape. Remove the beans from the heat and cool. Then remove them from the liquid and discard the garlic head.

To prepare the pimentos: Roast the peppers on a gas flame until seared black on all sides. Set aside, covered, for 15 minutes. Then peel and seed the peppers. Put them in a small saucepot and simmer with the white wine for 5 minutes. Remove from the heat and mash through a fine sieve. Let cool. Season with salt, white pepper, white truffle oil, and 2 tablespoons of the vinegar.

To finish the black beans: Toss them in the olive oil and the remaining vinegar, then season with salt and fresh chopped chives. Add the smaller pieces of shaved truffle and toss carefully. Serve the black beans and white truffles on a small pool of roast pimentos.

Garnish with the larger shavings of white truffle and the chive sticks.

To prepare the mushrooms: Cut the stems off the portobello mushrooms and reserve for other uses. Combine the white wine, garlic, olive oil, pepper, and salt. Marinate the portobello caps in this mixture for 30 minutes.

To cook the mushrooms: Heat the grill, preferably wood burning, and grill the mushrooms for about 3 minutes until cooked through, turning several times while cooking.

To assemble and serve: Peel and carefully slice the avocado very thin. Slice the yellow tomato very thin as well. Carefully cut the goat cheese with a hot knife blade, as thin as possible. Cut a grilled portobello mushroom into 3 pieces horizontally across the top. Stack the mushroom, tomato, avocado, and goat cheese slices alternately, finishing with a mushroom top. Make 3 more stacks in the same manner. Cut the stacks in half and serve on a bed of frisée.

GRILLED PORTOBELLO MUSHROOM, AVOCADO, AND GOAT CHEESE CLUB SANDWICH

SERVES 4

- 4 large portobello mushrooms
- 2 tablespoons white wine
- 1 tablespoon minced garlic
- 1 tablespoon olive oil
- 1/2 teaspoon fresh ground black pepper
- 1/2 teaspoon kosher salt
- 1 medium avocado
- 1 medium yellow tomato
- 1/4 pound fresh goat cheese
- 1 head frisée, washed

PURPLE EGGPLANT TIMBALE

SERVES 4

1   medium eggplant

1   tablespoon kosher salt, plus extra, to taste

1   cup olive oil

4   cloves garlic

1/2   medium Spanish onion, julienned

1/4   pound wild or button mushrooms, sliced thin

2   tablespoons dry white wine

1   medium ripe tomato, peeled, seeded, and roughly diced

1/2   bunch fresh basil (half chopped, half for garnish)

1   cup chopped fresh leaf spinach, washed

1/4   cup grated Parmesan cheese

Fresh ground black pepper

This is one of the first dishes I developed for Chef Allen's. It's easy to prepare and can be made ahead and kept refrigerated until you're ready to heat it up.

To prepare the eggplant: Slice the eggplant thinly on a diagonal, lengthwise. Salt the slices liberally. Let them set for 1 hour, then rinse under running cold water and pat dry. In a shallow, heavy pot, slowly heat 3/4 cup of the olive oil with 3 cloves of the garlic. When the oil is hot, remove the garlic cloves and cook the eggplant slices for 30 seconds on each side. Remove and cool on absorbent towels. Line 4 individual soufflé molds with the eggplant, crisscrossing 2 slices in each mold with the ends of the strips hanging over the mold edge.

To prepare the timbale filling: Sauté the onion in the remaining olive oil for 1 minute. Add the mushrooms. After 1 minute, add the remaining clove of garlic, minced, and then the white wine. Add the tomato, chopped basil, and spinach. Remove from the heat and drain the mixture in a colander. Add in the Parmesan and season with salt and pepper.

To assemble and serve: Preheat the oven to 350°. Fill the molds with the timbale filling and close the tops with the overlapping eggplant. Bake the timbales for 10 minutes to warm through.

Spoon a splash of Tomato Coulis (about 1 tablespoon) onto each of 4 serving plates. Invert the mold—the timbale will slide out easily—on top of the coulis. Garnish with the fresh basil leaves.

ACCOMPANIMENT:
TOMATO COULIS

To prepare the tomatoes: Peel the fresh tomatoes by scoring an **X** opposite the stem side, plunging them into a pot of boiling water for 30 seconds, then cooling them in an ice bath. The skin should peel off easily. Next cut the tomatoes in half crosswise, and squeeze out the seeds.

To make the coulis: In a food processor puree the garlic and basil with the olive oil. Add the tomatoes and continue to puree. Place the mixture in a saucepan and reduce over medium heat until it starts to thicken—about 5 minutes. Season with salt and pepper and remove from the heat.

TOMATO COULIS

MAKES 1 CUP
(MORE THAN ENOUGH
FOR 4)

2 large ripe tomatoes

2 cloves garlic

2 tablespoons chopped fresh basil

2 tablespoons extra-virgin olive oil

1 teaspoon kosher salt

$1/2$ teaspoon fresh ground black pepper

RADICCHIO RELLENOS WITH SPICY COUSCOUS

SERVES 6

2   radicchio heads

1   bunch chives

2   cups chicken broth

½   cup diced Spanish onion

½   cup diced carrot

½   cup diced zucchini

1   12-ounce box instant couscous

1   teaspoon kosher salt

1   tablespoon ground cumin

1   tablespoon ground turmeric

½   teaspoon dried red pepper flakes

¼   teaspoon ground allspice

¼   teaspoon ground cinnamon

2   tablespoons pine nuts

2   tablespoons currants

The texture and flavor of couscous make for a terrific stuffing. I may have been thinking about my grandmother's stuffed cabbage when I created this dish, but the radicchio and hot spices bring it out of the kitchen where I grew up and into the New World. I think Rose would have approved.

To prepare the radicchio and chives: Separate the leaves of the radicchio. Blanch the leaves for 30 seconds in a pot of boiling salted water, then plunge immediately into an ice bath. Pat dry and reserve these for later. Also blanch the chives following the same method.

To prepare the couscous: Warm the chicken broth in a small stockpot. Add the vegetables and simmer until tender, approximately 5 minutes. Bring the broth to a boil and add the couscous, stirring well. Add the seasonings. Let this cook together, stirring constantly, for 3 to 4 minutes. Remove from the heat and pour the mixture onto a sheet pan to cool. Quickly toast the pine nuts in a dry pan, either in the oven at 350° or on the stove top, until the nuts are golden brown. Remove from the heat and let the pine nuts cool. Combine the pine nuts and currants into the couscous mixture.

To assemble and serve: Individually spoon about 1 tablespoon of couscous into a radicchio skin. Place the couscous at one end of the skin. Fold the ends over as if you were rolling it into a package. Tie each package with 2 chives, as you would belt a sea trunk. Serve the radicchio packages either at room temperature or hot, by baking them for 5 minutes in a 325° oven.

To prepare the sweet potato puree: In a skillet sweat the onion in the corn oil until translucent. Add the sweet potatoes, yams, chicken stock, ginger, allspice, and garlic cloves. Cook the mixture for 30 minutes, until the potatoes and yams are soft. Puree and pass through a fine sieve. Return to the heat and continue to simmer for 5 minutes.

To prepare the corn: Roast the corn in the husk on an open flame or grill, turning it often, for 5 minutes. Remove from the heat and let cool. Cut the corn from the cob. Add to the simmering puree.

To finish the soup: After 5 minutes, add the Scotch bonnet, turmeric, and salt. Simmer for 3 more minutes. Adjust the seasoning and heighten the flavor with a squeeze of fresh lime.

SWEET POTATO SOUP WITH FIRE-ROASTED CORN

SERVES 6

1 medium sweet onion, julienned

1 tablespoon corn oil

1/2 pound sweet potatoes, peeled and diced

1/2 pound yams, peeled and diced

3 cups chicken stock

1/4 teaspoon peeled and well-chopped fresh ginger

1/4 teaspoon ground allspice

2 cloves garlic

1 large corn on the cob in its husk

1/2 teaspoon minced Scotch bonnet

1/2 teaspoon ground turmeric

2 teaspoons kosher salt

1 medium lime

COLD RED BANANA BISQUE WITH CINNAMON CROUTONS

SERVES 6

1   pound red bananas, chopped

3   cups chicken stock

1   vanilla bean, split open

1/2 cup sweet cream

1   teaspoon kosher salt

1/2 teaspoon fresh ground black pepper

1/4 teaspoon grated nutmeg

1   tablespoon Armagnac

1/2 cup 1/2-inch brioche cubes

1   teaspoon ground cinnamon

1   tablespoon clarified butter

Red banana is one of the more abundant "other banana" varieties. It has an intense banana flavor with a bit of vanilla aroma. When this banana is ripe, its skin is a deep chocolate-red, though the flesh is still creamy white. This bisque makes an excellent and unusual first-course soup.

To prepare the bisque: In a small stockpot combine the red bananas, chicken stock, and vanilla. Simmer for 20 minutes. Add the sweet cream, salt, pepper, and nutmeg. Continue cooking for 5 more minutes. Strain the bisque, add a dash of Armagnac, and set aside to cool. Refrigerate to chill well before serving.

To prepare the croutons: Dust the brioche cubes with the cinnamon. Drizzle with the clarified butter, then toast on a cookie sheet in a 350° oven for 5 minutes, turning once or twice, until golden brown. Set these aside to cool and use to garnish the bisque when served.

The classic French vichyssoise is a cold cream of potato soup made with leeks and onions. I've substituted boniato for the potatoes and added grated horseradish for kick.

To make the boniato and leek soup: In a large saucepot sweat the onions in the clarified butter. Add the bay leaves, thyme, chicken stock, leeks, and boniatos. Bring up to a boil and simmer slowly for 35 to 40 minutes, or until the boniato is soft. Season with salt and pepper. Remove from the heat and pass through a food mill. Let cool, then refrigerate overnight.

To assemble the vichyssoise: Combine the cold boniato mixture with the sour cream, horseradish, and sweet cream. Adjust the seasoning with salt and pepper. Serve chilled.

BONIATO VICHYSSOISE SPIKED WITH HORSERADISH

SERVES 6 (2 QUARTS)

1	large white onion, chopped
2	tablespoons clarified butter
2	bay leaves
3	sprigs fresh thyme
2	quarts chicken stock
1/2	pound leeks, white only, chopped roughly
1 1/2	pounds boniatos, peeled and diced
2	tablespoons kosher salt
1	tablespoon white pepper
3	tablespoons sour cream
3	tablespoons grated horseradish
1/2	cup sweet cream

SPICY GAZPACHO WITH BAKED BRIE WRAPPED IN PHYLLO

SERVES 6

2 cups chopped, peeled, and seeded tomatoes

1 cup chopped, peeled, and seeded cucumber

1 cup chopped onion

½ cup peeled, chopped celery

½ cup chopped, seeded red bell pepper

½ cup chopped, seeded Anaheim chili

2 cups tomato juice

½ teaspoon Scotch bonnet

1 teaspoon chopped garlic

1 teaspoon ground cumin

1 teaspoon dried oregano

2 teaspoons sea salt

3 tablespoons extra-virgin olive oil

1 small Brie wheel

3 sheets phyllo dough

1 tablespoon olive oil

To prepare the gazpacho: In a food processor equipped with a steel blade combine the vegetables, Anaheim chili, tomato juice, Scotch bonnet, and garlic. Run the processor until the ingredients are all well incorporated. Season with cumin, oregano, and sea salt. Then drizzle in the extra-virgin olive oil while the processor is running. Set this mixture aside.

To prepare the Brie: Cut the Brie into 6 small triangle wedges. Layer 3 phyllo sheets with a brush of olive oil between each. Cut the phyllo into 6 equal pieces and wrap a Brie wedge into each. Bake in a 350° oven for 10 minutes, until golden brown.

To serve: Strain the gazpacho through a sieve. It will be served at room temperature. Pour into 6 individual bowls and garnish each serving with hot baked Brie.

Mezuna, Fennel, and Green Mango

Jicama, Mango, and Watercress Salad
with Pecan Vinaigrette

Arugula, Romaine, and Almond Caesar Salad

Watermelon and Lychee Salad with Frisée

Wild Greens, Herbs, and Flowers

Bibb Lettuce, Pine Nuts, Yellow Raisins,
and Gorgonzola with Mustard Vinaigrette

Radicchio, Endive, Lemon, and Crab with Tomato Dust

Leaf Spinach with Oranges, Figs, and Bermuda Onion

Belgian Endive, Mustard Greens, and Black Truffles

CHAPTER 4
SALADS

My folks really believed that salads and vegetables were an integral part of dinner, so luckily these were on the table every day. We usually started with half a grapefruit, then had a salad before moving on to the main course. I remember what probably every American my age remembers—the ubiquitous iceberg lettuce with tomatoes and Russian dressing. Mayonnaise plus ketchup, something that Russians never dreamed of! Once in a while we had a variety of greens, but iceberg lettuce, along with shredded carrots, tomatoes, and cucumbers, were the mainstays of the sixties table.

The seventies brought us the American salad bar, which I must admit I don't understand—in terms of diet, sensible eating, or even delightful eating. It encourages people to gorge on a haphazard mixture of ingredients thrown together on a plate without thought or arrangement, and it's abundance in its worst guise. The classical version of salad, the way the French did and still do it, is a small salad with a light vinaigrette served after the main meal. At Chef Allen's we serve salads in two ways: as a course before the first that focuses mostly on different sorts of lettuces and wild greens, and as a first course, when the lettuce leaves and greens accent and give color and texture to focal items such as seafood, fruits, mushrooms, or vegetables.

Certainly there's nothing wrong with the familiar lettuces such as iceberg or romaine, but so many different types of greens are available now, it would be a shame not to experience them. If you were to taste the various leaves blindly, you'd discover different nuances ranging from grassy to peppery, sweet, herbaceous, minty, or reminiscent of licorice or anise. Radicchio and endive are assertive, while red oak leaf and butter or Bibb lettuces are soft and pleasant. If you haven't tried them yet, the readily available mesclun or baby lettuce mixes sold in supermarkets are not only convenient but lovely on a plate and to the palate.

I love to use edible flowers for color. I use them whole or chopped up. I cut them up into vinaigrettes or spread the petals on the salad leaves to endow them with a rainbow of hues. Lightly dressed, such a salad becomes not just a healthy choice, but a beautiful and exciting one.

MEZUNA, FENNEL, AND GREEN MANGO

SERVES 6

1   bunch mezuna

1   bunch arugula

1   head fennel

1   medium green mango

¼   cup lemon juice

½   cup extra-virgin olive oil

½   tablespoon sea salt

1   teaspoon fresh ground black pepper

Mezuna is a unique, sharp-edged peppery green with pointed triangular leaves. If you can't find it in your local market, dandelion greens will make a fine substitute.

To prepare the salad: Wash the mezuna leaves and the arugula, then dry them carefully. Pare away any blemishes from the fennel. Peel the mango and remove the flesh from the large center pit. Julienne both the fennel and the green mango, then toss them with a few tablespoons of lemon juice.

To make the vinaigrette: In a small bowl whisk together the remaining lemon juice and the olive oil. Season with the sea salt and black pepper.

To assemble and serve: Drizzle some of the vinaigrette on the salad leaves and arrange around the edge of the plate. Drizzle the remainder of the vinaigrette on the fennel and mango, and place them in the center.

On a recent excursion to Caracas, Venezuela, I cooked a New World Cuisine menu. This combination of jicama, mango, and watercress surprised—and delighted—the diners.

To prepare the salad: In a large bowl combine the jicama, mango, watercress, and red pepper. Toss with the Pecan Vinaigrette.

To serve: Divide the salad onto 4 chilled plates. Garnish each with 1 tablespoon toasted pecans and a pinch of fresh ground sea salt.

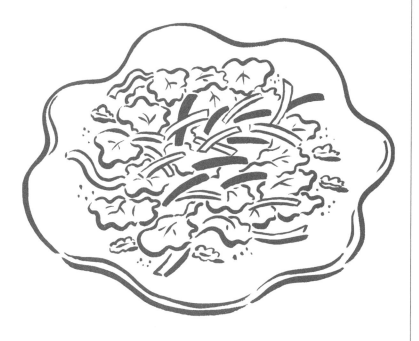

Combine the walnut and olive oils. In a steel bowl whisk together the oils and vinegar. Add the pecans, chives, parsley, and cilantro. Season with the salt and pepper.

JICAMA, MANGO, AND WATERCRESS SALAD WITH PECAN VINAIGRETTE

SERVES 4

- 1 cup julienned jicama
- 1 cup julienned mango
- 1 bunch watercress, cleaned
- 1 small red bell pepper, julienned
- 1/2 cup Pecan Vinaigrette (recipe follows)
- 1/4 cup toasted whole pecans
- 1/2 teaspoon fresh ground sea salt

PECAN VINAIGRETTE

MAKES 1/2 CUP

- 3 tablespoons walnut oil
- 3 tablespoons extra-virgin olive oil
- 3 tablespoons white vinegar
- 1 1/2 tablespoons chopped pecans
- 1 teaspoon chopped fresh chives
- 1 teaspoon chopped fresh flat-leaf parsley
- 1 teaspoon cilantro
- 1/4 teaspoon kosher salt
- 1/4 teaspoon fresh ground black pepper

ARUGULA, ROMAINE, AND ALMOND CAESAR SALAD

SERVES 6

1 bunch arugula

1 head romaine

1 clove garlic, halved

$1/2$ cup Parmesan cheese, $1/4$ cup grated, $1/4$ cup shaved

$1/4$ cup French bread croutons

$1/4$ cup Caesar Dressing (recipe follows)

3 tablespoons dry toasted almonds

CAESAR DRESSING

MAKES 1 CUP

1 large egg yolk

$1^1/2$ tablespoons Dijon mustard

$1/2$ large lemon, juiced

$1/2$ teaspoon chopped garlic

$1/4$ cup red wine vinegar

4 whole anchovies

$3/4$ cup extra-virgin olive oil

1 tablespoon chopped fresh chervil

To prepare the lettuce: Wash and carefully pat the lettuce leaves dry. The point is to preserve the shape and crispness of the leaves while drying them well enough so that the dressing is not watered down. Chill the dried leaves for 30 minutes in the refrigerator.

To prepare the salad: Rub the inside of a very large wooden bowl with the cut garlic clove. Add the chilled arugula and romaine. Add the grated Parmesan and the croutons and toss with the Caesar dressing.

To finish: Top the salad with the shaved Parmesan cheese and toasted almonds and serve.

In a food processor fitted with a steel blade combine the yolk, mustard, lemon, garlic, vinegar, and anchovies by pulsing them on and off. Through the top, add the olive oil in a steady drizzle with the machine running. Garnish with the fresh chervil.

This is a light, exotic, tangy, summery salad. To prepare the lychees, simply crack the leathery shells and the skin will peel off easily. Black sesame seeds are readily available in Oriental markets.

To prepare the salad: Cut the watermelon pieces into 1-by-1-inch cubes. Combine the watermelon, lychees, and frisée in a bowl.

To make the vinaigrette: Whisk together in a small bowl the tarragon, orange juice, lemon juice, olive oil, salt, and pepper.

To assemble: Toss the salad with the vinaigrette and garnish with the black sesame seeds.

WATERMELON AND LYCHEE SALAD WITH FRISÉE

SERVES 6

2   cups watermelon pieces

24 lychees, peeled

1   bunch frisée, torn

2   tablespoons chopped fresh tarragon

1/4 cup fresh orange juice

3   tablespoons fresh lemon juice

1/2 cup extra-virgin olive oil

1   teaspoon kosher salt

1   teaspoon coarse ground black pepper

2   teaspoons black sesame seeds

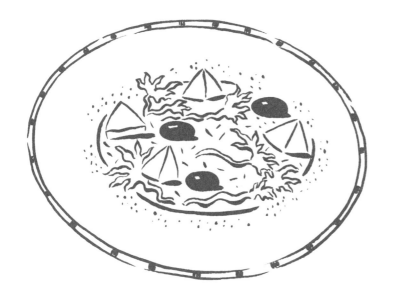

WILD GREENS, HERBS, AND FLOWERS

SERVES 6

3   cups wild greens, such as mustard greens, dandelion greens, frisée, tatsoi, or red oak leaf

2   tablespoons fresh tarragon leaves

2   tablespoons fresh chervil leaves

2   tablespoons snipped fresh chive

1   tablespoon fresh basil leaves

1   tablespoon fresh mint leaves

3   tablespoons petals of edible flowers

3/4 cup grape-seed oil

1/4 cup champagne vinegar

1/2 teaspoon kosher salt

1/2 teaspoon fresh ground black pepper

This is a splendid salad for early spring. The edible flowers—such as pansies, violets, hibiscus, and rose petals—together with the fresh herbs create an explosion of colors and aromas on the plate. Use the first-of-the-season wild greens, which are sweet, crisp, delectable.

To make the salad: Toss the greens, herbs, and flowers together in a bowl.

To make the vinaigrette: Whisk the grape-seed oil and champagne together in a small bowl with the salt and pepper.

Toss the salad with the vinaigrette and serve.

Because Bibb lettuce is grown in limestone sandy soil, it must be washed twice in cold water to remove all the sand and grit.

Wash the lettuce, place it in a bowl, and toss it with the mustard vinaigrette. Add the toasted pine nuts and raisins. Finish the salad by crumbling the gorgonzola in large pieces on its top.

In a stainless-steel bowl whisk the Dijon mustard and red wine vinegar together. Drizzle in the olive oil while whisking. Blend in the salt, pepper, and parsley.

BIBB LETTUCE, PINE NUTS, YELLOW RAISINS, AND GORGONZOLA WITH MUSTARD VINAIGRETTE

SERVES 6

2   heads Bibb lettuce

½   cup Mustard Vinaigrette (recipe follows)

3   tablespoons toasted pine nuts

2   tablespoons yellow raisins

2   tablespoons gorgonzola cheese

MUSTARD VINAIGRETTE

MAKES ½ CUP

1   tablespoon Dijon mustard

2   tablespoons red wine vinegar

6   tablespoons olive oil

¼   teaspoon sea salt

⅛   teaspoon fresh ground black pepper

1   tablespoon chopped fresh flat-leaf parsley

RADICCHIO, ENDIVE, LEMON, AND CRAB WITH TOMATO DUST

SERVES 6

1   head radicchio

1   head Belgian endive

3   tablespoons fresh lemon juice

1   tablespoon snipped fresh chives

1   tablespoon chopped fresh dill

1/2   cup crab meat, picked clean

1/2   teaspoon kosher salt

1/4   teaspoon dried red pepper flakes

3   tablespoons extra-virgin olive oil

1/4   cup tomato dust (see recipe head)

I make tomato dust with ripe red tomatoes. It's quite an easy process. Peel, seed, and slice the tomatoes. Using a dehydrator, slowly cook the sliced tomatoes at 110° for approximately 8 hours. Next, pulverize the dried tomatoes in a food processor, and then push them through a fine-mesh screen. Though the tomato dust adds a wonderful color, flavor, and texture to this dish, the salad can certainly be served proudly without it.

To prepare the salad: Cut the radicchio into a fine dice. Slice the endive crosswise into fine strips. Toss the lettuces with the lemon juice, chives, dill, and crab meat. Season with salt and pepper, and toss with a drizzle of olive oil.

To finish: Place the tossed salad in the center of an oversized, chilled plate. Dust the edge of the plate completely with the tomato dust.

Fresh figs are not available all year round, so I've composed this salad to work equally well with dried figs. The plump sweet figs of summer conjure up clear blue skies, warm grass, and long warm days in the shade; while the flavor of dried figs—wonderful in a winter salad—is about home, hearth, and the prolonging of our summer pleasures into cooler days.

To prepare the spinach: Wash the spinach leaves in several changes of cold water. Remove the fibrous stems and dry well.

To make the vinaigrette: In a small bowl whisk together the red wine vinegar, honey, walnut oil, salt, and pepper.

To prepare the figs: If you're using fresh figs, cut them into quarters. If dry figs are used, cut them into 10 to 12 small pieces.

To assemble: Combine the figs, spinach, oranges, and onions. Toss with the vinaigrette and serve.

LEAF SPINACH WITH ORANGES, FIGS, AND BERMUDA ONION

SERVES 6

2   cups leaf spinach

3   tablespoons red wine vinegar

1   tablespoon honey

5   tablespoons walnut oil

1/2   teaspoon kosher salt

1/2   teaspoon fresh ground black pepper

3   large fresh or dried figs

1   large orange, segmented

1   medium Bermuda onion, cut into rings

BELGIAN ENDIVE, MUSTARD GREENS, AND BLACK TRUFFLES

SERVES 6

2	medium fresh black truffles
4	heads Belgian endive
1	bunch mustard greens, cleaned
3	teaspoons lime juice
3	teaspoons extra-virgin olive oil
1/4	teaspoon sea salt
1/8	teaspoon fresh ground black pepper

The best, most aromatic, and flavorful fresh black truffles are available in late fall and winter and come from the Périgord region in France, although Italy has good black truffles as well. Summer truffles, which are one quarter the price, aren't nearly as rich. Although canned truffles are not nearly as aromatic as fresh ones, they're an acceptable flavor substitute here.

To prepare the truffles: Wash the truffles under cold running water. Using a small firm brush (I use a toothbrush), clean all the nooks and crannies. Dry the truffle well. With a very sharp French knife, cut very thin slices of truffle. If you like gadgets you can get a truffle cutter from a gourmet shop to shave the truffles thin. Then julienne these slices.

To prepare the salad: Julienne the Belgian endive crosswise. Separate the leaves and place them in a large wooden bowl. Add the mustard greens and truffles. Toss with the lime juice and olive oil. Season with sea salt and freshly ground black pepper.

GROUPER

Grouper Gravlax with Horseradish Cream
(first course)

Roasted Grouper Salad with Onion, Corn,
and Mustard Seeds (first course)

Roast Black Grouper with Mole Verde

Pistachio-Crusted Grouper with Rock Shrimp,
Leeks, and Coconut Rum

SNAPPER

Mangrove Snapper Brioche Cake (first course)

Blackened Red Snapper with Chayote and Plantains
served with Cool Orange Sauce

Yellowtail Snapper with Fennel, Orange, and Basil

TUNA

Tuna Carpaccio with Lime and Wasabi Cream
(first course)

Yellowfin Tuna Timbale with Ossetra Caviar
served with Lemongrass Crème Fraîche (first course)

Tuna Sashimi with Mango, Poblano,
and Toasted Pine Nuts (first course)

Citrus-Crusted Yellowfin Tuna
with Garlic, Ginger, and Lime

Charred Tuna and Moro Rice *served with* Mango Salsa

POMPANO

Pompano Mojo Creole (first course)

Pompano en Papillote with Fresh Black Truffle
served with Colorful Lime Butter

Grapefruit Barbecue Pompano with
Spicy Green Pigeon Pea Rice

COBIA

Cobia Ceviche with Papaya and Maui Onion
(first course)

Truffle-Roasted Cobia with Calabaza, Garbanzo Beans,
Wild Mushrooms, and Scotch Bonnet Broth

Pan-Roasted Cobia with Shallots,
Capers, and Boniato Lyonnaise

MAHIMAHI

Mahimahi Escabeche with Green Olives (first course)

Mahimahi with Sweet Corn Puree
and Fried Green Tomatoes

WAHOO

Grilled Wahoo with Caribbean Fines Herbes

Grilled Wahoo with Fricassee of Lobster, Mango,
and Fire-Roasted Peppers

SWORDFISH

Swordfish Escabeche *served with*
Preserved Lemon Zest (first course)

Swordfish with Conch-Citrus Couscous
and Macadamia Nuts

SHARK

Grilled Mako Shark and Shiitake Mushroom Brochette
served with Green Herb Pesto (first course)

Grilled Shark with Toasted Cumin and Celery Seed
served with Romesco Sauce

OTHER FISH

Parrot Fish with Hot Pepper Jelly and Cucumber Sticks
(first course)

Fish and Fruit Ratatouille (first course)

ish is my passion. Early mornings, when my purveyor arrives at the side door of Chef Allen's with a truckload of fish caught a few hours earlier, I can hardly wait to climb up the side of the cab to examine the bins of beautiful, bright-eyed species on ice. Now we all know that fish—whether or not it's a brain food—means smart and healthy eating, but my early experiences with fish did not turn me on to its possibilities.

In the fifties and sixties, one cooked fish until it flaked. Such overcooked fish—I remember in particular, halibut, flounder, gefilte fish, and dried-out fish sticks—was the reason I disliked it so much when I was a kid.

These days fish is what I sell most at Chef Allen's. When a customer says, "Your fish is so great, tell me what I'm doing wrong with mine," I ask, "How are you making it?" Usually the fillets are seasoned with fresh herbs and olive oil, which is fine, then put under a hot broiler for about twenty minutes, then turned over to continue broiling—which kills the fish a second time. "You're about fifteen minutes too late even before you turn the fish over," I say. Overcooking is the worst and most common crime home chefs commit against fish. Once you overcook it, the fish loses its texture and moisture and is never the same. James Beard advises ten minutes cooking time for every inch of thickness, which, to me, probably overcooks the fish, since it also continues to cook once you take it off the fire or out of the oven. It is better to allow only seven minutes for each inch of thickness, so that the fish is slightly underdone to preserve its natural oils and juices.

When you're cooking fish, you've got to use your hands. You need to touch the flesh to judge its firmness as the liquids and juices are being cooked out. It takes a little practice to be able to feel when a fish is done, but it's worth it. To put it simply, a cooked fish feels different from an uncooked fish.

Buy the freshest fish in the market, and that will help

you to decide what dish to make. How do you determine what's best, what's freshest? If you're looking at a whole fish, look for a glossy skin, clear eyes, intact red gills, good coloration without blemishes. Fillets should also be unblemished, bright and shiny. Ask to smell the fish—it should smell like fresh seawater. Fish should be stored on ice; if you're allowed to touch it, it should be cold. I'm not a fan of frozen fish, but if you're buying some, make sure it doesn't have any freezer burn, that it's well wrapped, and in good shape. Remember, you can only defrost frozen fish once. You can't defrost it, cut a piece, and refreeze it.

Fish spoils at home probably more often than in a fish store. You need to keep the fish cold while it's at home, and the best way to do that is to keep it on ice. If you wrap the fish in plastic wrap, then place it on ice in a deep pan and cover it with more ice, it will stay fairly fresh until you're ready to cook it that afternoon or the next day.

Nearly all white fish, such as grouper, snapper, and wahoo, are mild-tasting and tender, and their subtle flavors need to be either complemented or contrasted. Darker-fleshed fish tend to be richer and more assertive. As a broad generalization, thin fillets are usually white or light-fleshed, while thick fillets, as well as steaks, can be white, light, or dark.

People are looking for a lot more flavor from fish these days, which accounts for the popularity of the darker-fleshed fish such as tuna and salmon. The dark flesh that you sometimes see in tuna is the blood line that runs along the side of the center trunk (the loin) of the fish. These intensely colored areas aren't desirable for eating—although this is usually more as a matter of aesthetics than taste—and should be cut away.

As with red meat, cooking fish on the bone is another way to help maintain its flavor and integrity. I'm not talking about the little pin bones running along the ribs of a small snapper or grouper or salmon, which don't add flavor and should be removed before you cook the fish. If you have a choice between cooking a small fish whole or filleted, choose whole, and you'll wind up with a much more flavorful dish. Even with fish steaks, it's preferable to maintain the bone and remove it after cooking.

Fish is so flavorful in its natural state that I like to keep my recipes simple. The idea is to enhance and energize, rather than to smother its natural flavors. Once you understand the shapes of fish, the recipes in this book are pretty much interchangeable. First is the whole fish or round fish with the head on, including all the different varieties from red snapper to small groupers. Next is the steak, which is usually cross-cut to an inch or greater thickness. Finally there is the fillet, which is usually a thin cut along the length of the fish. If you work with these three shapes, you'll find it easy to substitute one fish for another in recipes. The way you cook a whole red snapper can be pretty much the way you cook a whole grouper or a whole yellowtail or a whole baby mackerel. Depending what's fresh and most available, most white pearly-fleshed fish can be substituted for one another, and the same goes for fish steaks.

Whether it's used for an hors d'oeuvre, first, or main course, fish is light, modern, healthy, simple to prepare, and delicious. It is elegant, satisfying, curiously purifying, and today lends itself to all sorts of marvelous inventions that your parents and grandparents never dreamed about. Taste the Blackened Red Snapper with Chayote and Plantains, for example; or the Yellowtail Snapper with Fennel, Orange, and Basil; or my Mahimahi with Sweet Corn Puree and Fried Green Tomatoes, and you will experience the best of what New World Cuisine has to offer.

Adventure, discovery, excitement, fulfillment, expansion. These are the ways that humans swim.

When you're working with the sweet white flesh of the grouper, a firm-textured fish, do not be afraid to pack it with assertive flavor.

To prepare the curing mixture: In a small bowl combine the black peppercorns, coriander seed, sugar, 2 tablespoons salt, and half the dill.

To prepare the gravlax: Rub the curing mixture onto the flesh sides of the grouper fillets. Drizzle with the vodka, then wrap the fillets with plastic wrap. Place the fillets in a flat pan under a weight in the refrigerator. After 12 hours turn the fillets, remove any liquid that has accumulated and let the fish cure for another 12 hours. After a full 24 hours, remove the fillets and scrape the curing mixture away. Coat with the rest of the fresh dill and slice the grouper thin across the grain (about 24 slices).

To prepare the horseradish cream: Combine the horseradish, sour cream, sherry vinegar, and the remaining salt. Let the flavors blend for 1 hour.

To assemble and serve: Spoon horseradish cream around the edge of each serving plate. Place 4 slices of gravlax fanned in the center of each plate. Garnish with sliced papaya.

GROUPER GRAVLAX WITH HORSERADISH CREAM

SERVES 6 AS A FIRST COURSE

1 tablespoon fresh ground black peppercorns

1/2 teaspoon ground coriander seed

1 teaspoon sugar

2 tablespoons plus 1/4 teaspoon kosher salt

1 bunch dill, chopped

1 pound grouper fillets, boned, skin on (about 1 or 2 large fillets)

3 tablespoons vodka

2 tablespoons horseradish

1 cup sour cream

3 tablespoons sherry vinegar

1 papaya, sliced

ROASTED GROUPER SALAD WITH ONION, CORN, AND MUSTARD SEEDS

SERVES 6 AS A FIRST COURSE

1   pound grouper fillets

2   teaspoons minced fresh thyme

2   teaspoons kosher salt

1 1/2   tablespoons olive oil

4   small onions, quartered

2   teaspoons whole mustard seeds

1   cup uncooked sweet yellow corn kernels

1   cup julienned radicchio

2   tablespoons fresh lime juice

1   tablespoon extra-virgin olive oil

2   tablespoons chopped fresh cilantro

The large white, flaky texture of cooked grouper lends itself well to this type of salad. The vegetables and grouper can be put into the oven at the same time but should be roasted separately so that their flavors remain distinct.

To roast the grouper: Preheat the oven to 325°. Season the grouper with 1 teaspoon of thyme and 1 teaspoon of salt, then coat it with the olive oil. Roast the fish for about 10 minutes, until the soft-flake stage.

To roast the vegetables: At the same time, season the onion with 1 teaspoon of thyme, 1 teaspoon of salt, and the mustard seeds and roast for 10 minutes. Add the corn to the onion and roast another 5 minutes. Remove from the oven and cool.

To combine the flavors: Hand-flake the grouper into a large bowl. Break apart the onion and add it to the fish together with the corn. Toss with the radicchio, add the lime juice, and toss once more. Mix well, though carefully, so as not to break up the fish. Cover and refrigerate for at least 3 hours but preferably for 24 hours.

To serve: Turn the whole salad mixture carefully and adjust the seasoning with extra-virgin olive oil and cilantro.

To season the grouper: In a small spice grinder grind the clove, allspice, peppercorns, and ½ teaspoon of the salt. Season the fish with the combination of dry spices.

To start the mole: Preheat the oven to 350°. In a dry hot sauté pan, toast the sesame and pumpkin seeds separately. Brown them evenly, developing a hearty aroma. This will add another layer of flavor to the mole. Roughly chop the romaine leaves and Swiss chard. Place the leaves in a small stainless-steel bowl and pour warmed white wine over them. Toss the leaves once or twice and then allow them to cool. Coat the poblano chilies with olive oil and roast them in the oven for 10 minutes to blister the skins. Remove from the oven and cool. Peel the skin and remove the seeds. Keep the oven on.

To finish the mole verde: Using a food processor, combine the wilted leaves, chilies, tomatillos, garlic, parsley, cilantro, and scallions. Add to this the toasted seeds and remaining salt. Pass the mixture through a fine sieve.

To roast the grouper: Coat the seasoned grouper with the mole verde. Roast the fish for approximately 6 minutes.

Serve with the Pigeon Pea Rice.

ROAST BLACK GROUPER WITH MOLE VERDE

SERVES 4

1	whole clove
3	whole allspice
6	whole black peppercorns
2	teaspoons kosher salt
4	6-ounce black grouper steaks
½	cup sesame seeds
½	cup pumpkin seeds
6	leaves romaine lettuce
6	leaves Swiss chard
½	cup dry white wine
2	large poblano chilis
1	teaspoon olive oil
6	medium tomatillos
2	cloves garlic
4	tablespoons fresh flat-leaf parsley
4	tablespoons fresh cilantro leaves
½	cup scallion pieces
2	cups Pigeon Pea Rice (see page 202)

PISTACHIO-CRUSTED GROUPER WITH ROCK SHRIMP, LEEKS, AND COCONUT RUM

SERVES 4

4   6-ounce grouper fillets

¼   cup pistachio nuts, whole, shelled and ground

1   tablespoon kosher salt

1   tablespoon coarse ground black pepper

3   tablespoons sweet butter

½   cup uncooked shelled rock shrimp

½   cup julienned leeks

½   cup peeled, chopped, seeded tomatoes

3   tablespoons coconut rum

¼   cup dry white wine

¼   cup coconut milk

3   tablespoons chopped fresh chives

This recipe calls for grouper fillets. I like to use black grouper but other varieties will work just as well. In fact, this recipe will be smashing with most white-fleshed fish.

To prepare the grouper: Roll the grouper fillets in the ground pistachio nuts. Season with 2 teaspoons each of the salt and pepper. Warm the butter in a sauté pan. When the butter is bubbling but before it begins to brown, place the crusted grouper in the pan. On medium heat, brown one side well for approximately 2 minutes, then turn and cook the other side an additional 2 minutes. Remove the fillets to a warm service platter. Be careful not to overcook the fish since it will continue to cook when it's removed from the pan.

To prepare the sauce: Add the rock shrimp to the pan. Sauté for 1 minute, then add the leeks, tomatoes, coconut rum, and white wine. Simmer the mixture for 2 minutes. Add the coconut milk and adjust the seasoning with the remaining salt and pepper. The sauce will have a broth-like consistency. Because of its richness, I like to keep it fairly thin. Finish with the chives.

Mangrove snapper is one of the many varieties available here in south Florida. Red snapper, gray snapper, or yellowtail snapper substitute beautifully for the mangrove snapper, but make sure to buy only the freshest fish available.

To prepare the cake mixture: In a skillet sauté the onion in 2 tablespoons of the clarified butter. Add the tomato, scallion, thyme, basil, cayenne, and garlic. Add the white wine and simmer until most of the liquid is evaporated, then remove from the heat. Combine the mangrove snapper and brioche crumbs with the vegetable mix. Add the orange zest and season with salt and pepper. Let this sit to incorporate the flavors for almost 1 hour. Shape into 12 cakes about 2 inches in diameter and ½ inch thick.

To finish and serve: In a pan sauté the snapper cakes in the remaining clarified butter, browning the first side well for 2 minutes before turning to cook the other side for about 1 more minute. Serve on a bed of fresh spinach leaves.

MANGROVE SNAPPER BRIOCHE CAKE

SERVES 6 AS A FIRST COURSE

1	small onion, diced
4	tablespoons clarified sweet butter
1	large tomato, peeled, seeded, and chopped
3	tablespoons diced scallion
½	teaspoon chopped fresh thyme
3	tablespoons chopped fresh basil
¼	teaspoon cayenne pepper
½	teaspoon minced garlic
¼	cup dry white wine
¾	pound boneless snapper fillets, finely diced
½	cup brioche crumbs
1	teaspoon orange zest
½	teaspoon kosher salt
¼	teaspoon fresh ground black pepper
2–3	cups fresh spinach leaves, washed and stemmed

BLACKENED RED SNAPPER WITH CHAYOTE AND PLANTAINS

SERVES 4

1   tablespoon fresh ground black pepper

1   tablespoon white pepper

1/2   tablespoon minced fresh basil

1/2   tablespoon minced fresh oregano

1/2   tablespoon minced fresh thyme

1/2   tablespoon fennel seed

3   tablespoons paprika

1/4   tablespoon cayenne pepper

2   tablespoons sea salt

4   6-ounce red snapper fillets, cleaned and deboned

4   tablespoons olive oil

1   medium chayote

2   ripe plantains

Bryan Miller, the former New York Times *food critic, thought so much of my blackened red snapper that he wrote in a review, "I would hop a Trailways local from New York to North Miami for another taste of Chef Allen's blackened red snapper with orange sauce. The picante spice mixture is offset beautifully by the semi sweet sauce."*

To prepare the snapper: Combine the seasonings in a small bowl. Generously season the snapper with some of the herb mixture. Drizzle the snapper with 2 tablespoons of the olive oil.

To prepare the chayote and plantains: Slice the chayote thin. Season the slices lightly with the herb mixture and drizzle with the remaining olive oil. Grill the chayote slices for 2 or 3 minutes, cooking them through. Roast the plantains in their skins for 20 minutes in a 350° oven. Remove the skins and slice the flesh thin, on a bias.

To cook the snapper: In a red-hot cast-iron pan sear the red snapper for 1 minute, then turn it and sear the other side. The fish should be cooked no longer than 2 minutes total.

To assemble and serve: Serve the fish with the plantains, chayotes, and Cool Orange Sauce.

ACCOMPANIMENT:
COOL ORANGE SAUCE

Zest the oranges and squeeze their juice. In a saucepan over medium heat combine the zest, juice, and sugar and reduce by one half. Add the Grand Marnier and reduce to a syrup. Remove from the heat. When cool, mix well with the yogurt.

COOL ORANGE SAUCE

MAKES ABOUT 1 CUP

- 2   large Florida oranges
- 2   tablespoons sugar
- 3   tablespoons Grand Marnier
- 1   cup low-fat plain yogurt

YELLOWTAIL SNAPPER WITH FENNEL, ORANGE, AND BASIL

SERVES 4

4   6-ounce yellowtail snapper fillets, skin left on

1   teaspoon sea salt

1   teaspoon fresh ground black pepper

2   tablespoons orange-fennel oil (see recipe head)

2   tablespoons diced shallots

3   tablespoons dark spiced rum

1   cup julienned fennel

2   large oranges, 1 juiced and the other segmented

½   cup clam broth

⅓   cup julienned fresh basil

The recipe calls for an orange-fennel oil that is very easy to prepare ahead: simply combine the zest of 2 oranges, 2 tablespoons dry toasted fennel seeds, 1 cup olive oil, and 1 cup extra-virgin olive oil, and set the mixture aside in a covered glass jar until ready to use.

To prepare the yellowtail snapper: Score the skin on the yellowtail so that it doesn't curl when you cook it. Season the fish with the salt and pepper.

To cook the yellowtail: In a heavy-bottomed sauté pan warm the orange-fennel oil. Place the yellowtail in the pan, skin side down, and cook over medium heat for about 2 minutes until the skin is browned and crispy. Turn the fish over and add the shallots. After a minute, deglaze with the rum. Remove the fish to a warm platter. Add the fennel and continue to sauté for 2 minutes. Add the orange juice and clam broth and continue to cook until the liquid is reduced by one half.

To serve: Place the sautéed fennel on a plate. Spread the julienned basil over the fennel, then place the yellowtail on top. Garnish with the fresh orange segments.

To prepare the tuna: Cut the tuna into four 2-ounce pieces. Carefully pound the tuna between 2 sheets of plastic wrap until it's thin enough to see through. It should form four approximately 6-inch circles. Refrigerate these in the plastic wrap.

To prepare the salad garnish: Very finely dice the arugula, endive, and red onion. Gently combine these with the flower petals, then set them aside.

To make the wasabi cream: Mix the wasabi, lime juice, and white vinegar to form a paste. Add this paste to the sour cream and season with salt. Put in a squeeze bottle.

To assemble and serve: Carefully remove the tuna carpaccios from the plastic and set them in the center of 4 serving plates. Garnish with the diced salad mixture and squeeze a wide back and forth swizzle of wasabi cream over all.

TUNA CARPACCIO WITH LIME AND WASABI CREAM

SERVES 4 AS A FIRST COURSE

1	8-ounce fresh yellowfin tuna steak
1/2	bunch arugula
1	head endive
1/2	medium red onion
2	whole edible flowers, separated into petals
1	teaspoon wasabi
1	teaspoon lime juice
1	teaspoon white vinegar
1/2	cup sour cream
1/2	teaspoon kosher salt

YELLOWFIN TUNA TIMBALE WITH OSSETRA CAVIAR

SERVES 6 AS A
FIRST COURSE

2   8-ounce fresh yellowfin tuna steaks

2   tablespoons chopped capers

2   tablespoons finely chopped red onion

1   tablespoon chopped fresh chives

1   tablespoon chopped fresh cilantro

1   teaspoon chopped jalapeño

1/2 teaspoon sea salt

1   ounce Ossetra caviar

1   small French bread, cut into points and toasted

To prepare the tuna: Clean the tuna and remove any silver skin and fiber from the meat. Chop very fine. Combine with the capers, red onion, chives, cilantro, jalapeño, and salt. Mix well. Fill six 3-ounce ramekin molds about three quarters full with the tuna tartare. Press and indent the center of the mold to form a small hollow. Fill this hollow with the caviar. Fill the rest of the mold with the remaining tuna, enclosing the caviar surprise in the center. Refrigerate until ready to use.

To serve: Ladle some crème fraîche sauce in the center of each serving plate. Unmold the tuna in the center of the sauce that is polka dotted with salmon caviar and chives. Garnish the tuna with warm French bread toast points.

ACCOMPANIMENT:
LEMONGRASS CREME FRAICHE

To prepare the sauce: In a medium saucepot combine the lemongrass, shallots, and white wine. Reduce over medium heat. Add the heavy cream after 2 minutes. Continue to reduce the liquid by half, approximately 5 minutes. Strain through a fine sieve. In a stainless-steel container, combine the sour cream, buttermilk, and lemongrass crème. Refrigerate this mixture for 2 hours.

To serve: Remove the sauce from the refrigerator and let it sit for 5 minutes. Add the chives and salmon caviar to garnish. Season with salt and pepper.

LEMONGRASS CRÈME FRAÎCHE

MAKES 1 CUP

1	bunch lemongrass, roughly chopped
2	large shallots, chopped
1	cup dry white wine
1	cup heavy cream
3	tablespoons sour cream
½	cup buttermilk
3	tablespoons chopped fresh chives
3	tablespoons salmon caviar
½	teaspoon kosher salt
½	teaspoon fresh ground black pepper

TUNA SASHIMI WITH MANGO, POBLANO, AND TOASTED PINE NUTS

SERVES 4 AS A
FIRST COURSE

½ pound tuna (bigeye tuna, sushi quality)

½ medium mango, diced fine

1 large plum, diced fine

1 medium poblano chili, diced

3 tablespoons toasted pine nuts

¼ cup grapefruit-ginger oil (see Note)

½ teaspoon fresh ground sea salt

Here's what happens when Japan and the Caribbean collide. The focus of this dish is the freshest possible tuna with condiments set around it to resemble a tartare platter.

To prepare the tuna: Nice and neatly, dice the tuna into very small cubes. Arrange the tuna in the center of a glazed enamel plate.

To finish the platter: Arrange the mango, plum, poblano, and pine nuts around the fish. Drizzle everything with grapefruit-ginger oil and sprinkle with the sea salt.

NOTE: To make grapefruit-ginger oil, combine the zest of 1 grapefruit, 1 tablespoon minced fresh ginger, and 1 cup extra-virgin olive oil in a small bowl. Set the mixture aside in a covered jar until ready to use.

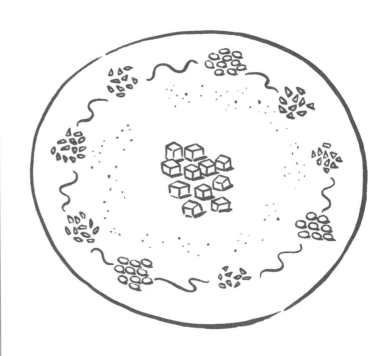

I try to undercook most fish a little because the flesh will continue to cook when removed from the heat. That's why I prefer to sear tuna, crusting the outside and leaving the center almost raw.

To prepare the crust: In a small saucepot combine the jalapeño, ginger, garlic, lime zest and juice, salt, peppercorns, sugar, and white wine. Simmer the mixture for 5 minutes on medium heat. Most of the liquid will be absorbed. Remove from the heat and cool.

To prepare the tuna: Pack the crust mixture onto the tuna steaks. Let them absorb some of the flavors for 20 minutes at room temperature before cooking. Preheat a heavy pan very hot for 5 minutes. Drizzle the tuna with olive oil, then sear for only about 30 seconds on each side. Serve.

CITRUS-CRUSTED YELLOWFIN TUNA WITH GARLIC, GINGER, AND LIME

SERVES 4

3   tablespoons finely chopped
     jalapeño

2   tablespoons finely chopped
     fresh ginger

1   tablespoon chopped garlic

3   tablespoons lime zest

3   tablespoons lime juice

1   tablespoon coarse salt

1   tablespoon crushed black
     peppercorns

2   tablespoons sugar

1   cup dry white wine

4   6-ounce tuna steaks,
     1½ inches thick

2   tablespoons olive oil

CHARRED TUNA AND MORO RICE

SERVES 4

4 6-ounce tuna steaks
2 teaspoons chopped lemon zest
2 teaspoons crushed black peppercorns
2 teaspoons peanut oil
1 tablespoon kosher salt
2 cups Moro Rice (recipe follows)

MORO RICE

SERVES 4

1 cup black beans
4 cloves garlic
1 medium carrot
2 bay leaves
1 teaspoon dried thyme
1 tablespoon kosher salt
1¹/₂ teaspoons coarse ground black pepper
1 cup white rice
3 teaspoons cider vinegar
2 tablespoons dry sherry

Charred rare tuna and Mango Salsa are naturals together. The little bit of heat and acid from the salsa perk up the tuna. Moro rice, which is made with black beans, is a staple of nearly every Cuban restaurant in Miami.

Coat the tuna with the lemon zest and peppercorns. Drizzle with peanut oil and season with salt. On the stove top, preheat a pan very hot for 5 minutes. Sear the tuna for only about 1 minute on each side. Remove from the heat and serve with Moro Rice and the Mango Salsa.

To cook the black beans: Wash the beans under running cold water. Place the beans in a large saucepot with enough water to cover, approximately 8 cups. Add the garlic, carrot, bay leaves, thyme, salt, and pepper. Bring the beans to a boil and reduce the heat to a simmer. Simmer for approximately 1³/₄ hours, until the beans are tender. Remove the garlic and carrot.

To cook the rice: Add the rice to the black beans and mix well. There should be enough liquid left for the rice to cook in; if not, moisten with another cup of water. Bring to a boil and reduce to a slow simmer. Cook for 20 minutes on this low heat. Add the cider vinegar and sherry, mix well, and remove from heat.

ACCOMPANIMENT:
MANGO SALSA

The popularity of salsa, we are told, has surpassed that of ketchup in America. This one uses mango and papaya instead of the more ordinary tomato for an intense tropical experience.

To prepare the fruit: Peel the mango and cut the flesh away from the center seed. Peel the papaya and clean away the black seeds. Dice both into small cubes.

To make the salsa: In a large bowl combine the mango and papaya cubes, red pepper, onion, jalapeño, and cilantro. Season with the cumin, olive oil, and fresh lime juice.

MANGO SALSA

SERVES 4 (1 CUP)

1	large mango
1/2	large papaya
1/2	medium red bell pepper, diced
1/2	medium red onion, diced
1	small jalapeño, diced fine
2	tablespoons chopped fresh cilantro
2	teaspoons ground cumin
2	tablespoons extra-virgin olive oil
2	tablespoons fresh lime juice

POMPANO MOJO CREOLE

SERVES 4 AS A FIRST COURSE

¼ cup olive oil

1 medium onion, diced

4 cloves garlic

1 teaspoon sea salt

1 cup sour orange juice (or see recipe head)

1 teaspoon fresh ground black pepper

4 4-ounce pompano fillets

1 lime, sliced

2 tablespoons fresh mint leaves

2 tablespoons fresh cilantro

The bittersweet taste of sour orange, which grows in many south Florida backyards, is an essential flavor in many Caribbean dishes. If you can't find fresh sour oranges, you can substitute ¼ cup lime juice plus ¾ cup orange juice for 1 cup sour orange juice.

To prepare the mojo: In a saucepot, warm together the olive oil, onion, garlic, and salt, and simmer this mixture for 10 minutes. Add the sour orange juice and black pepper. Simmer for 5 more minutes. Then remove from the heat.

To braise the pompano: Preheat the oven to 350°. Place the pompano fillets in a shallow oven pan. Spoon the mojo mixture over the pompano until the liquid comes halfway up the sides of the fish fillets. Braise the fish for about 5 minutes. Remove from the oven carefully.

To serve: Carefully transfer the pompano to a large serving plate. Spoon the mojo sauce over the fillets and garnish the plate with the lime slices, mint leaves, and cilantro.

Pompano is one of Florida's prized fish. In this recipe, pompano's rich yet delicate flavor combines with the rich flavor of truffles for a marvelous fusion of sea and earth.

To prepare the pompano: Season the pompano with ¹/₂ teaspoon of the salt and ¹/₄ teaspoon of the pepper.

To make the truffle mixture: In a bowl combine the leek, truffle, extra-virgin olive oil, white wine, and remaining salt and pepper.

To prepare the parchment: Using a pair of scissors, carefully cut a heart-shaped piece approximately 10 inches across out of each parchment sheet.

To assemble: Lightly butter a sheet of parchment paper. Put one pompano fillet in the center of the right half. Top with a quarter of the sliced tomatoes, alternating in red and yellow "shingles." Top this with a quarter of the truffle mixture. Seal the papillote by folding the left half over the right half. Crease and fold 2 inches of the upper corner of parchment together. Continue to crease and fold at 2-inch intervals, sealing the parchment as you work around and down the pompano, turning the last fold under the parchment. Repeat this for each of the fillets.

To bake: Preheat the oven to 350°. Bake the papillote for approximately 5 minutes. The parchment will be browned and puffed.

To serve: Cut through the center of the papillote. Roll back the edges to reveal the colorful interior and release the aroma. Place a medallion of Colorful Lime Butter on top of the fish so the butter is melted before serving.

ACCOMPANIMENT:
COLORFUL LIME BUTTER
SEE NEXT PAGE

POMPANO EN PAPILLOTE WITH FRESH BLACK TRUFFLE

SERVES 4

- 4 medium pompano fillets
- 1 teaspoon kosher salt
- ¹/₂ teaspoon fresh ground black pepper
- 1 large leek, julienned
- 1 medium truffle, julienned
- 2 tablespoons extra-virgin olive oil
- 1 tablespoon white wine
- 4 sheets parchment paper
- 1 tablespoon sweet butter
- 1 large red tomato, sliced thin
- 1 large yellow tomato, sliced thin

COLORFUL LIME BUTTER

SERVES 4

¼ pound sweet butter, softened

1 teaspoon snipped fresh chives

1 teaspoon chopped fresh tarragon

1 tablespoon julienned edible flowers

1 teaspoon pink peppercorns

¼ teaspoon kosher salt

1 small lime, freshly squeezed for juice

1 sheet parchment paper

The edible flowers, herbs, and pink peppercorns make this a wonderfully seasoned and beautifully colored butter that can be used to finish a variety of fish or seasoned dishes.

To prepare the ingredients: Combine all the ingredients except the parchment in a small bowl. Mix until well incorporated.

To roll the butter: Place the flavored butter in the parchment paper and roll it into a cylinder. Refrigerate for 1 hour before using. This may be kept refrigerated for days, or frozen for several weeks, if desired.

To serve: Remove the butter from the refrigerator and parchment paper. Cut into ⅓-inch-thick butter medallions.

Here is another of my barbecue favorites, one that is certain to dazzle.

To prepare the grapefruit: Put the grapefruit zest in a small saucepot, add cold water to cover and bring to a boil. Remove the zest. Boil it again in a fresh change of cold water. This removes the bitterness from the skin. Now cook the zest into a simple grapefruit syrup by combining it with the sugar and 1 cup water and simmering the mixture for 30 minutes. The liquid should be reduced to about 1/2 cup.

To prepare the grapefruit barbecue: Add to this grapefruit syrup the chili-garlic sauce, soy sauce, honey, lime and grapefruit juices. Continue to simmer for another 20 minutes until syrupy in consistency. Remove from the heat and cool. The sauce can be stored in a glass jar for 2 weeks.

To barbecue the pompano: Heat the grill for 10 minutes. Brush the pompano fillets generously with the sauce and grill for about 1 1/2 minutes on each side. (If you prefer to "barbecue" this pompano in the broiler on high heat, it will take about the same time.) Serve with the Spicy Green Pigeon Pea Rice.

GRAPEFRUIT BARBECUE POMPANO WITH SPICY GREEN PIGEON PEA RICE

SERVES 4

2 large grapefruits, zested and juiced.

1 cup sugar

1 cup water

4 tablespoons chili-garlic sauce (available in most Oriental markets)

3 tablespoons dark soy sauce

2 tablespoons honey

2 tablespoons lime juice

4 6-ounce pompano fillets

2 cups Spicy Green Pigeon Pea Rice (recipe follows)

SPICY GREEN PIGEON PEA RICE

SERVES 4

1/3 cup chopped sweet Spanish onion

1 1/2 tablespoons olive oil

1 teaspoon minced garlic

1 1/2 cups uncooked white rice

2 cups water

1 bay leaf

1/3 teaspoon minced fresh thyme

2 teaspoons kosher salt

2/3 teaspoon coarse ground black pepper

1 teaspoon ground cumin

1 Scotch bonnet

2/3 cup cooked pigeon peas

2 tablespoons chopped oregano leaves

3 tablespoons chopped parsley leaves

3 tablespoons chopped cilantro leaves

1 1/2 tablespoons extra-virgin olive oil

Pigeon peas are eaten as extensively in the Caribbean islands as in the American South. When I was introduced to them in a native Puerto Rican dish, I quickly adapted them to my New World Cuisine.

To cook the rice: In a large saucepot combine the onion and olive oil; cook until the onion is translucent. Add the garlic, then the white rice, water, bay leaf, thyme, salt, pepper, cumin, and Scotch bonnet. Bring the mixture to a boil, reduce the heat to low, and simmer for 20 minutes. Do not stir after it has boiled, and be careful later not to break the Scotch bonnet, which, cooked whole, has a wonderful hot citrus flavor. Remove the rice from the heat and take out the Scotch bonnet and bay leaf. Add the pigeon peas and stir.

To finish the rice: Add the oregano, parsley, cilantro, and extra-virgin olive oil. Mix well and serve.

Cobia is a fish indigenous to the Caribbean and the Gulf of Mexico. Its texture, with firm white meat and large white flakes, makes for an excellent ceviche. Chop the Scotch bonnet wearing plastic gloves and remove the ribs and seeds. And be forewarned: this is a dish with plenty of heat.

To prepare the cobia: Cut the fillets into evenly diced pieces about 1 inch long and ¹/₂ inch wide. It is important to prepare an even cut so they "cook" evenly—that is, so that the acid in the citrus juices penetrates the fish pieces evenly.

To "cook" the ceviche: In a large stainless-steel bowl marinate the cobia in the lime and lemon juices. Be sure there is enough juice to cover the fish completely. Let this sit for 1 hour. Add the Scotch bonnet, cilantro, Maui onion, and salt. Mix well, being careful not to break up the fish. Cover and refrigerate for about 3 hours, preferably for 24.

To serve: Turn the whole mixture carefully and adjust the seasoning with salt and pepper. Garnish with the freshly sliced papaya.

COBIA CEVICHE WITH PAPAYA AND MAUI ONION

SERVES 6 AS A FIRST COURSE

1   pound boneless cobia fillets

³/₄   cup fresh lime juice

³/₄   cup fresh lemon juice

¹/₂   medium Scotch bonnet, diced fine (see recipe head)

¹/₄   cup chopped fresh cilantro

1   cup julienned Maui onion

1   tablespoon sea salt

Fresh ground black pepper, to taste

1   large firm ripe papaya, sliced

TRUFFLE-ROASTED COBIA WITH CALABAZA, GARBANZO BEANS, WILD MUSHROOMS, AND SCOTCH BONNET BROTH

SERVES 6

2   pounds cobia fillets, boned and trimmed

7   tablespoons olive oil

½   bunch thyme

2   teaspoons cracked peppercorns

2   teaspoons kosher salt

4   tablespoons truffle dust (see recipe head, page 143)

1   cup fresh mixed wild mushrooms

½   teaspoon chopped garlic

1½   cups dry white wine

½   cup diced sweet onion

½   cup diced celery

To prepare the cobia: Rub the fillets with 2 tablespoons of the olive oil and season it with thyme sprigs (reserving 3 sprigs for the broth), 1 teaspoon of the cracked peppercorns, ½ teaspoon salt, and the truffle dust. Marinate for 1 hour.

To prepare the wild mushrooms: Clean the wild mushrooms and separate the stems from the caps. In a sauté pan warm 1 tablespoon of the olive oil with the garlic. Sauté the cleaned mushroom caps for 2 minutes, season with ½ teaspoon salt, and add ½ cup of the white wine. Set aside.

To prepare the Scotch bonnet broth: In a heavy stockpot sweat the onions in 2 tablespoons of olive oil for 5 minutes. Add the celery, leeks, and the remaining cup of white wine. Simmer this for several minutes, then add the bay leaf, reserved thyme, and the Scotch bonnet, being careful not to break the skin of the chili. Add 3 cups of water and bring the broth to a boil. Lower the heat and simmer for 45 minutes. Then strain, skim, and season with ½ teaspoon of salt. Two cups should be the yield.

To prepare the garbanzo beans: Using a pressure cooker, cook the garbanzo beans for 20 minutes in ½ cup of water, ½ teaspoon salt, and the remaining cracked peppercorns. (If you don't have a pressure cooker, cook the beans in a heavy-bottomed pot in 2 cups of water with the lid on.) Remove from the heat. When the pressure has dissipated, remove the garbanzo beans, toss with the remaining 2 tablespoons of olive oil, and set aside.

To prepare the calabaza: In a small sauté pot cook the calabaza in 1 cup of the Scotch bonnet broth for about 15 minutes, until tender. Remove from the broth and reserve.

To roast the cobia: Preheat the oven to 400°. Roast the cobia for 5 minutes, then turn the fish. Reduce the heat to 350° and continue to cook for another 5 minutes. Remove the fish.

To assemble and serve: To the roasting pan, add the sautéed mushrooms, the garbanzo beans, and the calabaza. Add enough broth (approximately 1 cup) to moisten the vegetables well. Add the cream, tarragon, and chervil. Simmer on top of the stove, reducing the broth for 3 minutes to incorporate the flavors and herbs. Generously ladle the calabaza, garbanzo, and wild mushroom–Scotch bonnet broth onto a plate. Slice the roast cobia into ½-inch-slices and serve on top of the broth.

½	cup diced leeks
1	bay leaf
1	Scotch bonnet
3½	cups water
1	cup garbanzo beans
¼	medium calabaza (Caribbean pumpkin), peeled and diced
2	tablespoons heavy cream
1	teaspoon chopped fresh tarragon
1	teaspoon chopped fresh chervil

PAN-ROASTED COBIA WITH SHALLOTS, CAPERS, AND BONIATO LYONNAISE

SERVES 4

2   cups peeled, thinly sliced boniato

1   cup julienned sweet onion

6   tablespoons olive oil

1   tablespoon kosher salt

1   teaspoon coarse ground black pepper

3   tablespoons chopped fresh cilantro

4   6-ounce cobia fillets

3   tablespoons diced shallot

1/4 cup dry red wine

3   tablespoons capers

When I was young, my mother always served us fish with potatoes. Even though I didn't appreciate the flavors then, somehow the sense of balance on my mother's plates was being stored in my taste banks.

To roast the boniato Lyonnaise: Preheat the oven to 350°. Season the boniato and onion with 3 tablespoons of the olive oil and 2 teaspoons of salt and 1/2 teaspoon pepper, then roast in the oven. When the vegetables begin to brown, after approximately 10 minutes, turn them over and roast for another 10 minutes. Remove from the oven, sprinkle with the chopped cilantro, and keep warm. Do not turn off the oven.

To pan-roast the cobia: Season the cobia with 1 teaspoon of salt and 1/2 teaspoon pepper. Warm the remaining olive oil in an ovenproof pan on top of the stove. Brown one side of the cobia fillets, then turn them over, add the shallots, and transfer the pan to the hot oven. After 3 minutes, add the red wine and capers. Roast for 2 more minutes and remove from the oven.

To serve: Serve the fish with its natural pan juices and the boniato Lyonnaise.

Since the escabeche is predominately white with green accents, I like to serve this on an orange or yellow platter with the onions and olives arranged in the center. Snapper or grouper can be substituted for the mahimahi.

To cook the fish: Season the fish with salt and pepper. In a skillet fry the fish over medium heat in just a few tablespoons of the olive oil, browning both sides for only about 1 minute. Remove the fish to an earthenware bowl to cool.

To prepare the escabeche mixture: In a heavy pan combine the onions, garlic, bay leaves, peppercorns, vinegar, and the remaining oil. Warm together for 5 minutes, then add the olives. Pour the mixture over the fish, and cover tightly overnight. Keep the bowl covered for up to several days in the refrigerator to allow the flavors to intensify.

MAHIMAHI ESCABECHE WITH GREEN OLIVES

SERVES 4 AS A FIRST COURSE

4	4-ounce mahimahi fillets
1/2	teaspoon sea salt
1/4	teaspoon coarse ground black pepper
1	cup extra-virgin olive oil
2	onions, sliced
2	cloves garlic
2	bay leaves
1	teaspoon whole peppercorns
1/2	cup white vinegar
20	green olives

MAHIMAHI WITH SWEET CORN PUREE AND FRIED GREEN TOMATOES

SERVES 4

3   ears sweet corn
2   cups chicken stock
1   bay leaf
1   clove garlic
1/2   cup whole milk
1   tablespoon kosher salt
1   teaspoon coarse ground black pepper
4   6-ounce mahimahi fillets
2   tablespoons olive oil
1/4   cup dry white wine
8   slices Fried Green Tomatoes (recipe follows)

FRIED GREEN TOMATOES

SERVES 4 TO 6

2   large green tomatoes
1   tablespoon kosher salt
1/2   tablespoon coarse ground black pepper
1   cup cornmeal
1 1/2   cups peanut oil for frying

Mahimahi, or as we used to call it here in Florida, dolphin, is one of our local fish. Make no mistake, it's the fish, not the mammal, that's used in this recipe. Flipper is still alive and well in Miami.

To prepare the sweet corn puree: Cut the corn kernels off the cob. We're using both corn and cob here. Place both in a medium saucepot. Add the chicken stock, bay leaf, and garlic clove, bring to a boil, and reduce the heat to a simmer. Cook for 20 minutes. Then add the milk, 1 teaspoon of salt, and 1/2 teaspoon pepper, and continue to simmer for 10 minutes. Remove the corn cobs and bay leaf. Puree the liquid in a food processor or with a processor wand. Adjust the seasoning. Keep warm until ready to serve.

To prepare the mahimahi: Season the fillets with the remaining salt and pepper. Warm the olive oil in a sauté pan and cook the mahimahi for 3 or 4 minutes on one side, browning it well. Turn the fish and continue to cook for another 2 minutes, then drain the oil. Add the white wine and sweet corn puree to the mahimahi and finish cooking for another minute.

Serve with crisp Fried Green Tomatoes.

Tart green tomatoes pan-fried with a crust of cornmeal add a great texture to many dishes.

To prepare the tomatoes: Cut the tomatoes into 3/4-inch-thick slices. Season with the salt and pepper, then dredge in the cornmeal.

To fry the tomatoes: Warm the peanut oil in a heavy-bottomed skillet; the oil should be about 1/2 inch deep. When the oil is hot, pan-fry the tomato slices, browning them well on both sides, overall about 1 minute. Drain the finished slices on paper towels.

Fines herbes—a classic in French cuisine—is a combination of fresh chives, parsley, chervil, and tarragon that is often used to enhance the flavor of fresh fish or to beautify butter. My Caribbean fines herbes are a combination of fresh oregano, tarragon, cilantro, and chives accompanied by the flavor of fresh citrus.

To prepare the Caribbean fines herbes: In a small bowl combine the herb leaves, orange juice, and extra-virgin olive oil. Set this aside.

To grill the wahoo: Preheat a grill. Season the wahoo with the salt and pepper and drizzle with the olive oil, then cook on a very hot grill. The wahoo is a fish that requires care to avoid overcooking. It takes only a few minutes for its flesh to firm and turn white. Remove from the grill and immediately top with the combined fines herbes.

GRILLED WAHOO WITH CARIBBEAN FINES HERBES

SERVES 4

1   teaspoon chopped fresh oregano

1   teaspoon chopped fresh tarragon

1   teaspoon chopped fresh cilantro

1   teaspoon snipped fresh chives

2   tablespoons orange juice

1   tablespoon extra-virgin olive oil

4   6-ounce wahoo steaks

1   teaspoon sea salt

1   teaspoon fresh ground black pepper

2   teaspoons olive oil

GRILLED WAHOO WITH FRICASSEE OF LOBSTER, MANGO, AND FIRE-ROASTED PEPPERS

SERVES 6

6   4-ounce wahoo steaks

5   tablespoons olive oil

1   tablespoon fresh thyme leaves

1   tablespoon cracked black peppercorns

1   teaspoon kosher salt

1   large red bell pepper

3   tablespoons diced sweet onion

1   12-ounce spiny lobster tail, split and diced fine, shell reserved

1   teaspoon chopped fresh ginger

1/2   teaspoon chopped garlic

1/4   cup dry white wine

1   cup Lobster Broth (recipe follows)

1   medium mango, peeled and diced fine

This preparation was one of my early New World creations. Its combination of flavors and textures helped to hook me on the tropical cuisine and island pleasures.

To marinate the wahoo: Marinate the wahoo in 2 tablespoons of the olive oil, the thyme, peppercorns, and kosher salt for at least 30 minutes at room temperature or 1 hour refrigerated.

To prepare the red peppers: Roast the red pepper on an open flame until seared black on all sides. Set aside in a bowl covered with a towel for 15 minutes. Then peel, skin, and seed. Dice evenly in 1/2-by-1/2-inch pieces.

To make the fricassee: Warm the remaining 3 tablespoons of olive oil in a large sauté pan. Sauté the onion until translucent, then add the lobster, ginger, and garlic and sauté over medium heat for 2 minutes. Deglaze the pan with the white wine, and then add the broth. After 30 seconds add the diced red pepper and mango. Bring to a simmer and lower the flame. Add the coconut milk and reduce the sauce for 3 minutes. Remove from the heat and add the chervil and cilantro.

To cook the wahoo: Preheat the grill. A wood-burning or gas grill would be best. A broiler will suffice. The fish should cook for no more than a total of 3 minutes.

To assemble and serve: Cover the bottom of a serving plate with the fricassee. Put the wahoo in the center, and garnish with the carambola slices.

2 tablespoons coconut milk

2 tablespoons fresh chervil
leaves

2 tablespoons fresh cilantro
leaves

1 large carambola, sliced

Put the water in a large stockpot and add the celery, onions, and leeks. Add the garlic, lobster shells, peppercorns, bay leaf, and white wine. Bring to a boil and lower the heat to a slow simmer. Cook for about 30 minutes. Strain and reserve the broth.

LOBSTER BROTH

3 cups cold water

$\frac{1}{2}$ cup diced celery

1 cup diced onion

$\frac{1}{2}$ cup chopped leeks, green
part only

3 cloves garlic

3 cups lobster shells (reserved
from lobster tail)

5 whole white peppercorns

1 bay leaf

1 cup dry white wine

SWORDFISH ESCABECHE

SERVES 6 AS A FIRST COURSE

1   pound swordfish

½   cup freshly squeezed lemon juice

½   cup freshly squeezed lime juice

2   bay leaves

2   cups white vinegar

1½   tablespoons coarse sea salt

2   tablespoons minced jalapeño

¼   cup finely diced red bell pepper

¼   cup finely diced yellow bell pepper

½   cup julienned onion

¼   cup chopped fresh chives

3   tablespoons chopped fresh cilantro

1   cup extra-virgin olive oil

1   head Bibb lettuce

PRESERVED LEMON ZEST

SERVES 6 (½ CUP)

2   ripe lemons

1   cup kosher salt

½   cup olive oil

I learned this version of escabeche from Alain Sailhac, my mentor during the seventies at Le Cirque in New York City. This is something of a cross between ceviche and escabeche and represents one of my earliest culinary exposures to "Latin" cuisine.

To prepare the swordfish: Cut the swordfish into a baton shape approximately 2 inches long and ½ inch thick. Place the swordfish in a stainless-steel bowl, cover it with the lemon and lime juices, and add the bay leaves. Let it "cook" for 1 hour at room temperature. Afterward, drain the swordfish in a colander. Wash the fish with the vinegar by pouring the vinegar over the draining fish.

To marinate the swordfish escabeche: Return the fish to the bowl. Season it with the salt and add the jalapeño, bell peppers, onion, chives, and cilantro. Toss well but carefully. Add the olive oil to cover the mixture completely. Cover with plastic wrap and refrigerate for 24 hours.

To serve: Arrange the Bibb lettuce on an oversized platter. Spoon the escabeche of swordfish onto the lettuce. Garnish with Preserved Lemon Zest.

ACCOMPANIMENT: PRESERVED LEMON ZEST

To preserve the lemons: Wash and dry the lemons well. Cut each into 8 wedges. Toss them with the salt. Place in a small glass jar and close tightly. Let the lemons cure at room temperature for 28 days. Shake the jar occasionally to incorporate the sediment.

To serve: When ready to use, remove the lemon wedges from the jar. Rinse well under running water and cut away the flesh. Julienne the skin. To store, add olive oil to cover and refrigerate. It will keep indefinitely.

Swordfish is one of the most versatile fish in the world. It's easy to handle, and its firm texture, both raw and cooked, makes it as simple to cook as a steak.

To prepare the couscous: Warm 2 tablespoons of the olive oil in a large sauté pan. Add the shallots and cook until translucent. Add the garlic and conch and cook for 1 minute. Add the lime zest and white wine, toss well, and add the couscous. Let this simmer for a minute, then add the macadamia nuts and scallion. Keep warm until ready to serve.

To prepare the swordfish: Preheat the broiler very hot. Season the swordfish with the thyme, salt, and pepper. Drizzle with the remaining olive oil. Broil the swordfish for 3 or 4 minutes on each side.

Serve the fish with the couscous, adjusting the seasoning with salt and pepper.

NOTE: Grind conch in a meat grinder (or you can finely chop it). If you ask your "fish guy," he will be happy to grind it for you.

SWORDFISH WITH CONCH-CITRUS COUSCOUS AND MACADAMIA NUTS

SERVES 4

4	tablespoons olive oil
2	tablespoons chopped shallots
1	tablespoon chopped garlic
¼	cup ground conch (see Note)
2	tablespoons lime zest
½	cup dry white wine
2	cups cooked couscous
2	tablespoons macadamia nut halves
2	tablespoons chopped scallion
4	6-ounce swordfish steaks
1	teaspoon minced fresh thyme
1	teaspoon kosher salt
½	teaspoon coarse ground black pepper

GRILLED MAKO SHARK AND SHIITAKE MUSHROOM BROCHETTE

SERVES 6 AS A FIRST COURSE

1 pound mako shark steak

2 tablespoons annatto oil (see page 9)

1 teaspoon chopped garlic

12 large rosemary branches, each approximately 3 inches long

12 medium shiitake mushrooms, stems removed

1 teaspoon sea salt

½ teaspoon fresh ground black pepper

Shark is one of those fish that cooks well in cubes on the grill or broiler. Other circular flaked fish, such as swordfish, wahoo, or tuna, can be substituted for the shark.

To prepare the shark: If the shark meat comes with its skin, remove it first. Cut the shark steak into 1-by-1-inch cubes (approximately 12 pieces). Place them in a stainless-steel bowl, and add the annatto oil and garlic.

To prepare the rosemary: The plan here is to use the rosemary branch as a brochette skewer. Remove the rosemary leaves from most of the branch leaving a few leaves on the end as decoration.

To make up the brochettes: Add the shiitake caps to the seasoned shark mixture—just to coat them lightly. Then alternately skewer 2 pieces of shark and 2 pieces of shiitake on each brochette. Season with salt and pepper.

To cook the brochettes: Preheat the grill or broiler very hot. Grill the brochettes quickly, turning them with a pair of kitchen tongs every 30 seconds. Try to keep the end with rosemary leaves out of the flame (or you may have to cover the rosemary leaves with aluminum foil while cooking) in order not to singe them. The brochettes should be finished after about 2 minutes of cooking. Remove from the heat.

To serve: Using about 1 cup total of Green Herb Pesto, spoon about 3 tablespoons of the pesto on each colorful individual plate, spreading it out just evenly with the back of the spoon. Serve 2 brochettes on top of each pesto-lined plate.

ACCOMPANIMENT:
GREEN HERB PESTO

In a food processor, using a metal blade, puree all the ingredients. Stored in a covered jar in the refrigerator, the pesto will keep for up to 3 weeks.

GREEN HERB PESTO

MAKES 3 CUPS

3   tablespoons chopped fresh chives

3   tablespoons chopped scallions

1   teaspoon chopped garlic

3   tablespoons chopped fresh cilantro

3   tablespoons chopped fresh basil

$^1/_2$ cup capers

$^1/_2$ cup grated Parmesan cheese

$^3/_4$ cup pine nuts

$^1/_3$ cup extra-virgin olive oil

GRILLED SHARK WITH TOASTED CUMIN AND CELERY SEED

SERVES 4

2   tablespoons cumin seed

2   teaspoons celery seed

1   tablespoon black peppercorns

1   teaspoon kosher salt

3   tablespoons olive oil

4   6-ounce shark steaks

Shark is an exceptionally flavorful fish. But because of its very dense flesh, care must be taken to avoid overcooking it, or the fish will lose its moisture.

To toast the spices: In a dry sauté pan over medium heat slowly toast the cumin, celery, and black peppercorns. This allows the rich aromatic oils to be released. Remove from the heat and add the salt and olive oil.

To grill the shark: Preheat a grill. Rub the shark steak with the spiced oil and grill over medium-high heat, searing both sides. A shark steak approximately 1 inch thick should grill for a total of 5 minutes.

To serve: Place the Romesco Sauce on a large oval platter and arrange the shark steaks on top of the sauce.

ACCOMPANIMENT:
ROMESCO SAUCE

In this recipe I use chipotle chili, which is a large, dried, sweet, smoked jalapeño with medium heat and a nutty finish. To prepare it for this recipe, roast the chili in the oven at 350° for just 3 minutes. Then transfer the chili to a pot with water and simmer for 5 minutes.

In a small ovenproof pan roast the tomato and garlic at 350° for 30 minutes.

While this is roasting, heat 1 tablespoon of the olive oil and fry the crusty bread until golden on both sides. Transfer this to a food processor. Add another tablespoon of olive oil and the toasted almonds to the processor. Process together, then add the roasted tomato and garlic, the vinegar, and the smoked chili pepper. While the machine is running, drizzle in the remaining olive oil. Season with salt and pepper, strain through a fine sieve, and serve at room temperature.

ROMESCO SAUCE

MAKES 1 CUP

1   large tomato, quartered

5   cloves garlic

1/2   cup olive oil

1   slice crusty bread

1/4   cup toasted almonds

1/4   cup sherry vinegar

1   large smoked chili pepper (see recipe head)

1   teaspoon kosher salt

1   teaspoon fresh ground black pepper

PARROT FISH WITH HOT PEPPER JELLY AND CUCUMBER STICKS

SERVES 6 AS A FIRST COURSE

1½ pounds parrot fish fillets

Kosher salt and fresh ground black pepper

2 tablespoons all-purpose flour

1 medium orange, zested and juiced

3 tablespoons sour orange juice

½ cup hot pepper jelly

2 tablespoons sweet butter

2 tablespoons Grand Marnier

2 tablespoons clarified butter

1 medium chayote, julienned

½ medium seedless cucumber, cut into batons (double matchstick size)

1 teaspoon chopped fresh thyme

½ teaspoon ground allspice

Parrot fish is not eaten often and is seldom fished commercially, but its colorful stripes make it one of the favorite fish of scuba divers in the Caribbean. Snapper or tile is a fine substitute for the parrot fish in this dish.

To prepare the parrot fish: Season the parrot fish with the salt and pepper and dust very lightly with the flour.

To prepare the pepper jelly mix: Combine the orange and sour orange juices and the hot pepper jelly in a saucepan over medium heat. Reduce the mixture to half its volume, about 4 minutes, and let cool.

To cook the parrot fish: Preheat the oven to 350°. In a hot ovenproof pan, melt the butter. Just before the butter starts to smoke slightly, place the fillets in the pan. Cook for 2 minutes, until well browned on one side. Turn the fillets, add the pepper jelly mix, and finish cooking the fish in the oven for 2 more minutes. When it's done, top with the orange zest and flambé with the Grand Marnier. Remove from the pan and transfer to a serving platter.

To sauté the cucumber and chayote: Heat the clarified butter in a skillet and sauté the chayote and cucumber for about 1 minute, until just softened. Season with the salt, pepper, thyme, and allspice.

To assemble and serve: Arrange the sautéed cucumber and chayote around the parrot fish in an orderly fashion.

Classical Mediterranean ratatouille is a vegetable dish consisting of eggplant, zucchini, onions, green peppers, and tomatoes. Fruit and fish bring the flavor of the Caribbean to this New World ratatouille, which can be served hot or cold.

To prepare the fish: Cut the swordfish into large cubes. Season the fish with 1 teaspoon of the salt and let it sit at room temperature for 1 hour. Then rinse the fish and dry the cubes well. Warm 2 tablespoons of the olive oil in a heavy skillet and sauté the fish, carefully browning it on all sides, for about 1 minute. Remove the fish from the pan.

To prepare the ratatouille: Sprinkle the eggplant with the remaining salt. Let it sit for 1 hour, then rinse and dry as you did the fish. To the same hot pan the fish cooked in, add the remaining olive oil and quickly sauté the eggplant. Add the papaya, plantain, and peppers. Finally, add the tomato, scallion, and the cooked fish. Season with the oregano, thyme, garlic, and fresh ground black peppercorns.

To serve: Remove the mixture from the heat and sprinkle with the extra-virgin olive oil. Serve immediately, or allow to cool and serve at room temperature.

FISH AND FRUIT RATATOUILLE

SERVES 6 AS A FIRST COURSE

- 1 pound swordfish steak
- 2 tablespoons kosher salt
- 4 tablespoons olive oil
- 1 small eggplant, diced fine
- 1 cup finely diced green papaya
- 1 cup finely diced green plantain
- 1 medium yellow bell pepper, diced fine
- 1 medium red bell pepper, diced fine
- 1 large tomato, peeled, seeded, and diced
- 2 tablespoons chopped scallion
- 2 teaspoons chopped fresh oregano
- 1 teaspoon chopped fresh thyme
- 1 teaspoon diced garlic
- 1 teaspoon fresh ground black peppercorns
- 3 tablespoons extra-virgin olive oil

CHAPTER 6
SEAFOOD AND SHELLFISH

ROCK SHRIMP
Rock Shrimp Hash *served with* Cayenne-Mustard Aioli
(first course)
Rock Shrimp Risotto

SHRIMP
Truffle-Dusted Shrimp with Calabaza, Saffron,
and Leeks (first course)
Citrus-Crusted Shrimp with Starfruit, Ginger,
and Rum (first course)
Shrimp Poached in Orange Juice, Ginger,
and Sauterne
Shrimp and Lychees with Passion-Fruit Sauce

PRAWNS
Grilled Prawns with Curry Oil *served with*
Gingered Tropical Fruit Paella (first course)
Caribbean Freshwater Prawns with Tarragon,
Tomato, and Mustard
Prawns Stuffed with Green Apple, Dill,
and Red Onion

STONE CRAB
Stone Crab Frappe (first course)
Stone Crab Salad with Tangerine, Grapefruit,
and Mustard Seeds (first course)
Stone Crab Cobbler with Coconut Milk, Chilies,
Key Limes, and Coriander

CRAB
Crab Tian with Potato, Tomato, and Citrus *served with*
Manzanilla Olive Tapenade (first course)
Soft-Shell Crabs with Three Nuts (first course)

LOBSTER

Smoked Spiny Lobster with Pickled Bermuda Onion
served with Boniato Salad (first course)

Martini of Lobster, Olives, and Lime (first course)

Lobster Scotch Bonnet Cake *served with*
Strawberry-Ginger Chutney (first course)

Crisp Lobster Strudel with Chayote and Almonds
(first course)

Roast Lobster with Chilies, Saffron, Vanilla, and Rum

Lobster Cassoulet with White Beans, Conch,
Orange Zest, and Seafood Sausage

Lobster and Yams à la Nage with Candied Lemon Zest

CALAMARI

Grilled Calamari with Hot Mango Salsa (first course)

Roast Calamari with Green Lentils *served with*
Orange Balsamic Syrup (first course)

MUSSELS

Red Hot Curried Conch and Mussels (first course)

Mussels and Mango Moquecas

SCALLOPS

Jumbo Sea Scallops with Jamaican Blue Mountain
Coffee and Vanilla Bean (first course)

Tournedos of Jumbo Scallops Wrapped in Leeks

SEAFOODS

Local Seafood Minestrone with Clams, Calamari,
and Rapini

Seafood Choucroute

Seafood Sausage

Back in Brooklyn, when I was growing up, my family kept a kosher household. During autumn, winter, and spring, we studied, worked, and attended to the traditions of our faith through ritual prayers and food. But summers, spent in a bungalow on Coney Island, we swam, played, idled away our days, and once a week went to the amusement park for the rides, and, of course, to Nathan's. Nathan's is where, at the age of ten, I tasted seafood for the first time. Liberated from the routine of school, on a warm seaside afternoon, I experienced the crunch, sweetness, and heat of Nathan's fried shrimp with cocktail sauce—a classic along with their hot dogs and French fries.

I first became aware of mussels and calamari in the Italian neighborhood around Sheepshead Bay, at a large, noisy eating establishment called Lundy's. I remember the waiters—who seemed enormous—running through the restaurant with huge sizzling platters of fried calamari and mussels. But it wasn't until I was a young adult in cooking school that I learned how to prepare mussels. We did them simply, with white wine, shallots, and garlic. I didn't really begin to appreciate what could be done with calamari until I traveled and sampled my way through the restaurants of Italy.

My initiation into crab meat came during my apprenticeship at the Bristol Hotel in Paris, where I had the task of preparing stuffed crab with shallots and brandy. This involved picking through the meat to remove the shells and cartilage, preparing the stuffing mixture, and then stuffing it back into the crabs. I must admit that the vast number I was required to prepare prevented me from falling instantly in love with the crabs, but I was more than ready for my first experience with conch, a large mollusk indigenous to Caribbean waters.

I was already possessed by the New World spirit when I found myself in a small restaurant on a back street in Nassau, near the straw market. I must have been hungry as well, because that afternoon I tried conch every way the restaurant prepared it—as ceviche, cracked conch, conch fritters, and conch chowder. So much conch is eaten in the Bahamas that just outside the Nassau harbor is a virtual island consisting of the conch shells thrown overboard by the people who process the conch meat on boats. In the United States, most of the available conch is frozen, though we are starting to see the fresh product from conch farms on the Turks and Grand Caicos Islands. The meat is tough until tenderized, but it has a sweet, dense, fresh seawater flavor. I prefer conch to snails—which I like—any day, especially when it's the star of dishes such as my Conch and Garbanzo Bean Chili with Fried Green Tomatoes.

Stone crabs, of course, are the quintessential south Florida seafood—and a pleasure accessible to people living beyond our balmy Caribbean climate only since jets have made travel fast, and the global village and New World Cuisine possible. Stone crabs are caught in traps that are hoisted up on fishing boats. The claws are pulled off for boiling and chilling on board, and the crabs are tossed back to regenerate new claws. Although stone crabs are fabulous served the way they are bought in the market, cold, with an accompaniment of mustard sauce, they are transcendent when cooked in a stone crab cobbler with chilies, tomatillos, corn, and coconut milk.

You'll find it easy to substitute one seafood for another in most of the recipes in this book. Lobster, whether Maine or Florida (also called Bahamian, spiny, or rock) is generally sweeter and firmer than shrimp, which is juicier and more flavorful. Because it is so perishable, shrimp is generally available only frozen, either individually or in blocks. Unless you are traveling through the Florida Keys, the shrimp you see in the fish markets have been defrosted, so you can't freeze them again. The lobsters you buy should be lively in the tank. The best and largest scallops come from the Northeast, particularly from the waters around Nantucket. Scallops, both the small bay and the larger sea, are plumply sweet. They offer a great salt brine flavor and a fabulous food surprise when prepared with Jamaican Blue Mountain coffee and vanilla bean.

Seafood is synonymous with luxury, but there is really no reason to avoid incorporating it into your weekly dining at home. It may be more expensive than fish, but it is so sweet and satisfying that a little goes a long way. If you remember that the dense flesh of seafood tends to continue cooking off the heat, and so aim for undercooking, nothing is quite as simple and quick to prepare. Seafood is also versatile enough to beg for bold invention. If you love shrimp cocktail, try my recipe for Warm Shrimp Cocktail with mashed potatoes and horseradish, or Rock Shrimp Hash with Cayenne-Mustard Aioli, which addicts in my restaurant have been known to order for dessert.

It's been a long time since I was a boy at Coney Island, biting into my first fried shrimp on an afternoon when all my senses were quickened by the sun and ocean air. The sea and what it has to offer has become my Emerald City: Toto, I guess I'm not at Nathan's anymore.

Hash is a real comfort food. The contrast between its crisp exterior and its warm, soft interior is delightful—and delightful too are all the different versions of hash that can be made, ranging from seafood to meat to vegetables. The only limit is your imagination.

Prepare the potato for hash: Preheat the oven to 350°. Bake the potatoes for 1 hour. Let them cool completely. Peel the potatoes and grate on the largest holes of a hand grater.

To make the rock shrimp mixture: In a stainless-steel bowl combine the rock shrimp, chives, tomato, garlic, basil, cayenne, egg whites, matzo meal, and cognac. Mix well. Add the grated potato.

To cook the hash: Form the hash into 12 ovals with a large kitchen spoon. Let these chill for 30 minutes. Warm the olive oil in a small cast-iron pan. Carefully cook the hash in the oil, browning one side for 2 minutes and then for 2 minutes on the other. Garnish a plate with ½ table-spoon of Cayenne-Mustard Aioli and place the hash in the center.

ACCOMPANIMENT: CAYENNE-MUSTARD AIOLI

Aioli is a French-style homemade mayonnaise infused with garlic, and a traditional accompaniment to bouillabaisse and cold French salads. I added the cayenne pepper for that special New World bite.

To prepare the garlic: Roast the garlic head whole for 1 hour in a 300° oven. Let it cool, cut it in half, and squeeze the pulp into a food processor fitted with a steel blade.

To prepare the aioli: Add the egg yolks, mustard, cayenne, and lemon juice. Pulse together. Drizzle the olive oil into the mixture with the machine running, and season with salt. Press the sauce through a fine sieve and chill for 1 hour before use.

ROCK SHRIMP HASH

SERVES 6 AS A FIRST COURSE

- ½ pound red potatoes
- ½ pound uncooked rock shrimp, peeled and deveined
- ½ bunch chives, snipped
- 1 medium tomato, peeled, seeded, and diced
- 1 teaspoon chopped garlic
- 1 tablespoon chopped fresh basil

Pinch cayenne pepper

- 2 large egg whites
- 1 tablespoon matzo meal
- 1 tablespoon cognac
- ¼ cup olive oil

CAYENNE-MUSTARD AIOLI

SERVES 6

- 1 head garlic
- 3 large egg yolks
- 2 tablespoons Dijon mustard
- 1 tablespoon cayenne pepper
- 1 large lemon, freshly squeezed
- 1 cup olive oil
- 1 teaspoon kosher salt

ROCK SHRIMP RISOTTO

SERVES 8

3 tablespoons annatto oil (page 9)

½ cup chopped Spanish onion

1½ cups arborio rice

¾ cup dry white wine

5½ cups warm clam broth

1 pound cleaned uncooked rock shrimp

1 tablespoon kosher salt

2 teaspoons coarse ground black pepper

2 teaspoons chopped garlic

3 tablespoons sweet butter, at room temperature

¼ cup freshly grated Parmesan cheese

3 tablespoons chopped fresh chives

Rock shrimp is one of our local Florida natives. Their sweet tender meat is protected against natural enemies by a rock-hard shell. Luckily, most shrimp today are sold shelled, so you don't have to worry about removing each and every rock coat.

To cook the risotto: In a heavy pot warm 2 tablespoons of the annatto oil. Add the onion and cook until translucent. Add the arborio rice and cook for another minute, stirring well. Add half a cup of the white wine and half a cup of the clam broth and stir. As the liquid is absorbed, add another half cup of broth. Continue to cook, stir, and add warm broth in this manner for 20 minutes.

To prepare the rock shrimp garnish: Warm the remaining annatto oil. Add the rock shrimp and sauté for a few moments, seasoning it with 1 teaspoon salt and 1 teaspoon pepper. Add the garlic and deglaze the pan with the remaining white wine. Add the rock shrimp mixture to the risotto. By this time almost all of the clam broth will have been added to the risotto. While continuing to mix the risotto, add the butter and Parmesan cheese. Season with the remaining salt and pepper and garnish with the chopped chives.

Oregon white truffles, dried in a slow oven over-night, can be transformed into a transcendent substance I call "truffle dust." When you cook the shrimp, the dried truffles are rehydrated with the flavor of the shrimp juices. The result is pure bliss. To make truffle dust, simply dry the truffles very well in a slow oven (200°) overnight. Then pul-verize them in a clean coffee or herb grinder until they are the texture of semicoarse ground pepper. Dry mushrooms such as porcini or chanterelles make a delicious substitution if truffles are not available.

To prepare the shrimp: Remove the shells, split the shrimp down the back, and clean them. Roll the shrimp in the truffle dust, season them with salt and pepper, and let sit for 1 hour at room temperature.

To infuse the saffron: To bloom the flavor and color of the saffron, warm the white wine in a small pot and add the saffron. Remove from the heat and let the mixture steep for 20 minutes.

To blanch the calabaza: Add the calabaza to a pot of boiling salted water. When the water returns to a boil, re-move from the heat and set the calabaza aside to cool still in the water.

To begin cooking: In a sauté pan melt 2 tablespoons of the butter. Add the shrimp and sauté them for 2 minutes over medium heat. Add the leeks and red pepper. Add the saffron/wine infusion and the calabaza. Remove the shrimp and set aside on a warm plate. Swirl in the re-maining tablespoon of butter. Serve the sauce under the truffle-dusted shrimp.

NOTE: If calabaza is not available use pumpkin.

TRUFFLE-DUSTED SHRIMP WITH CALABAZA, SAFFRON, AND LEEKS

SERVES 4 AS A FIRST COURSE

16	uncooked jumbo shrimp
2	tablespoons truffle dust (see recipe head)
1/4	teaspoon kosher salt
1/4	teaspoon fresh ground black pepper
1	cup dry white wine
1	teaspoon saffron
1	cup diced calabaza (see Note)
3	tablespoons sweet butter
1/2	cup diced leeks
1	medium red bell pepper, diced

CITRUS-CRUSTED SHRIMP WITH STARFRUIT, GINGER, AND RUM

SERVES 4 AS A FIRST COURSE

2 lemons, zested and juiced

2 limes, zested and juiced

2 tablespoons light brown sugar

1 tablespoon minced jalapeño

½ tablespoon crushed black peppercorns

½ teaspoon coarse salt

3 tablespoons olive oil

12 uncooked large shrimp

1 teaspoon chopped fresh ginger

1 medium starfruit, sliced crosswise

3 tablespoons rum

This is a marvelous first course with warm-weather flavors. The zest is removed from the fruit with a zester or vegetable peeler, then chopped fine to form a colorful crust for the shrimp, which become packed with concentrated citrus oils.

To prepare the citrus crust: In a small saucepan combine the lemon and lime juices with the brown sugar and simmer for 1 minute. Add the lemon and lime zests, the jalapeño, peppercorns, and salt. Cook for 1 minute more and remove from the heat. Moisten with 1 teaspoon of the olive oil and let cool.

To prepare the shrimp: Peel and devein the shrimp. Butterfly by cutting them lengthwise so that they open like a book and lie almost flat. Do not cut them all the way through. Press the cooled citrus crust onto both sides of the shrimp. Warm the remaining olive oil in a pan until just before it smokes. Sear the shrimp on both sides. Cook for 1 minute, then add the ginger and starfruit. Add the rum, swirling it around in the pan for a few seconds, and serve immediately.

This simple combination of flavor and technique is always a winner. Poaching, one of the easiest techniques to master, is too often overlooked for methods of sizzle and fire.

Place all the ingredients in a low-sided pan with a lid and slowly warm over low heat to just about a simmer. Cover the pan and let this easy simmer poach the shrimp for 3 or 4 minutes. The shrimp should be rosy pink and firm to the touch. Remove from the heat and serve with all the ingredients.

SHRIMP POACHED IN ORANGE JUICE, GINGER, AND SAUTERNE

SERVES 4

16	uncooked jumbo shrimp, peeled, cleaned, and butterflied
2	cups freshly squeezed orange juice
2	tablespoons julienned fresh ginger
1/2	cup sauterne wine
2	cups julienned shallot
2	cups julienned carrot
1	teaspoon kosher salt
1	teaspoon coarse ground black pepper

SHRIMP AND LYCHEES WITH PASSION-FRUIT SAUCE

SERVES 4

1   pound uncooked large shrimp

1   teaspoon kosher salt

2   tablespoons olive oil

24   fresh lychees, peeled

1   tablespoon chopped fresh ginger

1/2   cup dry white wine

1/2   teaspoon dried red pepper flakes

1/4   cup chopped scallion

4   passion fruit

Fresh lychees are in season for just a few weeks from late May through early June. But they retain their distinctive flavor even when frozen or canned, so buy these when you can't get the fresh fruit.

To prepare and cook the shrimp: Peel and devein the shrimp and season them with the kosher salt. Warm the olive oil in a saucepan. Add the shrimp and sauté for 2 minutes on medium heat until pink. Add the lychees, ginger, and the white wine, and cook for 30 seconds. Add the red pepper and scallion. Toss again and set aside off the heat after 1 minute.

To assemble and serve: Cut the passion fruit in half and scoop out the flesh onto 4 serving plates. Reserve 4 fruit shell halves, one for each plate. Serve the shrimp in the passion-fruit cup to one side of the passion-fruit pulp.

For this recipe I leave the shells on the shrimp to preserve their natural juices.

To prepare the curry oil: In a stainless-steel bowl moisten the curry powder with just enough water to form a paste. Add the olive oil and mix well. Pour the mixture into a clear glass jar and let it set overnight. The curry will settle to the bottom. Skim off the "curry oil" into another, smaller jar. Discard the sediment. The curry oil can be stored for up to 1 month.

To marinate the prawns: To infuse this terrifically hot and lively flavor, cut the prawns down the back but leave the shells on. Marinate them with 3 tablespoons of curry oil, the garlic, red pepper flakes, and salt for 30 minutes at room temperature or 1 hour refrigerated.

To grill the prawns: Heat the grill or oven broiler. Place the prawns on the grill and cook the first side for approximately 1 minute, then 1 minute on the other to finish. Baste with the marinade. Serve with the Gingered Tropical Fruit Paella.

ACCOMPANIMENT:
GINGERED TROPICAL FRUIT PAELLA
SEE NEXT PAGE

GRILLED PRAWNS WITH CURRY OIL

SERVES 4 AS A FIRST COURSE

- 4   tablespoons curry powder
- 1   cup olive oil
- 8   uncooked jumbo prawns or shrimp
- 1   tablespoon chopped garlic
- 1/4 teaspoon red pepper flakes
- 1/2 teaspoon kosher salt

GINGERED TROPICAL FRUIT PAELLA

SERVES 4 (2 CUPS)

1	medium onion, diced
4	tablespoons olive oil
1	teaspoon minced fresh thyme
½	teaspoon ground turmeric
1	teaspoon kosher salt
1	cup arborio rice
2½	cups chicken broth
1	tablespoon chopped garlic
2	tablespoons chopped fresh ginger
1	large red bell pepper, diced
½	small pineapple, diced
1	medium mango, diced
1	large starfruit, sliced crosswise
1	medium papaya, diced
4	large dates, diced
2	tablespoons rum

Think about the best paella you've ever eaten— and then dream on, to include ginger, pineapple, mango, starfruit, and papaya. This is what I'd want to eat it I were shipwrecked on an ocean island.

To prepare the rice: Cook the onion in 2 tablespoons of the olive oil until translucent, then add the thyme, turmeric, salt, and rice. Stir well. Add the broth, stir once, and set on low heat for 20 minutes.

To prepare the paella: In a large sauté pan warm the garlic and ginger in the remaining olive oil, then add the diced red pepper. Add the fruits and sauté for 1 minute. Add the rum to the hot pan and ignite the liquor to flambé before adding the cooked rice. Toss all together carefully until thoroughly incorporated and serve.

After dining in the French town of Dijon, I knew mustards would always be part of my cuisine. The French Old World influence is also exerted in this recipe by the tarragon, with its slight licorice scent. The New World is represented by some beautiful local Caribbean prawns.

To prepare the prawns: In a large sauté pan warm 2 tablespoons of the olive oil. Add the prawns, then season them with ½ teaspoon salt and ¼ teaspoon black pepper. Sauté for 2 minutes, then add 2 tablespoons of the Pernod, the tomato, and the Dijon mustard. Remove from the heat and sprinkle with 2 tablespoons of the tarragon.

To prepare the mushrooms: Brush and clean the mushrooms and cut them into quarters. Warm the remaining olive oil in another sauté pan and cook the mushrooms for about 2 minutes. Add the garlic, season with remaining kosher salt and black pepper, Pernod and tarragon.

To serve: Place the mushrooms in the center of an oversized serving platter and arrange the prawns around the platter's edge.

CARIBBEAN FRESHWATER PRAWNS WITH TARRAGON, TOMATO, AND MUSTARD

SERVES 4

4 tablespoons olive oil

12 uncooked prawns, peeled, cleaned, and deveined

2 teaspoons kosher salt

1 teaspoon fresh ground black pepper

3 tablespoons Pernod

1 cup peeled, seeded, and diced tomato

3 tablespoons Dijon mustard

3 tablespoons chopped fresh tarragon

3 cups wild mushrooms (your favorite)

1 tablespoon minced garlic

PRAWNS STUFFED WITH GREEN APPLE, DILL, AND RED ONION

SERVES 4

12 uncooked jumbo freshwater prawns in the shell

1   teaspoon kosher salt

1/2 teaspoon coarse ground black pepper

2   tablespoons cognac

1   cup peeled and finely diced green apple

1/2 cup finely diced red onion

1/4 cup chopped fresh dill

1   tablespoon sweet butter, at room temperature

2   tablespoons fresh French bread crumbs

I created this dish for a champagne dinner I held for Mumm's champagne. The green apple and onion add texture and excitement to the soft meat of the prawns, and the dill helps round out the flavor of all three ingredients. If you can't find freshwater jumbo prawns, you can substitute regular jumbo shrimp.

To prepare the prawns: Split the prawns open from head to tail in their shells. Clean out the vein and head portion. Season with 1/2 teaspoon of salt and 1/4 teaspoon of pepper and drizzle with the cognac.

To prepare the stuffing: In a small bowl combine the apples, onion, dill, butter, and bread crumbs. Season with the remaining salt and pepper. Stuff the head cavities of the prawns with the mixture. Use any remaining stuffing to fill in the tail portions.

To finish the prawns: Preheat the oven to 350°. Place the stuffed prawns in an ovenproof dish and bake for 6 to 8 minutes. The shells will turn bright red and the stuffing should be well browned.

Stone crab meat is rich but addicting, so buy at least two claws, preferably jumbo, for each person. Serve the claws cold with the mustard sauce, garnished with starfruit or Key limes. If Key limes are not available, use fresh lime juice, but do not attempt to substitute bottled lime juice—a pale version that lacks the acidity of the real thing.

To prepare the stone crab claws: Crack the stone crab claws with a wooden mallet by firmly tapping in the center of each knuckle and claw until the shell gives way. The meat should be removed carefully.

To prepare the mustard sauce: In a large glass bowl whisk together the sour cream, heavy cream, honey, Dijon and Pommery mustards. Season the mixture with the cayenne, Key lime juice, salt, and allspice. The sauce will be smooth and rich. Chill the sauce for 30 minutes.

To serve: Arrange the stone crab knuckle—meat and claws—in 4 chilled large stem goblets. Pour the sauce over the claws.

STONE CRAB FRAPPE

SERVES 4 AS A FIRST COURSE

8   jumbo stone crab claws

1   cup sour cream

¼   cup heavy cream

3   tablespoons honey

5   tablespoons Dijon mustard

3   tablespoons Pommery mustard

½   teaspoon cayenne pepper

¼   cup fresh Key lime juice

1   teaspoon sea salt

⅛   teaspoon ground allspice

STONE CRAB SALAD WITH TANGERINE, GRAPEFRUIT, AND MUSTARD SEEDS

SERVES 6 AS A FIRST COURSE

3 medium tangerines

1 large grapefruit

2 teaspoons fresh ground black pepper

1 medium jalapeño, ribs and seeds removed, chopped fine

1 large Anaheim pepper, ribs and seeds removed, chopped fine

1 medium red bell pepper, cut into thin strips

1/2 bulb fennel, cut into thin strips

2 tablespoons chopped fresh cilantro

2 teaspoons sea salt

1 tablespoon extra-virgin olive oil

1 tablespoon dry-toasted mustard seeds

1 tablespoon cider vinegar

18 large stone crab claws, shells removed (see page 151)

The popularity of stone crabs has increased dramatically in the United States and Japan, so we can be grateful for their unique biological trick. When they're caught, stone crabs can release their claws and survive to regenerate new ones—as many as three or four times.

Peel and segment the tangerines and grapefruit, removing the seeds.

In a stainless-steel bowl, combine the black pepper, jalapeño, Anaheim, red pepper, fennel, and the fruit and marinate for 1 hour. Add the cilantro, salt, olive oil, mustard seeds, and cider vinegar. Chill and serve with the stone crab claws.

Once you experience the aroma from this dish coming out of the oven, you'll know what angels would eat if they ate Caribbean. It combines the sweet richness of stone crab claws with coconut milk, the heat of the chilies, and sweet toasty corn beneath a cobbler crust.

To prepare the stone crab mixture: Crack the stone crabs and remove all the meat from the cartilage, but reserve the claws and knuckle meat separately. In a medium saucepan warm the olive oil. Sweat the shallots until translucent. Add the tomatillos, corn, and Anaheim chili. Flavor this mixture with the coriander, ginger, curry, rum, and ¾ cup of the coconut milk. Add the knuckle meat and simmer for 3 or 4 minutes; season with ¾ teaspoon of salt.

To prepare the cobbler top: In a stainless-steel bowl mix together the flour, ¼ teaspoon of salt, the sugar, and baking powder. Add the softened butter until the mixture is the consistency of fine pebbles. Add the key lime zest, cilantro, and the remaining coconut milk until it binds together into a lumpy paste—be careful not to overwork the dough. It should remain rough so that when it bubbles up on top of the cobbler, it develops a free-form crust.

To bake the cobbler: Preheat the oven to 350°. Place the mixture in a small ovenproof dish. Top with the stone crab claws and the cobbler topping. Bake for 8 minutes, or until the top begins to brown well. Serve immediately.

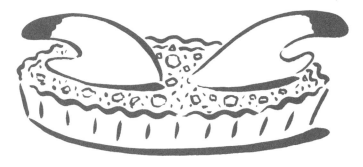

STONE CRAB COBBLER WITH COCONUT MILK, CHILIES, KEY LIMES, AND CORIANDER

SERVES 6

12	large stone crab claws
2	tablespoons olive oil
2	large shallots, diced
4	medium tomatillos, diced
1	cup corn kernels
1	large Anaheim chili, diced
½	teaspoon ground coriander seeds
½	teaspoon chopped fresh ginger
½	teaspoon curry powder
3	tablespoons dark Jamaican rum
1¼	cups unsweetened coconut milk
1	teaspoon kosher salt
1	cup all-purpose flour
1	teaspoon sugar
1½	teaspoons baking powder
3	tablespoons sweet butter, softened
1	tablespoon key lime zest
1	tablespoon chopped fresh cilantro

CRAB TIAN WITH POTATO, TOMATO, AND CITRUS

SERVES 6 AS A FIRST COURSE

1   pound jumbo lump crab meat

3   tablespoons snipped fresh chives

3   tablespoons lime juice

5   tablespoons extra-virgin olive oil

1/8 teaspoon dried red pepper flakes

3   tablespoons kosher salt

1   pound red potatoes

2   medium shallots, diced

3   teaspoons chopped black olives

1   teaspoon white pepper

1   medium red tomato

1   medium yellow tomato

1   medium seedless cucumber, sliced

A tian is normally a layered and molded French dessert. This savory New World tian would be ideal for lunch, a light supper, or as the first course in a more elaborate meal.

To prepare the crab meat: Pick through the crab meat to remove any particles of shell or cartilage. In a stainless-steel bowl combine the crab meat, chives, 1 tablespoon of the lime juice, 2 tablespoons of the olive oil, the dried red pepper flakes, and 1/2 teaspoon of the salt. Toss carefully to avoid crushing the crab meat.

To prepare the potatoes: Boil the potatoes in a large pot of water with 2 1/3 tablespoons of the salt for 15 minutes. Remove them from the water and let cool. Slice the potatoes with the skin on. In a stainless-steel bowl combine the potatoes, shallots, black olives, the remaining lime juice, and 2 more tablespoons of the olive oil. Season with 1 teaspoon of the salt and 1/2 teaspoon of the white pepper.

To prepare the tomatoes: Peel, seed, and dice the red and yellow tomatoes. Season with 1/2 teaspoon of the salt, 1/2 teaspoon of the white pepper, and the remaining olive oil.

To assemble and serve: Use a bottomless 3-inch-wide ring mold with sides about 3 inches high to mold the salads. Arrange the sliced cucumber inside the mold set in the center of a serving plate. Next add the potato salad, then the chopped tomato, and last the crab-meat salad. Carefully remove the mold ring and finish the presentation with 6 teaspoons of Manzanilla Olive Tapenade spooned on top of the tian.

ACCOMPANIMENT:
MANZANILLA OLIVE TAPENADE

On a recent trip to Spain, I discovered the terrific Spanish olives being farmed there. One of my favorite olives, the Manzanilla, is grown in the southwestern part of Spain, which also produces a local Manzanilla wine. According to local tradition in the coastal fishing village of Sanlúcar, to sip Manzanilla wine on the beach while watching the sun set over the Atlantic Ocean is an experience you'll never forget.

In a food processor with a steel blade combine the olives, garlic, anchovies, parsley, and cilantro. While the processor is running, drizzle in the extra-virgin olive oil.

Any leftover tapenade can be stored, covered, in the refrigerator, for up to 2 weeks.

MANZANILLA OLIVE TAPENADE

MAKES 2 CUPS

1½	cups pitted Manzanilla olives
2	tablespoons chopped garlic
10	anchovy fillets
¼	cup fresh flat-leaf parsley
¼	cup fresh cilantro leaves
¼	cup Spanish extra-virgin olive oil

SOFT-SHELL CRABS WITH THREE NUTS

SERVES 4 AS A FIRST COURSE

4   prime soft-shell crabs, cleaned

2   teaspoons minced garlic

½   teaspoon minced fresh oregano

½   teaspoon fresh ground black pepper

½   teaspoon coarse salt

½   teaspoon minced fresh thyme

4   tablespoons olive oil

1   small lime, juiced

1   medium tomato, peeled, seeded, and diced

3   tablespoons pistachios

3   tablespoons pecans

3   tablespoons pine nuts

3   tablespoons dry white wine

1   tablespoon chopped scallion

A blue crab will generally molt or shed when the water warms and remain in this delectable soft stage for only one 10-day cycle a year. Up north the molting season begins in May and continues through most of the summer. The water temperatures in south Florida, however, are warm enough for winter molting, so soft-shell crabs are available fresh virtually all year round.

When you buy live crabs they don't come clean, unless the fish store has cleaned them for you. To clean the crab you must first remove the tail flap under the belly and the membranes under the soft-shell flaps. Then simply snip the eyes with scissors. Shelf life is short. After cleaning, the crab must be cooked within a few hours or they start to dehydrate.

To prepare the crabs: Season the crabs with a mixture of 1 teaspoon garlic, the oregano, black pepper, salt, thyme, 2 tablespoons of the olive oil, and the lime juice.

To cook the soft-shell crabs: In a large sauté pan warm the remaining olive oil. Cook the soft-shell crabs, up side down first, for 3 minutes, browning the shells well, then flip them over and cook for another minute. Add to the pan the tomato, the remaining garlic, the pistachios, pecans, and pine nuts. Cook for 1 minute and add the white wine. Remove the crabs to a serving plate. Reduce the nut sauce for just a moment and add the scallion. Serve the crab with the nut sauce.

If you've never had smoked lobster before, you should try this recipe served with the Boniato Salad. A smoker is preferable, but a barbecue grill with a cover will do the trick here. Slow-cook the lobster with the lid closed and the rack placed as high as possible above the coals.

Tamarind is one of the basic flavors in Worcestershire sauce, and it adds a rich, tart tang to the flavors of this dish. It grows abundantly in south Florida and is available fresh in many Southeast Asian and Latin American markets. It's also carried frozen in many supermarkets.

To cure the lobster: Split the lobster in half and season it with 2 teaspoons of the kosher salt and 1 teaspoon of the sugar. Set it aside for 1 hour. Combine the ginger, cumin, pepper flakes, olive oil, 1/2 cup of the white wine, and the tamarind pulp. Rub this mixture onto the lobster tails and let them sit for 30 minutes. Smoke the lobster on a barbecue as described in the recipe headnote. Turn the tails every 3 or 4 minutes, basting with the marinade. They should be finished in about 10 minutes. Remove from the heat and let them chill for 1 hour.

To pickle the onion: Very finely julienne the Bermuda onion and place it in a stainless-steel bowl. Pour the cider vinegar over it and add the remaining white wine, salt, and sugar. Let this marinate for 1 hour. Drain.

To assemble and serve: Remove the lobster meat from the shells and slice it into medallions. Serve with the pickled onion and garnish with sliced starfruit.

ACCOMPANIMENT:
BONIATO SALAD
SEE NEXT PAGE

SMOKED SPINY LOBSTER WITH PICKLED BERMUDA ONION

SERVES 4 AS A FIRST COURSE

2	large spiny lobster tails
1	tablespoon kosher salt
1	tablespoon sugar
1	tablespoon minced fresh ginger
1	tablespoon ground cumin
1/2	teaspoon dried red pepper flakes
2	tablespoons olive oil
1	cup dry white wine
1	tablespoon tamarind pulp
1	large Bermuda onion
1	cup cider vinegar
1	large starfruit

BONIATO SALAD

SERVES 4

1 *pound boniato*

2 *tablespoons ground turmeric*

2 *tablespoons chopped fresh oregano*

2 *tablespoons extra-virgin olive oil*

1/2 *teaspoon dried red pepper flakes*

1 *teaspoon kosher salt*

1 *teaspoon cider vinegar*

Boil the boniatos with the skin on for 45 minutes, until cooked through but still firm. Drain the boniatos and put them aside until cool. Peel and slice them about 1/2 inch thick. Season with the turmeric, oregano, olive oil, pepper, salt, and finally the cider vinegar.

This is a heady cocktail for the lover of seafood: intoxication guaranteed. Although Florida lobsters will work here, Maine lobsters are my choice for this dish. They hold their flavor and texture well in a cold salad, and they're readily available already prepared in many markets.

To prepare the salad: Dice the Maine lobster meat into 1/2-by-1/2-inch pieces. Dice the red potatoes, skin on, in the same fashion. Add the minced shallot. Cut eight of the olives in half. Carefully toss these ingredients with the vermouth, dill, olive oil, the juice of 1 lime, and the salt and pepper.

To serve: Fill 4 martini glasses with lobster salad and garnish each portion with a skewer of 2 olives and a lime segment.

MARTINI OF LOBSTER, OLIVES, AND LIME

SERVES 4 AS A FIRST COURSE

1 1/2	cups cooked lobster meat
3	medium red potatoes, boiled
1	small shallot, minced
16	small cocktail olives
2	tablespoons dry white vermouth
1	teaspoon chopped fresh dill
2	tablespoons extra-virgin olive oil
2	medium limes, 1 cut in quarters
1/2	teaspoon kosher salt
1/4	teaspoon fresh ground black pepper

LOBSTER SCOTCH BONNET CAKE

SERVES 10 AS A FIRST COURSE

4	tablespoons olive oil
1	medium onion, minced
1	tablespoon minced garlic
2	tablespoons chopped fresh basil
1/2	teaspoon ground cumin
1/4	teaspoon minced Scotch bonnet
1	tablespoon minced fresh ginger
1	cup dry white wine
1	large tomato, peeled, seeded, and diced
1/4	bunch scallions, chopped
1 1/2	pounds spiny lobster meat or Maine lobster meat, diced
2	large eggs
1	cup fresh French bread crumbs
1	tablespoon kosher salt

Spiny lobster also known as rock lobster is available in many parts of the world, and is abundant here in the Caribbean and south Florida where our commercial lobster season begins in late summer and extends to early spring.

These lobsters do not have claws as the North Atlantic lobster does, although either would be appropriate for the recipe. The lobster cake will be much tastier if raw meat is used. But use cooked if you must. Just don't pass up this recipe!

To prepare the sofrito (a combination of cooked vegetables, seasoning, and spices): In a large, heavy sauté pan warm 3 tablespoons of the olive oil. Add the onion and cook until translucent. Add the garlic, basil, cumin, Scotch bonnet, and ginger. After 1 minute add the white wine, tomato, and scallions. Mix together carefully to avoid breaking the tomato too much. Remove from the heat and let this sofrito cool.

To prepare the lobster cake: Add the cooled sofrito mixture to the lobster meat. Fold in the eggs. Add enough bread crumbs to bind the mixture, and season with salt. Chill for 1 hour.

To cook the cakes: Shape the mixture into 10 oval patties approximately 3 inches each. Sauté the lobster cakes in the remaining olive oil, browning them well for 2 minutes on each side.

Serve immediately with 1 cup of Strawberry-Ginger Chutney on the side.

ACCOMPANIMENT:
STRAWBERRY-GINGER CHUTNEY

Florida strawberries peak in February and March. In the rest of the country, the best strawberries are available from early to midsummer.

To prepare the fruit: Clean the strawberries under cold running water. Remove the stems and cut any very large berries in half. Peel the mango and dice the meat into ½-inch pieces.

To make the sauce: In a pan heat the olive oil and sauté the onions until they start to caramelize. Add the red pepper, ginger, red wine, and vinegar and cook for 3 minutes until the liquid is reduced to half its volume. Add the brown sugar and cumin. Cook until the mixture is smooth, then add the strawberries and mango. Continue cooking for 15 minutes and spoon out the fruit from the mixture. Reserve the fruit and return the liquid to the heat and reduce to thicken. Adjust the seasoning with more vinegar if necessary and the salt.

To assemble and serve: Pour the sauce over the fruit and let it cool. Prepare the chutney at least a day ahead to allow the flavors to develop fully. Store in the refrigerator for up to 2 weeks.

STRAWBERRY-GINGER CHUTNEY

MAKES 2 CUPS

3	cups strawberries
2	large mangos
3	tablespoons extra-virgin olive oil
1	medium Spanish onion, diced fine
1	teaspoon cracked red pepper
1	tablespoon minced fresh ginger
½	cup dry red wine
¼	cup red wine vinegar
½	cup light brown sugar
1	tablespoon ground cumin
1	tablespoon kosher salt

CRISP LOBSTER STRUDEL WITH CHAYOTE AND ALMONDS

SERVES 6 AS A FIRST COURSE

  1   pound lobster meat, chopped
 1/4 cup julienned shallots
 1/4 cup julienned celery
 1/4 cup julienned red bell pepper
  2   tablespoons brandy
  2   teaspoons kosher salt
1 1/2 teaspoons fresh ground black pepper
  9   sheets phyllo dough
  5   tablespoons olive oil
 1/2 cup julienned chayote
 1/2 cup julienned Anaheim chilies
 1/2 cup julienned mango
 1/4 cup slivered almonds

To prepare the lobster stuffing: In a stainless-steel bowl combine the lobster meat, shallots, celery, red pepper, brandy, 1 teaspoon of salt, and 1 teaspoon of pepper. Mix well. Set aside.

To prepare the strudel: Layer 3 phyllo sheets on top of one another, brushing olive oil in between each layer. Set up 3 sets of sheets, then cut each in half lengthwise. Divide the lobster stuffing mixture among the 6 half sheets, placing the lobster at one end and then spreading it out over a third of the phyllo. Roll up the strudel jelly-roll style, enclosing the lobster filling. Brush each finished strudel with olive oil (each strudel should be about 2 inches thick and 6 inches long).

To bake the strudel: Preheat the oven to 375°. Bake the strudel on a cookie sheet in the center of the oven for 6 or 7 minutes, until golden brown.

To serve with vegetable garnish: Warm a sauté pan with the remaining olive oil. Sauté the chayote for 1 minute, then add the Anaheim chilies, mango, and almonds. Season with the remaining salt and pepper. When warmed throughout, place a portion on each plate with the finished lobster strudel.

This is an elegant dish consisting of lobster, island spices, dark rum, and fire. In flambéing, the rum flavors are absorbed by the lobster, most of the alcohol is cooked away, and the sauce is slightly, tantalizingly caramelized, adding depths of flavor. My only word of caution is this: because of the chilies and rum keep this dish away from children.

To prepare the vanilla, saffron, and chili glaze: In a small saucepan cook the shallots, vanilla, Scotch bonnet, and white wine together for 5 minutes, until the liquid is reduced by half. Strain through a fine sieve and add the saffron.

To roast the lobster: Split the lobster tails open. Season them with thyme, salt, and pepper, coat with olive oil, then roast in a 350° oven for 3 minutes. Brush the lobster tails with the vanilla, saffron, and chili glaze and continue to roast for another 5 minutes.

Now for the flambé: Remove the pan from the oven, place it on the stove top over medium heat, and pour in the rum. The pan juices should be hot enough so that the rum will flame. If it isn't, touch a match to the surface of the liquid. When the flames die out, brush the tails again with the pan juices and serve immediately.

ROAST LOBSTER WITH CHILIES, SAFFRON, VANILLA, AND RUM

SERVES 4

2	shallots, diced
1	vanilla bean, split open
1	teaspoon finely diced Scotch bonnet
1	cup dry white wine
1/2	teaspoon whole Spanish saffron threads
4	6-ounce lobster tails
1	teaspoon chopped fresh thyme
1	teaspoon kosher salt
1/2	teaspoon fresh ground black pepper
2	tablespoons olive oil
3	tablespoons Myers's dark rum

LOBSTER CASSOULET WITH WHITE BEANS, CONCH, ORANGE ZEST, AND SEAFOOD SAUSAGE

SERVES 4

- 2   large spiny lobster tails
- 1   tablespoon chopped fresh thyme
- 1   teaspoon saffron
- 3   teaspoons chopped garlic
- 2   tablespoons olive oil
- 1   large orange
- 1   cup cold water
- ½   cup fresh bread crumbs
- 6   tablespoons chopped fresh flat-leaf parsley
- 1   tablespoon chopped fresh mint
- ¼   pound pancetta, diced
- ½   teaspoon kosher salt
- ½   teaspoon coarse ground black pepper
- 3   teaspoons diced shallots
- ½   cup dry white wine

This is a Caribbean spin on the classic French cassoulet. The orange is used in two ways in this recipe: for its zest, which garnishes the cassoulet, and for its juice, to simmer the seafoods.

To prepare the lobster: Split the lobster tails, but do not remove the meat. Combine the thyme, saffron, 1 teaspoon of the garlic, and the olive oil. Rub the mixture on the tails and let them marinate for 30 minutes.

To prepare the orange: Zest the orange with a zester. Squeeze the juice and reserve it for later. In a small pot combine the zest with the cold water. Bring to a boil, then drain the zest and turn it out onto paper towels to dry. Dice the zest and combine it with the fresh bread crumbs, 1 teaspoon of garlic, the parsley, and mint.

To begin the cassoulet: Place the pancetta in a heavy-bottomed pan over medium heat and render until most of the fat is cooked away. Remove the meat from the pan and set it aside. Season the marinated lobster with salt and pepper. Place the lobster tails, shell side up, in the pan and, over high heat, brown the lobster meat on both sides. Turn down the heat and add the shallots. Cook over medium heat until the shallots are translucent, then remove the lobster and deglaze the pan with the white wine. Add the conch, shrimp, calamari, and seafood sausage, then the reserved orange juice and the fish stock. Continue to simmer for 3 minutes. Remove the shrimp and sausage. Add the white beans and the reserved pancetta, stir well and remove from heat.

To finish the cassoulet: Preheat the oven to 350°. Layer the bottom of a large Crockpot with the bean mixture. Remove the lobster meat from the shells and slice it into medallions. Layer the lobster, shrimp, and sausage on the bean-calamari mixture. Top this with the orange zest mixture and generously dollop the top with butter. Bake for 10 minutes, until golden brown.

NOTE: To prepare calamari for cooking, see recipe head on page 167.

½ cup ground conch (see page 17)

4 uncooked jumbo shrimp

6 large calamari, cleaned and sliced crosswise into rings (see Note)

4 pieces Seafood Sausage (page 175)

¼ cup Fish Stock (page 22)

2 cups cooked white beans, warmed

2 tablespoons sweet butter

LOBSTER AND YAMS À LA NAGE WITH CANDIED LEMON ZEST

SERVES 4

1 medium Spanish onion, diced

1 large red bell pepper, diced

6 tablespoons chopped fresh flat-leaf parsley

1/4 cup lime juice

2 tablespoons plus 1/2 cup sugar

1/3 cup white vinegar

1/4 teaspoon diced Scotch bonnet

1 tablespoon julienned fresh ginger

1 quart plus 1/2 cup cold water

4 6-ounce lobster tails

2 medium yams

2 tablespoons lemon zest

2 medium limes, segmented

4 sprigs fresh cilantro

1/2 tablespoon kosher salt

Pinch fresh white pepper

Nage *means "swimming" in French. In this dish, the lobster is swimming in a very light sweet-and-sour broth.*

To prepare the nage: In a large saucepan combine the onion, red pepper, parsley, lime juice, 2 tablespoons of sugar, the white vinegar, Scotch bonnet, ginger, and 1 quart cold water. Simmer for 20 minutes.

To cook the lobsters: Split the lobster tails in half and simmer in the *nage* for 5 to 8 minutes.

To prepare the yams: Cook the yams in a pot of boiling salted water for approximately 30 minutes. Peel and dice in medium cut.

To candy the lemon zest: Place the lemon zest in a small pot with cold water to cover. Bring to a boil and strain. Cool the lemon zest. Cook the zest again in a simple syrup of 1/2 cup sugar and 1/2 cup water. Simmer until almost no liquid remains. Remove from the heat and cool.

To assemble and serve: Remove the lobster to a serving platter. Place the yams, lime segments, and cilantro with the lobster. Strain the *nage* over the yams and lobster. Adjust the seasoning with salt and fresh white pepper. Garnish with the candied lemon zest.

To clean the calamari, separate the body from the tentacles. The long slender body needs to be rinsed under cool running water. Slice along the side from top to bottom with a small sharp paring knife to open up the squid like a book. Remove the cartilage and any other body materials from the inside. Lay the squid flat on a cutting board and mark it very lightly with the point of the knife to create a small checkerboard pattern. This helps tenderize and shape the squid when it is grilled. Clean the tentacles by squeezing the "eye" and removing the ink. Cut away any hard cartilage that remains.

To marinate the squid: Marinate the cleaned squid in ½ cup of the white wine, 2 tablespoons of the olive oil, the garlic, cracked pepper, thyme, and ½ teaspoon of the salt.

To prepare the mango: Peel and cut the mangos into medium dice. Cut the jalapeño in half. Remove the seeds and ribs. Cut into very fine dice. Carefully pick the leaves of the cilantro. Reserve some for garnish and roughly chop the rest. Combine the mango, jalapeño, and cilantro in a stainless-steel bowl. Season with the lime juice and ½ teaspoon of salt. Stir in the remaining olive oil. Let sit in the refrigerator for an hour or more.

To prepare the Vidalia onion garnish: Finely julienne the Vidalia onions and soak them in lightly salted cool water for 5 minutes. Drain and shake dry. Season with the remaining salt and the pepper, cumin, and the remaining white wine.

To grill the calamari: Heat a grill until the coals are hot. (You can also use the broiler of your oven.) Quickly grill the marinated squid. It should be done in approximately 1 minute; be careful not to overcook it.

To compose this platter with great eye appeal: Arrange the onions on the outer edge of the platter. Just inside the onions arrange the mango salsa. Place the hot grilled calamari in the center, and garnish with the reserved cilantro leaves.

GRILLED CALAMARI WITH HOT MANGO SALSA

SERVES 6 AS A FIRST COURSE

1	pound fresh calamari
¾	cup white wine
3	tablespoons extra-virgin olive oil
1	tablespoon minced garlic
1	tablespoon cracked black peppercorns
½	teaspoon chopped fresh thyme
1½	teaspoon sea salt
2	large ripe mangos
1	large jalapeño
¼	bunch cilantro
	Juice of 1 medium lime
2	medium Vidalia onions
½	teaspoon fresh ground black pepper
¼	teaspoon ground cumin

ROAST CALAMARI WITH GREEN LENTILS

SERVES 6 AS A FIRST COURSE

- 3 tablespoons herbes de Provence
- 1 tablespoon chopped garlic
- 2 tablespoons olive oil
- 1 teaspoon kosher salt
- 1/2 teaspoon fresh ground black pepper
- 18 pieces calamari head and tentacles, cleaned (see recipe head, page 167)
- 2 cups cooked green lentils

To roast the calamari: Combine the herbes de Provence, garlic, olive oil, salt, and pepper. Toss the calamari in the herb mixture. Place the calamari in a small roasting pan in a 375° oven for approximately 2 minutes. Baste with the herb mixture, turn over, and finish roasting for approximately 2 more minutes.

To serve: Warm the green lentils and arrange them on an earthenware service platter. Place the hot calamari in the center of the lentils. Drizzle with 6 tablespoons of Orange Balsamic Syrup.

ACCOMPANIMENT:
ORANGE BALSAMIC SYRUP

ORANGE BALSAMIC SYRUP

MAKES 1 CUP

- 6 oranges, freshly squeezed
- 1 quart balsamic vinegar

This is a very flavorful condiment that I think you will use over and over again. Try this over any roasted or grilled fish or vegetable.

In a small saucepot combine the orange juice and balsamic vinegar and reduce over a medium heat until only 1 cup remains of liquid. Take care not to burn the liquid by reducing it too quickly. The process should take about 45 minutes. Strain the syrup through a fine sieve into a glass jar. Let cool and cover. This will keep, refrigerated, for up to 4 weeks.

You can adjust the heat of this assertive dish by adding more or less Scotch bonnet pepper.

To prepare the seafoods: Rinse the conch under cold running water. Trim any of the thick dense muscle—mostly in the cylindrical end part—with a small paring knife. Crack the conch several times with a mallet, then chop it fine and set the meat aside. Clean the mussels by removing the beards, scraping the barnacles (if you're using wild mussels), then rinsing and swirling them first clockwise, then counter-clockwise, in salted water. Discard any mussels that float to the top of the water.

To steam the mussels: In a medium saucepot warm the olive oil. Add the shallots and cook until translucent. Add the garlic and mussels, stirring, then add the white wine. Cover for 2 minutes. Add the vegetables, spices, and Scotch bonnet. Mix well and simmer for another 2 minutes. Add the conch and coconut milk, then bring back to a simmer. Cook for 3 minutes. Season with sea salt, then stir in the chervil and fresh lime juice.

To make the crispy noodle garnish: In a deep fryer or heavy pan heat the peanut oil to 425° and deep-fry the cellophane noodles for 3 seconds. They should blow up and triple in size to a large white nest. Remove and drain. Arrange the mussels around the edge of a service platter and pour the broth and vegetables in the middle. Garnish with the crisp cellophane noodles.

RED HOT CURRIED CONCH AND MUSSELS

SERVES 4 AS A FIRST COURSE

½	pound conch
20	large mussels
2	tablespoons extra-virgin olive oil
4	large shallots, diced
1	tablespoon minced garlic
1	cup dry white wine
½	cup corn kernels
½	cup diced red bell pepper
½	cup diced yellow bell pepper
1	tablespoon curry powder
1	tablespoon ground turmeric
1	tablespoon ground cumin
¾	teaspoon minced Scotch bonnet
½	cup coconut milk
1	tablespoon sea salt
1	tablespoon chopped fresh chervil

Juice of 1 large lime

2	cups peanut oil for frying
1	bunch cellophane noodles

MUSSELS AND MANGO MOQUECAS

SERVES 6

36 large mussels

2 tablespoons olive oil

4 large shallots, diced

1 tablespoon chopped garlic

1 cup Chardonnay

1 cup diced green plantain

½ cup diced red bell pepper

1 tablespoon ground cumin

1 teaspoon diced Scotch bonnet

1 medium firm mango, diced

2 teaspoons sea salt

1 tablespoon chopped fresh chervil

Moquecas is a Latin American seafood stew. This is a unique combination that brings North and South American flavors together.

To prepare the mussels: Clean the mussels and remove the beards with a small paring knife.

To cook the stew: In a medium saucepan warm the olive oil. Add the shallots and cook until translucent. Add the garlic and mussels. Mix thoroughly and add the Chardonnay and green plantain. Cover for 2 minutes. Add the red pepper, cumin, and Scotch bonnet. Mix well and simmer for another 2 minutes. Add the mango and bring back to a simmer. Cook for 3 more minutes, until all the mussels open. Season with sea salt and garnish with the chervil.

To assemble and serve: Arrange the mussels around the edge of a service platter and pour the broth and vegetables in the middle.

Jamaican Blue Mountain coffee is one of the finest in the world. The beans are carefully selected at their peak of ripeness, then roasted. The resulting aroma is full-bodied yet not overpowering. In this recipe I suggest that you start with whole beans and use the freshest that are available. If you can't find Jamaican Blue Mountain coffee, substitute another full-flavored, fresh-roasted coffee bean. The trick here is to use the freshest beans available.

To prepare the scallops: Pare the muscles from the scallops with a small knife. Process the Blue Mountain coffee in a coffee grinder to a very coarse grind. Next grind the black pepper separately. Season the scallops with the coffee (reserving 2 tablespoons for garnish), the pepper, and salt. Set the scallops aside.

To prepare the vanilla bean sauce: Cut the vanilla bean into quarters, then dice the shallots. In a small saucepot combine these with the white wine. Reduce on medium heat for 10 minutes until only 3 tablespoons of liquid remain. Add the vinegar and cream and reduce the sauce still further until only 4 tablespoons remain. Whisk in 4 tablespoons of sweet butter piece by piece to keep the mixture emulsified. Strain through a fine sieve and keep warm until ready to serve.

To cook the scallops: In a very hot sauté pan put the remaining sweet butter and quickly cook the scallops for 30 seconds on each side, browning them well.

To assemble and serve: I like to present this dish on a round glass platter with a wide rim. The scallops should be arranged in a small circle in the center of a puddle of vanilla bean sauce. Then dust the rim of the platter with some freshly ground coffee.

JUMBO SEA SCALLOPS WITH JAMAICAN BLUE MOUNTAIN COFFEE AND VANILLA BEAN

SERVES 6 AS A FIRST COURSE

12 *jumbo sea scallops*

¼ *cup Jamaican coffee beans*

2 *tablespoons whole black peppercorns*

½ *teaspoon coarse salt*

1 *whole vanilla bean*

3 *medium shallots*

1 *cup dry white wine*

1 *tablespoon white vinegar*

3 *tablespoons heavy cream*

5 *tablespoons sweet butter, at room temperature, cut up*

TOURNEDOS OF JUMBO SCALLOPS WRAPPED IN LEEKS

SERVES 4

12   extra-jumbo sea scallops

1   tablespoon chopped garlic

1   teaspoon coarse salt

½   teaspoon coarse ground black pepper

½   teaspoon chopped fresh thyme

3   tablespoons sweet butter, at room temperature

4   leeks, soft green part only

I created this dish for Paul Bocuse on the occasion of Chef Allen's restaurant's seventh anniversary. The scallop tournedos with a Boniato Vichyssoise sauce is a marvelous synthesis of American products and classic French ideas.

To prepare the scallops: Season the scallops with the garlic, salt, pepper, and thyme. Coat each scallop with butter. Over medium-high heat, preheat a heavy, buttered pan until the butter starts to brown. Sear the scallops for 30 seconds on each side, then remove from the pan. The scallops will still be raw on the inside.

To prepare the tournedos: Preheat the oven to 350°. Cut strands of leek approximately 8 inches long and ½ inch wide. Blanch these in a pot of boiling water for 1 minute, then plunge immediately into cold water. To form the tournedos, tie 3 seared scallops securely together with a leek wrapper. Place the tournedos in a pan and bake for 5 minutes. With a spatula, carefully transfer the tournedos to a large, deep serving plate and serve with 2 cups of Boniato Vichyssoise sauce.

ACCOMPANIMENT:
BONIATO VICHYSSOISE (PAGE 79)

This soup, with its Caribbean and European flavors, was influenced by my travels in both the south of France and along the Adriatic coast of Italy.

To begin the seafood preparation: In a deep stockpot sweat the shallots in the olive oil. Add the clams and mussels. Cover the pot for a minute. Add the saffron, garlic, and then the white wine and calamari. Let these steam, covered, for 5 minutes as you prepare the vegetables.

To prepare the vegetables: In another pot combine the broccoli rab, tomato, and fish stock. Bring to a boil and add the angel hair pasta. Let this cook for a few minutes, until the pasta is done.

To finish the minestrone: Add all the seafoods and cooking liquid to the vegetable pot. Continue to simmer the minestrone for 1 minute and finish with fresh oregano, lime juice, salt, and pepper.

LOCAL SEAFOOD MINESTRONE WITH CLAMS, CALAMARI, AND RAPINI

SERVES 6

4 tablespoons chopped shallots

2 tablespoons olive oil

12 clams, washed and cleaned

12 mussels, washed and cleaned

1/2 teaspoon saffron

1 tablespoon chopped garlic

1/2 cup dry white wine

12 calamari (see recipe head, page 167)

1 cup chopped broccoli rab

1/2 cup peeled, seeded, and chopped plum tomato

1 1/2 cups Fish Stock (page 22)

1/2 cup angel hair pasta, broken into 2-inch pieces

1 tablespoon chopped fresh oregano

1 tablespoon lime juice

1 teaspoon kosher salt

1/2 teaspoon fresh ground black pepper

SEAFOOD CHOUCROUTE

SERVES 6

12 uncooked medium shrimp, peeled and cleaned

12 medium scallops, cleaned

1 pound snapper or grouper fillets, cut in 3-inch pieces

12 Seafood Sausages (recipe follows)

1 tablespoon kosher salt

1 teaspoon coarse ground black pepper

1 tablespoon coriander seeds

1 tablespoon whole juniper berries

1/2 cup dry white wine

3 tablespoons olive oil

2 small sweet onions, julienned

6 small turnips, peeled and quartered

2 cups Chicken Stock (page 21)

1 pound fresh sauerkraut, drained

2 tablespoons gin

3 tablespoons chopped fresh flat-leaf parsley

One of my favorite dishes is sauerkraut. My taste for the pickled, shredded cabbage started with hot dogs and mustard, but after my travels through Alsace, my taste advanced to France's national favorite, choucroute—a combination of duck, meats, and potatoes cooked in sauerkraut. My New World version transforms this classic combination with—what else?—seafood.

To prepare the seafood: Season all the fish and seafood with 2 teaspoons of salt, 1/2 teaspoon of pepper, coriander seeds, juniper berries, and white wine.

To prepare the choucroute: In a deep stockpot, warm the olive oil and cook the onions until translucent. Add the turnips and chicken stock. Bring the mixture to a boil and let simmer for 5 minutes, then remove from the heat. Add the sauerkraut and top with the fish, seafood, and marinade. Return to the heat and bring to a simmer on medium with a cover on the pot. Do not stir. Let the seafood steam on top of the sauerkraut. It should probably take 6 or 7 minutes to finish cooking.

To finish the choucroute: Remove the seafood to a warm serving platter, splash with the gin, sprinkle with the flat-leaf parsley, and adjust the seasoning with up to 1 teaspoon of salt and 1/2 teaspoon pepper. Serve the hot sauerkraut and turnips alongside the seafood.

These seafood sausages can be used in a variety of preparations: grilled with a guava barbecue sauce, roasted with a green herb pesto, baked in the seafood cassoulet, or chilled with the Caribbean antipasto.

To begin the filling: Roughly chop the snapper and half of the shrimp in a food processor fitted with a steel blade. Pulse it on and off several times. Add 3 of the eggs. Now run the processor and add the other eggs and half the cream. Season with the salt and white pepper. Using a rubber spatula, scrape down the sides of the processor. Continue to incorporate the remaining cream.

To prepare the stuffing: In a stainless-steel bowl fold together the stuffing, lobster, the remaining shrimp, the herbs, peppers, and Armagnac. Mix well.

To stuff the sausage: Set up your sausage maker. Wash the casing inside and out since it is usually preserved in salt brine. Then pull the casing on the appropriate-size nozzle. Stuff the sausage using even pressure to fill the casing. If you don't have a sausage machine, a pastry bag may be used, though it's a little more difficult. Using a pastry tube, carefully stuff the casing while maintaining even pressure on the pastry bag. This is a slow process. It's very important to avoid air pockets when stuffing the casing. You can also individually shape sausage in plastic wrap and tie to shape.

To finish the sausage: With butcher twine, tie the sausage into links at intervals of approximately 3 inches. Poke the casing of each individual sausage 2 or 3 times with a pin to allow some liquids to escape while cooking. The sausage can be grilled, sautéed, or poached according to your needs. It can also be saved raw if kept on ice or frozen immediately, layed out individually, allowing for a quick freeze. You can also make sausage patties, but that would limit the cooking method.

SEAFOOD SAUSAGE

MAKES 24 SAUSAGES

1	pound red snapper fillets
1	pound uncooked shrimp, diced
5	large eggs
2/3	cup heavy cream
2	teaspoons kosher salt
1	teaspoon white pepper
1/2	pound lobster meat, chopped
2	tablespoons chopped fresh chives
1	tablespoon chopped fresh tarragon
1/4	cup fine-diced red bell pepper
1/4	cup fine-diced yellow bell pepper
2	tablespoons Armagnac
1	hank sausage casing

CHAPTER 7

MEATS

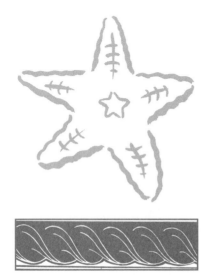

LAMB
Creole Barbecue Leg of Lamb *served with*
Yams and Smoked Onions

Lamb Chops with Dijon Crust and Saratoga Fries

Lamb T-Bone Steaks in Red Wine Mojo
with Garlic and Lime

VEAL
TriBeCa Veal Chops with Double Mustard Sauce
and Wild Mushrooms

BEEF
Delmonico Steaks with Homemade Tamarind-
Worcestershire Sauce *served with* Yuca Steak Fries

Palamillo Steak *served with* Roquefort
and Toasted Nut Salsa

Herb-Roasted Beef Tenderloin *served with*
Wild Mushroom Salsa

BUFFALO
Buffalo Steaks with Rosemary *served with*
Sweet Potato Hash

Red meat is not something I eat every day, but sometimes the carnivore awakens in my soul and demands to be fed. Lamb is my particular favorite of the red meats, and my young daughter Deanna's as well: she loves to pick up a lamp chop and chew around the bone. Many adults still love that kind of primal satisfaction. We sell a lot of meat, particularly lamb, at Chef Allen's.

My mom always prepared meats when I was growing up. We loved lamb chops, simply broiled, and roast beefs for special occasions. Looking over the edge of the kitchen counter when I was small and seeing a big roast beef, tied and ready to be carved, was a visual treat right out of a Dutch kitchen painting. I loved to chew on the string, to get the beefy juices while the meat rested. In those days we used to go to the kosher butcher, which was down the block from the fish, fruit, and live-chicken markets. The kosher butcher would grind and cut meat to our special order. But by the time I was ten, the supermarkets were becoming bigger, a new technology swept the country, and most meats were prepackaged. The small markets began vanishing.

The supermarket chains have transformed the nature of meat buying and eating in this country from those days when the small butcher cut you your piece of meat to order, then trimmed and prepared it. My wife Judi's grandfather was one of those butchers who worked until he was ninety-four, just cutting and preparing meats in a small neighborhood store in Pittsburgh.

That's still very much what you find in the markets in France and Italy. In many parts of Europe, big hunks of meat hang behind the counter waiting to be cut to order. One market will sell whole hanging sides of pork, another beef, another lamb. The dry-aging, which dries the blood, lends the meat a much more intense flavor than that of precut and plastic-wrapped meats. Unfortunately, most of what is available in supermarkets is cut, butchered, and prewrapped at a central plant before being shipped out across the country.

But just as there seems to be a trend back to fresher, dry-aged hanging meats, there is also a transformation, for health reasons, in our sense of the proper proportion of meat to the rest of the plate. In the Orient, the proportion of meat to starches and vegetables has been traditionally small. Until recently our American appetite has demanded meat—often in the form of a huge slab of steak—dominating the plate.

Moderation allows us to enjoy all foods, and in the New World Cuisine meat may still be the focus of a meal, but it's served in smaller portions and shares the plate with starches such as yuca fries. Buffalo is a New World red meat that's a healthy alternative to beef. It is low in fat and cholesterol and makes, among other dishes, a fabulous burger.

You'll see that I love barbecued meats. Meats charred on a barbecue or wood-burning grill offer us the pleasure of cooking outdoors in the fresh air and anticipating, as the smoke and aromas rise, the simple and wonderful flavors to come.

Meat, I think, is a treat we all need from time to time. It offers us a barbaric pleasure that answers our ancient yearnings. Sometimes there is nothing quite as satisfying as responding to the cave or jungle dweller that still exists in our bones.

I'm all for expanding the menu of the typical American barbecue. Next time you're in the mood for firing up the grill, try this winning combination.

To prepare the lamb: Have your butcher butterfly the lamb (remove all the bones and spread the meat flat). Also trim the fat and sinew from inside and out. In a small bowl combine all the seasonings and rub the lamb with this dry mixture, then with the onions, lime, and olive oil. Let marinate for 30 minutes.

To cook the lamb: Preheat your barbecue or gas grill. (Or you can use an oven broiler.) All the coals or the grill should be red hot. Sear the outside of the leg of lamb on both sides, then lower the heat by spreading the coals, raising the grill, or lowering the gas burners. Continue to grill, turning the meat regularly. It should take 20 to 25 minutes to cook to medium rare. After it's cooked, remove the lamb from the grill and let it rest for 5 minutes before slicing. Using a sharp slicing knife, cut it across the grain on a slight bias. Serve the leg of lamb with Yams and Smoked Onions.

ACCOMPANIMENT: YAMS AND SMOKED ONIONS

To smoke the onions: Cut the Bermuda onion into ½-inch rings. Place in a hot smoker for 10 minutes until softened (see Note).

To prepare the yams: In a large saucepot boil the yams in their skins for 30 minutes, until cooked through but still firm. Drain the yams and put them aside to cool. Peel the yams and slice them ½ inch thick. Season the yams with the remaining ingredients and toss gently.

To assemble and serve: Garnish the seasoned yams with the smoked onions.

NOTE: Although the authenticity of this dish would be changed, you could caramelize the onions in about the same amount of time, using a hot sauté pan with a tablespoon of extra-virgin olive oil.

CREOLE BARBECUE LEG OF LAMB

SERVES 6

1   6-pound butterflied leg of lamb

2   tablespoons kosher salt

2   tablespoons ground cumin

1   tablespoon ground allspice

1   teaspoon ground turmeric

2   tablespoons fennel seeds

2   tablespoons crushed black peppercorns

1   cup chopped Spanish onions

½   cup fresh lime juice

½   cup olive oil

YAMS AND SMOKED ONIONS

SERVES 6

2   large Bermuda onions

2   pounds yams

1   teaspoon ground turmeric

1   tablespoon chopped fresh oregano

½   tablespoon kosher salt

1   tablespoon extra-virgin olive oil

LAMB CHOPS WITH DIJON CRUST AND SARATOGA FRIES

SERVES 4

8 large lamb chops (rib)

2 teaspoons kosher salt

1 teaspoon coarse ground black pepper

4 tablespoons olive oil

2 teaspoons minced fresh rosemary

2 teaspoons minced garlic

3 tablespoons fresh French bread crumbs

4 teaspoons Dijon mustard

4 large Idaho potatoes

2 quarts peanut oil for deep frying

A big favorite of my customers in the restaurant, this dish is easy to prepare—the trick is to wait until the last minute to cook the chops so they're served hot and juicy.

To start the lamb: Preheat the broiler. Season the lamb with ½ teaspoon of salt and ½ teaspoon of pepper, then drizzle with 2 tablespoons of the olive oil. Grill the lamb chops for about 3 minutes on each side. Remove from the broiler.

To crust the lamb: In a small bowl combine the rosemary, garlic, and bread crumbs. Drizzle the bread crumbs with the remaining olive oil and season with ½ teaspoon of salt and ½ teaspoon of pepper. Liberally cover one side of each lamb chop with mustard, then pack the bread-crumb mixture on top. Reduce to oven temperature of 350° and return the lamb chops to the oven to brown the crust.

To prepare the Saratoga fries: Wash the potatoes well and dry them. Cut the unpeeled potatoes into very thin large julienne. A mandolin cutter will make the job very easy, but a sharp French knife and patience will work too. Deep-fry these potato sticks in hot (375°) peanut oil until crisp, approximately 3 minutes. Drain well on paper towels and sprinkle with 1 teaspoon of salt. Serve with the lamb chops.

Lamb is my favorite red meat because of its great depth of flavor. A mojo is like a warm vinaigrette. Here it is unique because of the addition of red wine that helps it match the flavors of the lamb.

To broil the lamb T-bone: Preheat your broiler. Season the lamb with ½ teaspoon of salt, ½ teaspoon of pepper, and thyme. Drizzle the steaks with 2 tablespoons of the olive oil. Broil the lamb 3 to 4 minutes on each side.

To prepare the mojo: In a medium saucepot sauté the onion with the remaining olive oil. When the onion is translucent, add the garlic. Continue to cook for 1 minute, then add the red wine, orange and lime juices. When the mixture comes to a boil, reduce the heat to a simmer for 5 minutes. Remove from the heat and add the cilantro and parsley. Adjust the seasoning with the remaining salt and pepper.

To serve: Pour the sauce over the T-bone steaks and serve on a large platter.

LAMB T-BONE STEAKS IN RED WINE MOJO WITH GARLIC AND LIME

SERVES 4

4	*8- to 10-ounce lamb T-bone steaks*
1	*teaspoon kosher salt*
1	*teaspoon coarse ground black pepper*
½	*tablespoon minced fresh thyme*
4	*tablespoons olive oil*
½	*cup diced Spanish onion*
1	*tablespoon chopped garlic*
½	*cup dry red wine*
½	*cup freshly squeezed orange juice*
2	*tablespoons freshly squeezed lime juice*
2	*tablespoons chopped fresh cilantro*
2	*tablespoons chopped fresh parsley*

TRIBECA VEAL CHOPS WITH DOUBLE MUSTARD SAUCE AND WILD MUSHROOMS

SERVES 4

4	12-ounce rib veal chops
1	tablespoon kosher salt
1	tablespoon coarse ground black pepper
2	tablespoons olive oil
1	teaspoon chopped garlic
1½	cups wild mushrooms (shiitakes, oyster, crimini, or white button), cleaned
½	cup red wine
5	medium shallots, diced
1	cup dry white wine
3	tablespoons Dijon mustard
3	tablespoons Pommery mustard
½	cup heavy cream

I call these chops "TriBeCa" to pay tribute to the old meat-packing houses whose products stocked the shops on the lower west side of Manhattan where I used to buy my meats. I miss those lost times and places, since today most of the meat America eats comes out of the Midwest, already packaged.

To prepare the veal chops: Preheat the oven to 350°. Season the veal chops with 1 teaspoon of salt and 1 teaspoon of pepper. Warm the olive oil in a large sauté pan with an ovenproof handle on the stove top. Just before it starts to smoke, place the veal chops in the pan. Sear the first side, browning it, then turn and sear the other side. This should take 4 to 5 minutes total on the stove top.

To finish the veal: Place the sauté pan in the preheated oven and roast the chops for 5 more minutes. Add the garlic and wild mushrooms and cook for 5 minutes. Remove from the oven, deglaze the pan with the red wine and then remove the veal chops. Let the chops rest for 5 minutes. Reduce the red wine with the mushrooms on top of the stove on medium heat for about 3 minutes. Season with 1 teaspoon of salt and 1 teaspoon of pepper.

To prepare the double mustard sauce: In a saucepan cook the shallots and white wine together until the liquid is reduced by half, about 10 minutes. Add the Dijon and Pommery mustards and the cream. Continue to reduce the mixture until the consistency is thick enough to coat the back of a spoon, about 5 minutes. Season with 1 teaspoon of salt and 1 teaspoon of pepper.

To serve: Place a portion of the wild mushrooms on each plate with a little bit of the sauce. Place a veal chop on top of the mushrooms and serve with the rest of the sauce on the side.

DELMONICO STEAKS WITH HOMEMADE TAMARIND-WORCESTERSHIRE SAUCE

SERVES 4

2   16- to 18-ounce Delmonico steaks

1   tablespoon crushed black peppercorns

1   teaspoon chopped garlic

1/2 teaspoon chopped fresh thyme

2   tablespoons olive oil

1   tablespoon kosher salt

1/2 cup Tamarind-Worcestershire sauce (recipe follows)

A Delmonico steak is cut from the prime rib. It can be any of the first 5 steaks cut about 2½ inches thick so that the eye is full. The name Delmonico comes from the first famous restaurant family of New York City, who became established in the 1890s. The steak really should be cooked on an open grill, either wood-burning or charcoal, to enhance the flavors of the meat.

To cook the steak: Preheat the grill. Season the steak with black peppercorns, garlic, and thyme, and drizzle with the olive oil. Grill the steak for 3 to 4 minutes on each side for medium rare. Turn the meat over with steak tongs. Never use a fork because it pokes holes in the surface and allows the juices to run from the meat.

To assemble and serve: It is also important to let the meat rest for several minutes before serving. Slice the steaks across the grain and serve with the Tamarind-Worcestershire Sauce on the side and 12 crisp hot Yuca Steak Fries.

ACCOMPANIMENT:
YUCA STEAK FRIES

To begin the process: Warm the olive oil in a large saucepot. Add the onion and cook until translucent. Add the horseradish, jalapeño, garlic, anchovy, and lemon. Let these cook together for 5 minutes. Add the water, white vinegar, molasses, tamarind, and cloves. Reduce the liquid by a third, about 10 minutes, and remove from the heat. Pour all the ingredients together into a stainless-steel container and refrigerate overnight.

To finish the Worcestershire: Put the whole mixture into a large saucepot and return to a boil. Simmer for approximately 30 minutes to achieve a syrupy consistency. Remove the mixture from the heat and strain. It can be stored refrigerated for up to 3 weeks in a sealed glass jar.

NOTE: If tamarind is not available you may use equal parts of dark corn syrup and lime juice to replace the tart-sweet taste of tamarind.

Why this recipe? Because people all over the globe have developed an insatiable appetite for fries, and because the texture of fried yuca is superior to that of potatoes. The fries are crisp outside and creamy inside—enough said?

To prepare the fries: Peel the skin from the yuca and cut it into 3-inch sections. Add the water and salt to a pot and simmer the yuca for 25 minutes, until soft through the center. Remove from the heat, Add ice to stop the cooking, and let cool completely; drain. Cut the parboiled yuca into steak fries approximately 3 inches long by ³⁄₄ inches wide. Roll the fries in the cornmeal.

To cook the yuca: Preheat a deep fryer to 375° and fry the yuca until golden brown, approximately 4 minutes.

TAMARIND-WORCESTERSHIRE SAUCE

MAKES 2 CUPS

4	tablespoons olive oil
1½	cups chopped sweet onions
5	tablespoons freshly grated horseradish
2	tablespoons chopped jalapeño
1	tablespoon chopped garlic
1	tablespoon chopped anchovy
2	tablespoons peeled and chopped lemon
1	cup water
2	cups white vinegar
½	cup molasses
1	cup tamarind pulp (see Note)
2	whole cloves

YUCA STEAK FRIES

SERVES 4 TO 6

1	1-pound yuca
1	quart water
3	tablespoons kosher salt
2	cups ice cubes
½	cup fine cornmeal
2	quarts peanut oil for deep-frying

PALAMILLO STEAK

SERVES 4

4 10-ounce sirloin steaks, well
  trimmed and butterflied (see
  recipe head)

1 tablespoon chopped garlic

2 tablespoons olive oil

1 teaspoon kosher salt

1 teaspoon fresh ground black
  pepper

A minute steak of sorts, palamillo steak is found on most Latin menus here in Miami. My favorite cut is a sirloin steak about 1½ inches thick. I butterfly the steak, cutting it in half horizontally through almost three quarters of it. Then, using plastic wrap to sandwich the meat, I pound it with a mallet until its uniform thickness is about ½ inch.

To prepare the steak: Rub the steaks with a combination of garlic and olive oil. Season them with salt and pepper.

To cook the steak: On the stove top, preheat a heavy cast-iron skillet very hot. This thin, large steak will cook quickly, so be alert. Place a steak in the pan, searing the first side for about 45 seconds. Turn it over and sear the second side for about 45 seconds more. Remove from the heat. Repeat with the remaining steaks.

To serve: Serve the steaks hot with ¼ cup of Roquefort Toasted Nut Salsa spread generously across each one.

ACCOMPANIMENT:

ROQUEFORT AND TOASTED NUT SALSA

To prepare the nuts: Preheat the oven to 300°. Dry toast each type of nut separately on a cookie sheet, shaking them often and baking until golden brown, about 6 minutes. Combine all the nuts together in a stainless-steel bowl and let cool.

To begin the salsa: In a another stainless-steel bowl combine the garlic, honey, mustard, rice vinegar, chives, and jalapeño. Mix well. Fold in the nuts.

To finish the salsa: Crumble the Roquefort into the mixture and combine well. Adjust the seasoning with salt.

ROQUEFORT AND TOASTED NUT SALSA

MAKES 1 CUP

⅓ cup whole pecans

⅓ cup whole pine nuts

⅓ cup whole macadamia nuts

⅓ teaspoon minced garlic

2 tablespoons honey

1 tablespoon Dijon mustard

1 ½ tablespoons rice wine vinegar

2 tablespoons chopped fresh chives

2 tablespoons chopped jalapeño

4 ounces Roquefort cheese

⅔ teaspoon kosher salt

HERB-ROASTED BEEF TENDERLOIN

SERVES 4

2 tablespoons mustard seeds

1 tablespoon fennel seeds

½ tablespoon cumin seed

1 tablespoon black peppercorns

1 tablespoon chopped fresh thyme

2 tablespoons olive oil

1 tablespoon coarse salt

4 8-ounce filets mignons

To roast the herbs: Heat a dry sauté pan on top of the stove. Add the mustard, fennel and cumin seeds, and black peppercorns. Toast these for 1 minute on medium heat. Remove the mixture from the heat and let it cool. Crush the spices in a small mortar with a pestle. Add the thyme. Moisten with the olive oil.

To prepare and cook the beef: Preheat the oven to 375°. Season the filets mignons with the salt and rub them with the herb mixture. In a hot ovenproof pan sear the filets on both sides. Pan-roast the filets in the oven for 3 to 4 minutes on each side.

To assemble and serve: Serve the roast filets with a generous helping of Wild Mushroom Salsa.

ACCOMPANIMENT:
WILD MUSHROOM SALSA

You can use any combination of wild or domestic mushrooms for the salsa, but I think it's important to use at least 3 different kinds for depth of flavor and texture.

To prepare the mushrooms: Clean each of the mushrooms and cut them in a small even dice. Warm the olive oil in a sauté pan. When the oil is hot, sauté the mushrooms quickly. Be careful not to overfill the pan. If necessary, sauté them in 2 batches and season with salt and pepper. Transfer the mushrooms to a stainless-steel bowl to cool.

To finish the salsa: Add the remaining ingredients to the bowl with the cooled mushrooms, and combine well. This can be made ahead and stored refrigerated for up to a day ahead.

WILD MUSHROOM SALSA

MAKES 2 CUPS

1   cup shiitake mushrooms

1   cup crimini mushrooms

1   cup chanterelle mushrooms

3   tablespoons olive oil

1   teaspoon kosher salt

1   teaspoon fresh ground black pepper

1   teaspoon ground cumin

3   tablespoons chopped Cubanelle chili

3   tablespoons chopped scallions

3   tablespoons chopped black olives

2   tablespoons chopped fresh cilantro

3   tablespoons lime juice

BUFFALO STEAKS WITH ROSEMARY

SERVES 4

4   8-ounce buffalo strip loin steaks

2   tablespoons minced fresh rosemary

2   tablespoons chopped garlic

1   tablespoon cracked black peppercorns

2   tablespoons olive oil

1   tablespoon kosher salt

Buffalo steak is a great alternative for those beef cravings. This delicious and full-flavored red meat has about half the fat and less than 50 percent the cholesterol of beef. Because buffalo is so lean, it's important not to overcook it so it doesn't get tough.

To prepare the steaks: Season the steaks with the rosemary, garlic, black peppercorns, and olive oil.

To cook the steaks: Preheat a grill or the broiler. It's essential to cook this meat over very high heat. One of the arts of steak cooking is to mark or brand the steak with the cross hatchings of the grill. This is done very easily. Begin by grilling the steak on the first side for 2 minutes, then turn the steak 45° (like a half left-hand turn) and continue grilling the same side for another 2 minutes. This will result in the cross-hatch marks. Turn the steak and grill the other side in the same manner. Remove the steak from the grill and season with the salt. Serve with Sweet Potato Hash.

ACCOMPANIMENT:
SWEET POTATO HASH

Sweet potatoes remind me of the crisp, cool days of autumn in New York, and of desires created by the chill in the air. Hash was, and still is, one of those desires.

To prepare the sweet potatoes: Preheat the oven to 350°. Wash and dry the sweet potatoes. Place the potatoes directly on the oven rack and bake them for 45 minutes, They should be slightly soft to the touch. Remove from the oven and let them cool completely. Peel the sweet potatoes and dice them into ½-inch cubes.

To prepare the hash: In a large, flat pan warm the olive oil on medium heat. Add the shallots and cook until they're caramelized, 3 or 4 minutes. Add the garlic and the diced sweet potato. Toss together and cook for another minute. Then add the star anise, red pepper, serrano chili, and parsley. Sauté together for another minute and season with salt.

SWEET POTATO HASH

SERVES 4 (2 CUPS)

- 4 medium sweet potatoes
- 3 tablespoons olive oil
- ½ cup julienned shallots
- 2 teaspoons chopped garlic
- ½ teaspoon ground star anise
- ½ cup diced red bell pepper
- 1 tablespoon diced serrano chili
- 1 tablespoon chopped fresh flat-leaf parsley
- 1 teaspoon kosher salt

CHAPTER 8

BIRDS

AND

POULTRY

CHICKEN
Chicken and Yams with Gingered Figs

Fufu-Crusted Chicken with a Black Bean Puree

Cumin-Baked Chicken *served with*
Puree of Three Latin Root Vegetables

Chilled Fricassee of Chicken, Chayote, and Cilantro

Poussin with Sour Orange–Oregano Mojo
served with Pigeon Pea Rice

TURKEY
Turkey Paillard with Toasted Cumin Seed *served with*
Green Papaya Slaw

QUAIL
Grilled Quail with Plantains, Apple, and Breadfruit

Tangerine Barbecued Homestead Quail
with Mango and White Bean Salsa

SQUAB
Tamarind-Glazed Squab *served with*
Ginger-Baked Calabaza

Lime-Grilled Squab *served with*
Green Onion Polenta

DUCK

Pecan Wood–Grilled Duck Breast
with Grapefruit and Juniper Berry Glaze

Honey-Chili Roast Duck *served with*
Stir-Fry Wild Rice

RABBIT

Medallions of Rabbit and Fire-Roasted Pepper Coulis
served with Papaya Corn Fritters

Roasted Rabbit with Crisp Orange Skin
served with Sun-Dried Fruit Relish

hicken seems to be the universal comparison. We talk about rabbit tasting like chicken, frog's legs tasting like chicken, and rattlesnake tasting like chicken. How can so many things resemble chicken? I don't know, but my love of it has its roots in my family's Friday night traditions, when my mother, father, and we four kids sat down at the table for supper. We'd begin by saying a prayer for the wine and a prayer for the bread. Then my mother served her chicken soup with noodles. The steam from the bowls rose with our contentment, and we'd move on to the salad, and finally the roast chicken with green vegetables. My mother cooked the chicken well but simply: seasoned with paprika, garlic, salt, a touch of pepper, and a little corn oil.

Americans love chicken for very good reason: it's versatile, lending itself to a wide range of preparations; it's economical; and it represents the fulfillment of the 1930s America's dream: a chicken in every pot. Although Americans have become accustomed to their taste, I'd stay far away from supermarket chickens, which are factory produced and have very little flavor. I prefer the more pronounced flavors of free-range or kosher chickens, which are easy to find, still economical, and will make a New World of difference in these recipes.

Turkey is a New World bird whose place in American cuisine has been pretty much confined to Thanksgiving and Christmas, because, until relatively recently, it was only available whole. Now that it's available in pieces or quick-cooking paillards, it's a lean, healthy, and flavorful alternative all year round.

Quail is easy, approachable, and delicious. You can buy the birds already boned, and the meat is very subtle and nicely flavored. Quail, squab, and pigeon might require a bit of attitude adjustment to eat, but I promise you they're wonderful. You eat them medium rare, with a little pink to the bone, so that their very lean flesh doesn't dry out. In the classical French tradition, chefs usually wrap the breasts with bacon or lard so that when they roast they maintain their moisture. The quick cooking methods I suggest for these game birds will guarantee their succulence on the plate.

Don't forget poussin either, or game hens. Fresh Cornish hens—frozen, if you must—are a delicious change of pace from chicken, as is the meat of the creature that is always included in the poultry section of cookbooks: rabbit.

Many Americans have an aversion to the idea of eating this marvelous meat, but in France rabbit is very popular and hangs, freshly skinned, in marketplaces all over the country. The prospect of eating rabbit was not the surprise I'd imagined it would be to my first-term cooking students at Florida International University, since the Latinos, in particular, ate it often. But there was a time, not too long ago, however, when my wife Judi was a rabbit virgin.

We were in Champagne, visiting Charles Heidsieck, who owns one of the oldest champagne houses in France. After a tour of his facility and his fantastic old home overlooking the cathedral of Reims, where all the kings were anointed with holy oil, the four of us—Monsieur and Madame Heidsieck, Judi, and I—went out to his country club to dine under the trees. Judi doesn't speak French, so when, after the first few courses, we were served what looked like chicken and were told in French, "This is a rabbit course," she picked up her fork without hesitation and ate.

"Do you like it?" I asked.

She said she did—very much.

"You know you just ate rabbit," I told her.

That evening, in France under the trees, Judi blushed and put down her fork, but since that time she eats and enjoys rabbit. That's one of the aims of New World Cuisine—to open up a world of possibilities for pleasure in foods that may have been unfamiliar.

CHICKEN AND YAMS WITH GINGERED FIGS

SERVES 4

1   tablespoon chopped fresh cilantro

3   tablespoons plus 1 teaspoon olive oil

1   teaspoon kosher salt

½   teaspoon coarse ground black pepper

4   boneless, skinless chicken breasts

2   large yams

¼   teaspoon ground allspice

¼   teaspoon grated nutmeg

2   large egg whites

12 fresh figs

1   tablespoon chopped fresh ginger

1   vanilla bean

1   cup dry white wine

2   cups arugula leaves

3   tablespoons extra-virgin olive oil

1   tablespoon balsamic vinegar

This is a light but wonderfully rich and flavorful supper dish that fuses lettuce, protein, fruits, and vegetables. Fresh figs are available summer and fall, but you can also make this recipe with dried figs for a different, more wintry flavor.

To marinate the chicken: In a small bowl combine the cilantro, 1 teaspoon of olive oil, ½ teaspoon of salt, and ¼ teaspoon of pepper. Marinate the chicken in the herb mixture for 30 minutes.

To prepare the yams: Peel the yams. On a box grater, using the largest holes, grate the yams. Season with the remaining salt and pepper, the allspice, and nutmeg.

To prepare and cook the chicken: Place the egg whites in a shallow bowl. Dip the chicken breasts in the egg white, then into the seasoned yams. Pack the yams on the chicken to encrust it completely. Set this aside in the refrigerator for 10 minutes. Warm the 3 tablespoons of olive oil in a sauté pan and cook the chicken until well browned, turn, and cook through; approximately 5 minutes. Remove from the heat and set aside.

To prepare the figs: In a shallow pan poach the figs with the ginger, vanilla bean, and white wine over very low heat for 5 minutes.

To assemble and serve: Toss the arugula with the extra-virgin olive oil and balsamic vinegar. Arrange on a plate with the chicken. Cut the figs in half and arrange them around the chicken.

"Fufu," a mashed plantain mixture, is served in the Caribbean as a side dish or stuffing. In this recipe I've used it to form a crust for the chicken to seal in its moisture and succulence.

To prepare the fufu: Preheat the oven to 350°. Place the plantains directly on the oven rack and roast them for 35 to 40 minutes, until cooked through and soft to the touch. Remove them from the oven and cool slightly before peeling. Place the plantains in a large mixing bowl and mash them with a wooden spoon. Add the garlic, 2 tablespoons of the olive oil, the cumin, 1 teaspoon of salt, and 1 teaspoon of black pepper. Mix together well and let cool completely.

To cook the chicken: Season each chicken breast with 1 teaspoon of salt and ½ teaspoon of pepper. Pack the fufu mixture on top of the chicken breasts to create a ⅓-inch crust. Warm a large skillet with the remaining olive oil. When the oil is hot, place the breasts fufu side down. Cook the breasts for 4 minutes on medium heat until well browned. Then turn and cook the other side for another 2 minutes, until cooked through. Remove from the pan and set aside for 1 minute.

To prepare the puree: Warm the black beans with a half cup of their cooking liquid, then transfer them to a food processor and puree. Add the sherry vinegar and extra-virgin olive oil and continue to process together until smooth. Season with 1 teaspoon of salt and ½ teaspoon of pepper, then pour the puree back into the saucepot and warm it. Add the cilantro just before serving. If the black beans are too thick to pour, dilute them with a little more of the cooking liquid.

To assemble and serve: Spread the black bean puree on the base of the plate. Slice the fufu-crusted chicken on a bias, and fan the slices over the puree.

FUFU-CRUSTED CHICKEN WITH A BLACK BEAN PUREE

SERVES 4

2   large green plantains, unpeeled

1   teaspoon minced garlic

6   tablespoons olive oil

1   teaspoon ground cumin

3   teaspoons kosher salt

2   teaspoons coarse ground black pepper

4   10-ounce boneless, skinless chicken breasts

1½ cups cooked black beans

2   tablespoons sherry vinegar

2   tablespoons extra-virgin olive oil

3   tablespoons chopped fresh cilantro

CUMIN-BAKED CHICKEN

SERVES 4

1   3-pound chicken

2   tablespoons ground cumin

1   tablespoon chopped fresh oregano

1   tablespoon fresh ground black pepper

1   tablespoon kosher salt

3   tablespoons white wine

2   tablespoons olive oil

The combination of cumin and oregano composes one of my favorite seasonings for poultry. Here it is served with a puree of Latin vegetables for a knockout effect. Flavors like these inspired me to learn everything I could about the creations of the Latin kitchen.

To prepare the chicken: Cut off the wing tips of the chicken. In a small bowl, combine the remaining ingredients. Coat the chicken with this mixture inside and out. Plump the chicken together so the legs and wings are set back toward the bird.

To bake the chicken: Preheat the oven to 350°. Place the chicken breast side up in a shallow baking dish and set it in the center of the oven. Bake for 25 minutes, then lower the temperature to 325° and continue to bake for 30 minutes more. The chicken should be finished and golden brown after 55 minutes of cooking. Remove from the oven and let it rest in the baking pan for 5 minutes before you cut it.

To serve: Carve the chicken and serve the purees separately.

ACCOMPANIMENT:
PUREE OF THREE LATIN ROOT VEGETABLES

Root vegetables are a staple of the Latin diet, and any of these starchy vegetables, familiar or newly available in this country, can be used for this recipe. In Miami, 4 or 5 Latin root vegetables are available in the major grocery chains. You can adjust the recipe with those that are available in your area.

To prepare the vegetables: The key here is to cook each of the root vegetables separately. Peel each of the vegetables. Place them in 3 separate pots, cover with cold water, and then add about 1 tablespoon of salt to each pot. Put the pots on the heat and bring to a boil. Lower to a simmer and cook for approximately 40 minutes, until cooked through and soft.

To puree the vegetables: Drain the malanga, yuca, and boniato separately and put them into 3 large mixing bowls. Using a ricer or a food mill, push the vegetables through into a second set of bowls. Add enough olive oil to each to smooth the mixture. Adjust the seasoning of each with the remaining salt and white pepper.

To flavor the root purees: The amount and type of fresh herbs to be added to each root puree is a matter of personal preference. To the malanga I add chives. I like yuca seasoned with tarragon, and the boniato with cilantro. Keep each puree warm on the stove top.

PUREE OF THREE LATIN ROOT VEGETABLES

SERVES 6

$^1\!/_2$ *pound malanga*

$^1\!/_2$ *pound yuca*

$^1\!/_2$ *pound boniato*

5   *tablespoons kosher salt*

6   *tablespoons extra-virgin olive oil*

3   *tablespoons white pepper*

2   *tablespoons chopped fresh chives*

2   *tablespoons chopped fresh tarragon*

2   *tablespoons chopped fresh cilantro*

CHILLED FRICASSEE OF CHICKEN, CHAYOTE, AND CILANTRO

SERVES 4

2 8-ounce skinless, boneless chicken breasts

3 cups chicken stock

2 medium chayotes, diced

2 medium shallots, peeled and diced

1 teaspoon ground turmeric

1/2 teaspoon minced fresh oregano

1/4 teaspoon ground cumin

1 1/2 teaspoons kosher salt

1/2 teaspoon fresh ground black pepper

2 tablespoons extra-virgin olive oil

2 teaspoons chopped fresh cilantro

Juice of 1/2 lime

1/8 teaspoon cayenne pepper

This is a perfect dish to follow a long hot day at the beach, because you can prepare it the day before and serve it cold.

To make the fricassee: In a large pot poach the chicken breasts in the stock with the chayotes, shallots, 3/4 teaspoon of turmeric, oregano, and cumin for 15 minutes, until the chayotes are soft. Remove the chicken and 1/2 cup of the chayotes. Season with the salt and black pepper. Puree the rest of the chayotes with the cooking liquid. Pass the puree through a fine sieve and let cool for 30 minutes. Add the olive oil and chill for at least 2 hours. This can be prepared the day before. Store the chicken, chayote, and puree separately in the refrigerator. When ready to serve, mix 1 teaspoon of the cilantro, the lime juice, and the cayenne into the puree.

To assemble and serve: Dice the cooled chicken. Divide the chicken and chayote garnish into 4 low-sided bowls. Pour about 3/4 cup of the cold chayote puree into each bowl. Garnish with a shake of turmeric and the remaining cilantro.

Poussin, or baby chicken, is very tender and sweet, and roasting keeps it moist and juicy. I marinate the bird in the mojo for about 1 hour to infuse herb and fruit flavors, but you can leave it marinating for as long as 24 hours. Then simply roast the chicken until it's crisp and golden brown, and serve with Pigeon Pea Rice.

To prepare the poussins: Cut the wing tips from the wings. Wash the birds in cold water and dry well. Combine the remaining ingredients in a large bowl and mix thoroughly. Coat the poussins inside and out with the marinade. Set aside for at least 1 hour at room temperature, covered with plastic wrap or in a plastic bag.

To roast the poussins: Preheat the oven to 350°. Set a roasting pan with a rack just larger than the poussins in the oven to preheat also. Remove the poussins from the marinade. Now "shape" the birds before you roast. To do this, place the birds on a work surface. Plump the breast by tucking the wings slightly under the bird and pushing the legs back close to the bird. Carefully place the poussins in the center of the hot roasting pan with the breast up. Ladle 2 tablespoons of marinade over the birds and place in the oven. After 15 minutes, baste again with 2 tablespoons of marinade and turn the birds over, taking care not to pierce the skin. Roast on the back side for 10 minutes and turn over one more time. Baste with another 2 tablespoons of marinade, and continue roasting approximately 15 more minutes, until golden brown.

To serve: Cut the birds in quarters and serve with the Pigeon Pea Rice under the poussin pieces in the center of the plate.

ACCOMPANIMENT:
PIGEON PEA RICE
SEE NEXT PAGE

POUSSIN WITH SOUR ORANGE-OREGANO MOJO

SERVES 4

4   22- to 24-ounce baby chickens

3   large sour oranges

3   tablespoons chopped fresh oregano

1   tablespoon ground cumin

1/2   cup julienned sweet onion

1   tablespoon minced garlic

2   tablespoons olive oil

1/2   tablespoon coarse ground black pepper

1   tablespoon kosher salt

PIGEON PEA RICE

SERVES 4 (4 CUPS)

½	cup chopped Spanish onion
2	tablespoons olive oil
1	teaspoon minced garlic
2	cups raw white rice
2½	cups water
1	bay leaf
1	teaspoon minced fresh thyme
2	teaspoons kosher salt
½	teaspoon coarse ground black pepper
1	teaspoon ground cumin
1	whole Scotch bonnet
¾	cup cooked pigeon peas
2	tablespoons chopped fresh cilantro

To cook the rice: In a large saucepot combine the onion and olive oil; cook over medium heat until the onion is translucent. Add the garlic, then the white rice, water, bay leaf, thyme, salt, pepper, cumin, and Scotch bonnet. Bring the mixture to a boil and reduce the heat to low. Cover and simmer for 20 minutes. Do not stir the rice after it has boiled, and be careful later not to break the Scotch bonnet, which imparts a wonderful hot citrus flavor when cooked whole. Remove the rice from the heat and take out the Scotch bonnet and bay leaf.

To finish the rice: Add the pigeon peas and cilantro. Mix well and serve.

A paillard is a thinly sliced and pounded piece of meat. To pound the turkey, place a thin slice between 2 large pieces of plastic and flatten it carefully with a mallet or the back of a flat pan. Remember that the lean, low-fat turkey paillard will cook quickly.

Toasting the cumin seed: Warm a dry, heavy pan until it's hot. Add the cumin seed and black peppercorns to the pan and toast them to bring out their natural oils. Remove from the heat, put them in a plastic bag, and crush with a mallet or the back of a cool, flat pan.

To cook the paillards: Heat the grill or broiler very hot so that the paillards cook quickly yet maintain their juices. Season the paillards with the fresh crushed cuminseed and peppercorns, the thyme, and salt. Drizzle with the olive oil. Grill the first side of the paillards for just about 1 minute, then turn and cook the other side for about 30 seconds. Remove from the heat and serve the Green Papaya Slaw on the side.

ACCOMPANIMENT:
GREEN PAPAYA SLAW

Papaya is eaten green or unripened throughout Latin and South America. The green fruit is crisp, juicy, firm, yet almost starchy in character. Green papaya can be used cooked, raw, or pickled in various recipes.

To prepare the papaya: Peel the skin from the papaya. Cut the flesh into quarters and discard the green seeds. Using a grater or mandolin, julienne the papaya pieces.

To make the slaw: Combine all the ingredients in a bowl and toss well. Let the flavors mature for an hour before serving.

TURKEY PAILLARD WITH TOASTED CUMIN SEED

SERVES 4

2	tablespoons cumin seed
1	tablespoon whole black peppercorns
1½	pounds turkey breast, cut and pounded into 4 paillards
1	teaspoon minced fresh thyme
1	teaspoon kosher salt
2	tablespoons olive oil

GREEN PAPAYA SLAW

SERVES 4 (2 CUPS)

1	medium green papaya
1	medium red bell pepper, julienned
1	small carrot, julienned
1	small white onion, julienned
2	tablespoons julienned fresh ginger
	Juice of 1 large lime
2	tablespoons olive oil
2	teaspoons celery seeds
1	tablespoon kosher salt
1	teaspoon white pepper

GRILLED QUAIL WITH PLANTAINS, APPLE, AND BREADFRUIT

SERVES 4

8 large quail (see recipe head)

2 teaspoons minced garlic

1 teaspoon minced fresh thyme

1 tablespoon kosher salt

1 teaspoon coarse ground black pepper

5 tablespoons olive oil

1 medium breadfruit

1 medium sweet onion, julienned

1 large green plantain, peeled, and sliced

1 medium green apple, peeled and sliced

Quail are immensely flavorful, and grilling helps maintain their earthy character. They're simple to handle and can be bought from specialty markets and gourmet shops "European style"—that is, with all the bones removed except those in the wings and the legs. The breast meat takes a little less time to grill than the legs. To prepare the quail for grilling, just sever the breast from the legs with a sharp knife.

To prepare the quail: Season the separated breasts and legs with 1 teaspoon of garlic, ½ teaspoon of thyme, 1 teaspoon of salt, and ½ teaspoon of pepper. Drizzle with 2 tablespoons of the olive oil. Preheat the grill or broiler until very hot.

To prepare the breadfruit: Peel the breadfruit and cut it into quarters. Cook the breadfruit as you would a potato in plenty of salted water, bringing it to a boil and reducing the heat to a simmer for 15 minutes. Remove from the heat and strain. Rinse the breadfruit under cold running water to cool. Then slice the quarters ¼ inch thick.

To finish the vegetables: In a large sauté pan warm the remaining olive oil. Start with the sweet onion and sauté until translucent. Add the sliced plantains and cook for 3 or 4 minutes. Add the green apple and sliced breadfruit and season with the remaining garlic, thyme, salt, and pepper.

To grill: Preheat a grill or broiler. Grill the quail breasts and legs separately. The breasts should be grilled on high heat for 3 or 4 minutes turning each minute; the legs should be cooked on slightly lower heat for 5 or 6 minutes, also turning each minute. When finished grilling, set aside to rest for a minute.

To assemble and serve: Arrange the vegetables in the center of a large, rustic, ceramic platter. Place the legs along the edge of the platter, and on top of each pair of legs place one breast.

TANGERINE BARBECUED HOMESTEAD QUAIL WITH MANGO AND WHITE BEAN SALSA

SERVES 6

12 large quail

1 cup Tangerine Barbecue Sauce (recipe follows)

2 tablespoons kosher salt

1 tablespoon coarse ground black pepper

1 large mango, firm (not ripe), diced

½ cup diced red onion

1 cup cooked white beans

1 teaspoon minced serrano chili

3 tablespoons chopped fresh cilantro

3 tablespoons chopped fresh flat-leaf parsley

½ teaspoon minced garlic

2 teaspoons lime juice

1 tablespoon extra-virgin olive oil

Let's say you're in the mood for a barbecue, but upscale, one that's different and sophisticated. Maybe the weather is fine, great friends are coming over for dinner, or maybe it's just you and your family, celebrating being together. For those times when barbecued chicken seems nearly right—but too mundane—choose quail, the freshest available in your region. It's elegant but easy to prepare, and you can use my Tangerine Barbecue Sauce or a commercial preparation. The Homestead in this recipe refers to a local farm area that is known for raising quail.

To barbecue the quail: Preheat the barbecue grill on medium for 30 minutes. (You can also use an oven broiler.) At the same time, marinate the quail in the Tangerine Barbecue Sauce. Season the quail with salt and pepper just before cooking. Barbecue the quail carefully, avoiding charring the bird by frequently turning it until it is crisp-skinned and cooked throughout. This should take 7 to 8 minutes overall.

To make the mango and white bean salsa: In a large stainless-steel bowl combine the remaining ingredients. This can be prepared one day ahead and stored in the refrigerator. Before serving allow to come to room temperature.

To serve: Set the salsa in the center of a large oval platter and arrange the barbecued quail around the platter.

Combine all of the ingredients in a food processor. Transfer the mixture to a heavy saucepot and cook on medium heat for 30 minutes or until thick enough to coat the back of a spoon. Strain though a fine sieve, cool, then cover and refrigerate until ready to use.

TANGERINE BARBECUE SAUCE

SERVES 6

Juice of 10 tangerines

³/₄	cup molasses
¹/₂	cup Dijon mustard
2	tablespoons diced garlic
1	cup tomato ketchup
¹/₂	cup diced onion
¹/₄	cup red wine vinegar
2	large chipotles (smoked, dried jalapeños)
¹/₂	teaspoon ground cinnamon
2	whole cloves

TAMARIND-GLAZED SQUAB

SERVES 4

½   cup tamarind pulp

1   tablespoon minced garlic

1   tablespoon mustard seeds

2   tablespoons honey

1   teaspoon minced fresh thyme

2   cups dry red wine

4   whole squabs

1   teaspoon kosher salt

½   teaspoon coarse ground black pepper

2   tablespoons olive oil

I was a guest chef on Cunard's cruise ship Sea Goddess, sailing in the Mediterranean from Ibiza, when I developed this dish to demonstrate my New World Cuisine to the European passengers. They loved this classic bird roasted in a very modern way.

To prepare the glaze: In a medium saucepan warm together the tamarind, garlic, mustard seeds, honey, thyme, and red wine. Simmer for 30 minutes and strain. Return the mixture to the heat and continue to cook for approximately 15 minutes until it thickens to a syrupy consistency.

To roast the squab: Preheat the oven to 375°. Set the squabs in a roasting pan, season them with salt and pepper, then drizzle with olive oil. Roast breast side up for 5 minutes. Brush the birds with the tamarind glaze and turn them over. Reduce the heat to 350° and roast for 5 more minutes. Turn the squabs back to breast side up, glazing again with the tamarind. Finish roasting for just a few minutes, until golden brown. The squab should be cooked until pink in the middle.

To serve: Arrange the glazed squab and 8 wedges of Ginger-Baked Calabaza on a large oval platter.

ACCOMPANIMENT:

GINGER-BAKED CALABAZA

Calabaza is a type of West Indian pumpkin. Its flesh is just a little firmer than that of the pumpkins we are used to, and it's available all year round in local south Florida supermarkets. If calabaza is unavailable where you live, substitute sweet pumpkin or Hubbard squash.

To prepare the calabaza: Trim the top and bottom off the calabaza. Cut into 8 large wedges approximately 3 inches wide. In a bowl combine the ginger, soy sauce, garlic, honey, and lemon juice. Toss the calabaza in this mixture and lay the pieces out on a flat pan to roast.

To cook the calabaza: Preheat the oven to 350°. Season the flavored calabaza with salt and pepper. Roast for 30 minutes turning halfway through, until golden brown and soft to the touch. Remove from the oven and serve.

GINGER-BAKED CALABAZA

SERVES 4

1   small calabaza
2   tablespoons chopped fresh ginger
2   tablespoons soy sauce
1   teaspoon minced garlic
2   tablespoons honey
2   tablespoons lemon juice
1   teaspoon kosher salt
1/2 teaspoon course ground black pepper

LIME-GRILLED SQUAB

SERVES 4

4   large squab

2   tablespoons fresh thyme
    leaves

1   tablespoon fresh rosemary
    leaves

1   tablespoon chopped garlic

1   teaspoon kosher salt

1   teaspoon ground black pepper

2   tablespoons olive oil

2   large limes, halved

2   tablespoons snipped fresh
    chives

GREEN ONION

POLENTA

SERVES 4 (2 CUPS)

2   tablespoons sweet butter

1   teaspoon chopped garlic

2   cups chicken broth

1   cup instant polenta

1   teaspoon kosher salt

1/2   teaspoon fresh ground black
      pepper

3   tablespoons sour cream

3   tablespoons chopped
      scallion (green onion)

Squab may be a little difficult to find in the market, but your butcher can order it for you. Cornish hens will also work perfectly well in this recipe, though their flavor isn't as exotic, and the cooking time will be a few minutes longer for the bigger bird. Remember, game birds are usually cooked pink at the bone, while other poultry is cooked though.

To prepare the squab: Cut the wing tips away. Split the squabs in half crosswise, separating the breasts from the legs. Sever the legs, leaving the squab cut in 3 pieces (the double breast and 2 separate legs). Season all the squab parts with the thyme, rosemary, garlic, salt, and pepper. Put the pieces into a stainless-steel bowl and drizzle with olive oil. Coat the squab well.

To grill or broil the birds: Preheat the grill to medium or let the fire of a wood-burning grill die down. Begin by cooking the leg parts because they take a few minutes longer. After 2 minutes, turn the legs and move them to lower heat. At this point put the breasts on the grill. Continue grilling, turning all the pieces at 1-minute intervals, for 4 or 5 minutes, until the exterior is crisp and the meat inside is just tinged pink.

To finish the squab: Remove from the heat onto a warm serving platter and squeeze fresh lime juice over the pieces. Sprinkle with the chives. Serve with the hot Green Onion Polenta on the side.

ACCOMPANIMENT: GREEN ONION POLENTA

In a large saucepot warm the butter and add the garlic. As the garlic turns translucent, add the chicken broth and bring to a boil. Whisk in the polenta and season with salt and pepper. Continue to stir the polenta until it thickens, 5 or 6 minutes. Remove from the heat and add the sour cream and green onion. Mix well and serve.

To marinate the duck breast: In a ceramic dish combine 1 tablespoon of the garlic, the chopped rosemary, olive oil, and 2 tablespoons of the gin with the duck breasts for 2 hours prior to grilling.

To prepare the grapefruit syrup: Combine the grapefruit juice with the sugar and water. Simmer this mixture until 1 cup of grapefruit syrup remains.

To prepare the gin sauce: In a saucepan simmer the Zinfandel with the shallots, juniper berries, peppercorns, thyme, and the remaining garlic. Reduce this on medium heat for 10 minutes, until ¾ cup of liquid remains. Add the duck or chicken stock and continue to reduce the mixture for 10 more minutes, until ¾ cup of liquid is left. Add the grapefruit syrup. Strain the sauce through a fine sieve and return to the heat. Bring back to a simmer. Season with salt and pepper, add the remaining gin, and reduce to the thickness of a glaze.

To cook the duck: Prepare a wood-burning grill with pecan wood, or prepare a charcoal grill 1 hour ahead, or preheat a gas grill or oven broiler. Place the duck breasts skin down on the grill and grill slowly and carefully for about 20 minutes, until the skin is crisp and the fat is cooked away. Turn the breast, being careful not to puncture the flesh. Cook this side for only 1 minute.

To assemble and serve: Cover half the plate with the grapefruit sauce. Slice the breasts, skin side down, on an angle across the 2 halves. Fan out the meat on the plate. Garnish with a fresh rosemary sprig and a few grapefruit segments.

PECAN WOOD-GRILLED DUCK BREAST WITH GRAPEFRUIT AND JUNIPER BERRY GLAZE

SERVES 4

2	tablespoons chopped garlic
½	teaspoon chopped fresh rosemary, plus 1 sprig
2	tablespoons olive oil
4	tablespoons gin
3	large Florida grapefruits, 2 juiced, 1 cut into segments
1	cup sugar
1	cup water
4	whole duck breasts, skin on
2	cups red Zinfandel wine
2	tablespoons chopped shallots
10	juniper berries
6	peppercorns
2	sprigs thyme
2	cups duck stock or Chicken Stock (page 21)

Kosher salt and fresh ground black pepper

HONEY-CHILI ROAST DUCK

SERVES 6

3   4-pound ducks
1   tablespoon minced fresh thyme
2   tablespoons chopped garlic
2   tablespoons kosher salt
1   tablespoon fresh ground black pepper
2   tablespoons olive oil
1/4   cup honey
2   tablespoons Thai garlic-chili sauce
1   tablespoon lemon juice
2   tablespoons Dijon mustard
1/2   cup dark rum

Duck is one of those dishes that many people enjoy eating but feel are too complicated to make at home. I would encourage those of you who love to cook not to be intimidated. It's actually very easy to handle.

To start the duck: Cut the first 2 joints from the wing. Wash the ducks well inside and out. In a small bowl combine the thyme, garlic, salt, pepper, and olive oil. Rub the ducks with the seasoning mixture inside and out. Preheat the oven to 425°.

To roast the duck: Preheat the roasting rack and pan. When it is very hot, place the ducks toward the center of the oven. Roast for 20 minutes, then lower the oven temperature to 350° for 45 more minutes. At this point remove the ducks from the oven and let them rest for 10 minutes. Pour the hot duck fat off to cool and discard later. Keep the oven on.

To glaze the duck: In a small bowl combine the honey, garlic-chili sauce, lemon juice, Dijon mustard, and rum. Baste the ducks with this mixture, then return them to the oven still set at 350°. This final process will crisp the skin as well as intensify the flavor. Roast the ducks for another 15 minutes, brushing every 5 minutes with the honey-chili sauce. When the skin is crisp and golden brown, remove the ducks from the oven and let them rest for a few moments.

To serve: Separate the breast from the leg meat. Working quickly, tear the leg meat from the bones, then julienne any large pieces of dark meat. Place this dark meat on top of the Stir-Fry Wild Rice. Remove the bones from the breast and serve whole on top of the leg meat.

ACCOMPANIMENT:
STIR-FRY WILD RICE

To prepare the rice: In a saucepot simmer the wild rice in the chicken broth for 20 minutes covered, until just tender. Be sure not to burst the grains by overcooking. Remove from the heat and allow to set for 10 minutes.

To stir-fry: In a hot wok or a high-sided sauté pan begin by stir-frying the bok choy in the sesame oil. Add the garlic and ginger and stir-fry for another few moments. Add the red pepper, poblano chili, bean sprouts, and scallions. Now add the wild rice. Season with the hoisin sauce, cilantro, and lime juice.

STIR-FRY WILD RICE

SERVES 6 (3 CUPS)

1	cup wild rice
2	cups chicken broth
½	cup chopped bok choy
¼	cup sesame oil
1	tablespoon chopped garlic
1	tablespoon chopped fresh ginger
¼	cup julienned red bell pepper
¼	cup diced poblano chili
¼	cup bean sprouts
¼	cup chopped scallions
2	tablespoons hoisin sauce
2	tablespoons chopped fresh cilantro
1	teaspoon lime juice

MEDALLIONS OF RABBIT AND FIRE-ROASTED PEPPER COULIS

SERVES 4

4 medium rabbit loins
½ head garlic
1 sprig rosemary
1 whole bay leaf
1 cup grape-seed oil
1 bundle baby leeks
3 medium red bell peppers
⅛ teaspoon minced Scotch bonnet
2 tablespoons sherry vinegar
1 teaspoon kosher salt
½ teaspoon fresh ground black pepper
1 medium papaya

A saddle is the flavorful back portion of the rabbit, which contains the 2 rabbit loins. I used to think that rabbit was very much a French-influenced culinary treat, but now I've discovered it's very common in Latin cookery as well.

To marinate the rabbit: Clean any sinew that remains on the loin. Marinate the loin fillets in 4 whole cloves of garlic, the rosemary, bay leaf, and grape-seed oil. If possible, prepare this a day ahead.

To prepare the leeks: In a pan blanche the baby leeks. Trim to 3-inch lengths. These will be used to wrap around the medallions.

To prepare the red peppers: Roast the red peppers over an open flame until all sides are well charred. Remove from the heat and cover. When cooled, peel off the skin and remove the seeds. Puree the roasted peppers with 1 clove of garlic and the Scotch bonnet. Stir in the sherry vinegar and ½ teaspoon of salt.

To cook the rabbit: Sear the rabbit fillets in an oven-proof pan on top of the stove to brown all sides. Then transfer them to a 350° oven for 5 minutes to finish the cooking. Remove from the pan, season with the remaining salt and fresh black pepper, then cut each fillet into 3 medallions 1½ inches thick. Wrap each medallion in a baby leek white.

To assemble and serve: Cover the bottom of each plate with the fire-roasted pepper coulis, then place a Papaya Corn Fritter in the center. Arrange the medallions of rabbit wrapped with the leeks, 3 to a plate, around the edge of the corn fritter. Garnish with slices of papaya.

ACCOMPANIMENT:
PAPAYA CORN FRITTERS

To prepare the corn: Put the corn in a pot of boiling water with the garlic cloves until it's cooked but still firm, about 6 minutes. Cool and cut the corn off the cob.

To make the batter: In a large bowl sift together the cake flour, baking powder, dry mustard, salt, and cayenne. Add the eggs and mix. Add the buttermilk until the mixture is thick but still pourable. Add the corn and papaya and adjust the seasoning with additional salt.

To cook the fritters: In a sauté pan warm the clarified butter over medium heat. For each fritter, ladle 2 tablespoons of batter into the pan. Brown well, cooking for approximately 2 minutes on each side. Remove the fritters from the pan and drain on paper towels.

PAPAYA CORN FRITTERS

SERVES 4

1	*medium corn on the cob*
2	*cloves garlic*
1/2	*cup cake flour*
1	*tablespoon baking powder*
1	*teaspoon English dry mustard*
1	*teaspoon kosher salt, plus extra to taste*
1/8	*teaspoon cayenne pepper*
2	*large eggs*
1/4	*cup buttermilk*
1	*small papaya, diced*
2	*tablespoons clarified butter*

ROASTED RABBIT WITH CRISP ORANGE SKIN

SERVES 6

1   large orange

2   tablespoons kosher salt

2   tablespoons cracked black peppercorns

2   3-pound rabbits, each cut into 6 pieces

1   teaspoon chopped garlic

1   teaspoon chopped fresh ginger

3   tablespoons olive oil

Rabbit is a very flavorful but lean meat, perfect for the modern fat-wary diner.

To prepare the orange seasoning salt: Using a vegetable peeler, remove all of the orange rind and dry it on a cookie sheet in a 200° oven for 40 minutes. Remove from the oven, cool, then chop. Combine the chopped rind with the salt and cracked peppercorns. This orange seasoning salt can be prepared ahead and kept in a sealed jar for weeks.

To prepare the rabbit: Wash the rabbit pieces and dry them well. Season with the orange salt, garlic, and ginger. Drizzle with the olive oil.

To roast the rabbit: Preheat the oven to 350°. Place the rabbit in a roasting pan and roast for 15 minutes. Brush with the pan drippings. Turn the pieces, continuing to roast for 15 minutes, until cooked through and crisp.

To serve: Place the rabbit pieces on a large serving platter and present with a cup of Sun-Dried Fruit Relish on the side.

ACCOMPANIMENT:
SUN-DRIED FRUIT RELISH

As the word implies, a relish is a condiment intended to enhance the pleasure of a dish. Dried fruits, with their intensely concentrated flavors and fabulous texture, are combined here in a relish that is sublime with roast meat, game, or poultry. It will keep for weeks tightly covered in the refrigerator.

To begin the relish: In a large sauté pan warm the olive oil. Add the onion and cook until caramelized, about 5 minutes. Add the garlic, cumin, and salt; cook the mixture on low heat for another minute. Add the white wine and bring to a boil. Remove from the heat.

To incorporate the dried fruits: Place all of the dried fruits in a large bowl and pour the hot onion mixture over them. Let the fruits soften together. Cover until completely cooled.

To finish the relish: Mix in the cilantro, scallions, and Anaheim chilies.

SUN-DRIED FRUIT RELISH

MAKES 4 CUPS

2   tablespoons olive oil
1   cup diced onions
1   tablespoon chopped garlic
1   teaspoon ground cumin
1   teaspoon kosher salt
2   cups dry white wine
1   cup chopped dried figs
1   cup chopped dried mango
1   cup chopped dried pineapple
1/2 cup dried cranberries
1/2 cup chopped fresh cilantro
1/2 cup chopped scallions
1/2 cup chopped Anaheim chilies

CHAPTER 9
DESSERTS

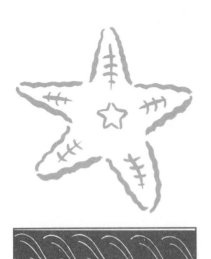

CHOCOLATE DESSERTS
Double Chocolate Coconut Cake

Bittersweet Chocolate Passion-Fruit Torte

Kahlúa Milk Chocolate Cheesecake
with a Crispy Hazelnut Crust

White Chocolate Macadamia Nut Bombe

Chocolate Cappuccino Brownies

Rocky Mango Brownies

Chocolate Pecan Pie

Godiva Chocolate Truffle Soufflé

Fallen Chocolate Soufflé Roulade

Chocolate Pots de Crème

White Chocolate and Tea Pavé

Chef Allen's Derby Pie

Flourless Tiramisu Torte

White and Dark Chocolate Chip Cookies

Milk Chocolate Hazelnut Bars

FRUIT AND SPICE DESSERTS
Mango Pot Pie with Praline Topping

Mango Tarte Tatin

Banana Bonbons with Spiced Rum Sauce

Red Banana–Almond Strudel

Key Lime Pie with Lime Curd

Floating Island with Mango-Ginger Sauce
and Fresh Summer Fruit

Papaya-Carrot Cake

Mamey Cheesecake

Blueberry-Starfruit Cobbler

West Indian Pumpkin Waffles

Baked Granny Smith Apples
Wrapped in Phyllo Cocoa Leaves

Apple Pie Timbale

Candied Lemon Slice Cookies

Guava Thumbprint Cookies

Pineapple Cake *served with*
Warm Ginger-Pineapple Salsa

Coconut Crème Brûlée

Pineapple Rice Pudding

Kumquat, Nutmeg, and Allspice Bread Pudding

Sweet Ginger Flan

Pain Perdu (French Toast)

FROZEN DESSERTS
Frozen Grapefruit Soufflé

Key Lime–Chocolate Napoleons

Mango Parfait

Chocolate Espresso Ice

Iced Cappuccino Float

Café con Leche Parfait

Frozen Jamaican Blue Mountain Sabayon

Blood Orange and Kumquat Sorbet

Grapefruit Sorbet

During my childhood, desserts were a treat and a reward. If I did something right, I'd get a cookie. When we got home from school and before we went to bed, my mother gave us milk and cookies. I remember an occasional sundae—and then I'd always eat the cherry first. Very rarely did we have dessert with dinner, except on weekends. I didn't really become initiated into the myriad possibilities of desserts until I began dining out and waiting for them—as so many people do—at the end of a meal. Dessert is the carrot at the end of the stick, a sweet and often decadent luxury. For some people, dessert is synonymous with chocolate.

People love chocolate desserts, the richer the better. Such as chocolate ice cream and chocolate sorbet, chocolate tortes and chocolate tarts, and chocolate soufflés with names like Chocolate Decadence, Chocolate Devastation, and Death by Chocolate. I'm happy to say that chocolate is one of the ingredients that were discovered in our New World. But desserts don't have to be limited to chocolate.

One of the more marvelous aspects of New World Cuisine is its use of tropical fruits in all fashions and in all stages of ripeness. Like most people, I love bananas—from the standard yellow to the intensely flavored red to the citrus-scented finger banana. Many tropical fruits are very rich, sweet, and custardy. Mangos, coconuts, papayas, pineapples, guavas, mamey, and sapote can be eaten fresh or in simple-to-make desserts. When lychees are in season in south Florida, I like to put a big iced bowl of them on the table. There is nothing more refreshing, involving, juicy, sweet, and lush.

Frozen desserts are also very popular. People love ice cream, and ice cream is easy to make in machines that range from thirty dollars and up, which allow you to control the natural goodness of the ingredients rather than depending on those mass-produced for a supermarket box.

Hot desserts are also terrific, and soufflés are among my favorites. Contrary to popular belief, they are easy to make, once you master the simple technique. There is nothing quite as impressive as a soufflé coming out of the oven baked high and aromatic. If you really want to be decadent, add some fresh, slightly whipped cream.

Many people plan what they are going to eat and how they're going to cook around the dessert. Dessert becomes the star, the climax of the meal. Desserts, which ought to be served with a fabulous coffee like Jamaican Blue Mountain or Kona, make the final impression. First impressions are absolutely important to set the mood for a dinner, but that last bite of dessert, whether beautifully lavish or beautifully simple, will be what people last remember and dream about.

DOUBLE CHOCOLATE COCONUT CAKE

SERVES 8 TO 10

1	cup sweet butter, softened
2	cups granulated sugar
1	teaspoon coconut extract
1/2	cup unsweetened cocoa powder
5	large eggs
2 1/2	cups all-purpose flour
1	teaspoon baking powder
1/2	teaspoon baking soda

Pinch salt

1	cup buttermilk
1	cup flaked coconut
1	recipe Double Chocolate Fudge Frosting (recipe follows)
1	cup flaked coconut, toasted

Chocolate and coconut are indigenous to the New World and together create a rich tropical delight.

To prepare the batter: In a large bowl beat the butter and sugar together with an electric mixer on medium speed until light and fluffy, approximately 2 minutes. Add the coconut extract and cocoa; beat until well blended. Add the eggs, one at a time, beating well after each addition.

In a separate bowl sift the dry ingredients—flour, baking powder, baking soda, and salt—together. Turn the mixer on low and alternately add the dry ingredients and the buttermilk to the chocolate mixture. Stop when they are completely incorporated. Stir in the flaked coconut.

To bake: Preheat the oven to 350°. Grease two 9-inch round cake pans. Dust with flour then tap out the excess. Divide the batter between the 2 prepared pans. Bake for 30 to 35 minutes, or until a cake tester inserted into the center of the cake comes out clean. Let cool in the pans for 15 minutes, then unmold to cool completely on a rack.

To finish the cake: Using a serrated knife, level off the 2 cake rounds. Spread one third of the frosting on top of each round, then top with toasted coconut. Stack the cake rounds on top of each other, and finish the sides with the remaining frosting and toasted coconut. Refrigerate until ready to serve.

In a medium bowl with an electric mixer beat together the butter and melted chocolate on medium speed until combined, about 1 minute. Beat in the cream. Add the sugar and vanilla and beat on high speed until the frosting is smooth and fluffy.

DOUBLE CHOCOLATE FUDGE FROSTING

MAKES 3 CUPS

1/4 cup sweet butter, softened

4 ounces bittersweet chocolate, melted

1/4 cup heavy cream

2 cups confectioners' sugar

1 teaspoon vanilla extract

BITTERSWEET CHOCOLATE PASSION-FRUIT TORTE

SERVES 6

 1 *pound good-quality bittersweet chocolate, such as Lindt*

 1 *cup plus 1 tablespoon sweet butter*

10 *large eggs*

½ *cup granulated sugar*

 3 *ripe passion fruit, pulp only*

Pinch salt

This is a very dense and seductive chocolate dessert, perfect for Valentine's Day on a table set with long-stemmed roses.

To prepare the bittersweet torte: In a double boiler melt the chocolate and 1 cup of the butter together. Beat 6 of the eggs and fold them into the mixture. Pour the batter into two 8-inch buttered springform pans. Bake these at 350° in a water bath (using a pan large enough to place the 2 spring molds, fill with water halfway up the edge) for 5 minutes covered, and 10 minutes uncovered. Remove the cakes from the oven and cool. The cakes don't rise but remain flat, like disks. When cooled completely, remove the cakes from the spring molds.

To prepare the passion-fruit curd: In a double boiler whip the remaining eggs with the sugar until ribbons form. Add the passion-fruit pulp, the remaining butter, and the salt. Cook until thickened, about 5 minutes, but do not let the mixture boil. Strain the curd through a fine sieve and cool in a stainless-steel bowl.

To assemble and serve: Trim the chocolate disks flat with a serrated knife. Spread the curd on top of the first disk. Then place the second disk on top and finish with another layer of curd. Let the torte set for 30 minutes in the refrigerator before serving.

This dessert is as fabulous as its name suggests.

To prepare the cheesecake mixture: In a large mixing bowl with a paddle attachment cream together the cream cheese, sugar, and sour cream, scraping down the sides of the bowl often. In a medium-size bowl combine the eggs and Kahlúa, whisking them together. Once the cream cheese mixture is softened and lump free, add the eggs in 3 parts, scraping down the sides of the bowl after each addition. In another medium-size bowl place the melted milk chocolate, then slowly whisk in a little of the cheesecake mixture, whisking constantly to create a smooth mixture. Add the milk chocolate mixture back into the cheesecake mixture and stir until completely blended.

To bake the cheesecake: Preheat the oven to 300°. Butter a round springform pan. Pour the mixture into the teflon pan and place in a water bath (a pan holding the cheesecake pan, filled halfway with water). Bake the cheesecake until the center is solid, about 1½ hours. Remove from the water bath and let the cake cool completely. Then chill in the refrigerator.

To prepare the hazelnut crust: In a double boiler melt the milk chocolate and butter and stir until completely dissolved. Remove from the heat, and fold in the hazelnuts and cornflakes. Take the cheesecake out of the refrigerator and pour the milk chocolate crust on top. Place back in the refrigerator and allow to set overnight.

To serve: When ready to serve, remove the cheesecake from the refrigerator and take it out of the springform pan. Invert the cake onto a large serving plate so the crust is on the bottom and serve.

KAHLÚA MILK CHOCOLATE CHEESECAKE WITH A CRISPY HAZELNUT CRUST

SERVES 10

CHEESECAKE:

- 1 pound cream cheese, softened
- 1 pound granulated sugar
- 1 cup sour cream
- 7 large whole eggs
- ½ cup Kahlúa
- 4 ounces good-quality milk chocolate, such as Godiva, melted

CRUST:

- 3 ounces good-quality milk chocolate
- 3 tablespoons sweet butter
- ¼ cup ground hazelnuts
- ¼ cup crushed cornflakes

WHITE CHOCOLATE MACADAMIA NUT BOMBE

SERVES 10

FOR THE WHITE CHOCOLATE MOUSSE:

10	large egg yolks
1	cup granulated sugar
1	pound white chocolate
½	tablespoon gelatin
2	tablespoons kirsch
3	cups heavy cream, whipped

FOR THE CHOCOLATE MACADAMIA FILLING:

1	cup sweet butter
½	cup granulated sugar
6	ounces chopped semisweet chocolate
3	ounces chopped unsweetened chocolate
4	tablespoons strong coffee
3	tablespoons Kahlúa
½	cup roughly chopped macadamia nuts
6	large eggs

FOR THE GANACHE:

2	cups heavy cream
8	ounces bittersweet chocolate

You'll need to start preparing this sumptuous dessert the day before you plan to serve it. But its 2 layers of white chocolate mousse, separated by a rich chocolate macadamia-nut layer and spread with chocolate ganache, make it well worth the planning.

To prepare the mousse: In a large bowl with an electric mixer whip the egg yolks and sugar together at a high speed until ribbons form. In a double boiler carefully melt the white chocolate. Off the heat fold the yolk mixture into the white chocolate. Dissolve the gelatin with the Kirsch. Add the gelatin to the chocolate mixture and finish by folding in the cream. Let the mixture set in the refrigerator for 30 minutes while you prepare the other parts of the bombe.

To prepare the filling: Preheat the oven to 350° and butter an 8-inch springform pan. In a saucepan melt the butter and sugar together. Bring to a simmer and remove from the heat. Add the chocolates and stir until completely uniform. Add the coffee and Kahlúa and continue to stir. Add

the nuts. Finally, add the eggs while stirring. Pour into the prepared pan and bake for 10 to 12 minutes. Remove from the oven and cool on a baker's rack for 1 hour. Release the baked layer from the springform pan.

To prepare the ganache: In a saucepot warm the heavy cream, being careful not to boil it. Chop the chocolate into small pieces. Add the warmed cream, mixing well until smooth and thick. Set aside.

To assemble and serve: Using an 8-inch springform pan, layer the bottom with the white chocolate mousse to fill a third of the mold. Top this with the chocolate macadamia disk. Finish filling the mold with white chocolate mousse. Let set in the freezer for 24 hours. Remove from the pan. Warm the ganache in a double boiler until liquefied. Cover the bombe carefully with the ganache. Return the bombe to the freezer for at least 1 hour before serving. The bombe can be held frozen for up to a week.

CHOCOLATE CAPPUCCINO BROWNIES

MAKES 16 BROWNIES

4   ounces unsweetened chocolate
1/2 cup sweet butter
1   cup granulated sugar
2   large eggs
1/2 teaspoon vanilla extract
1/4 cup all-purpose flour
2   teaspoons instant espresso powder
1   teaspoon ground cinnamon
1/4 teaspoon salt

If brownies are one of the delights of childhood and cappuccino one of the delights of adulthood, this dessert offers ecstasy for all ages.

To prepare the brownies: Preheat the oven to 325°. Lightly grease an 8-inch square baking pan. In a heavy saucepan dissolve the chocolate with the butter over low heat, stirring until both are completely melted. Remove from the heat and stir in the sugar. Beat in the eggs, one at a time, then add the vanilla and mix well. Stir in the flour, espresso powder, cinnamon, and salt, mixing well.

To bake: Spread the batter into the prepared pan and bake for 40 minutes, until cooked through. Remove from the oven, allow to cool, and cut into squares.

To prepare the batter: In a large bowl combine the unsweetened chocolate and butter. Melt over simmering water, stirring until smooth. Remove from the heat and whisk in the sugar, corn syrup, vanilla, and eggs until well blended. Stir in the flour, nuts, chocolate chips, and mango.

To bake: Preheat the oven to 350°. Grease an 11-by-17-inch jelly-roll pan with butter and spread the mixture evenly into it. Bake for 30 to 35 minutes, or until set. Do not overbake; a skewer inserted will come out clean. Let cool and then cut into 24 squares.

ROCKY MANGO BROWNIES

MAKES 24 BROWNIES

5	ounces unsweetened chocolate
1	cup sweet butter
1¾	cups granulated sugar
⅓	cup light corn syrup
1	teaspoon vanilla extract
4	large eggs
1	cup all-purpose flour
½	cup chopped walnuts
¾	cup semisweet chocolate chips
½	cup diced dried mango

CHOCOLATE PECAN PIE

SERVES 6

FOR THE SWEET PIE DOUGH:

- 1/2 cup sweet butter
- 2/3 cup granulated sugar
- 1 large egg, plus 1 egg yolk
- 1 teaspoon vanilla extract
- 2 1/4 cups all-purpose flour

FOR THE FILLING:

- 1 cup granulated sugar
- 2 tablespoons all-purpose flour

Pinch salt

- 3/4 cup dark corn syrup
- 3 large eggs
- 3/4 cup chopped pecans
- 5 ounces semisweet chocolate, chopped

FOR THE WHITE CHOCOLATE WHIPPED CREAM:

- 8 ounces high-quality white chocolate
- 1 cup heavy cream

Peel of 1/2 lemon

- 1 vanilla bean

FOR THE TOPPING:

- 3/4 cup pecan halves

The white chocolate whipped cream topping for this pie is as sweet and luxurious as a Caribbean cloud.

To make the dough: In an electric mixer combine the butter and sugar on medium speed until smooth. Add the egg and egg yolk separately until each is incorporated. Flavor the mixture with the vanilla. Add the flour all at once and mix slowly until the dough binds together. Remove from the bowl and refrigerate, covered, at least 1 hour before use. Roll out the dough to 1/2 inch thickness. Place it in a 9-inch tart pan and gently mold it to the pan.

To prepare the filling: In a mixing bowl combine the sugar, flour, salt, and corn syrup. Add the eggs, one by one, then stir in the chopped pecans and the chocolate.

To prepare the white chocolate whipped cream: Melt the chocolate in a double boiler over hot water. In a separate pot bring the cream, lemon peel, and vanilla bean slowly to a simmer. Strain the cream over the chocolate and stir until completely smooth. Cool completely. Whip as you would whipped cream.

To bake and serve: Preheat the oven to 325°. Pour the filling into the shell and bake for 40 minutes. Remove from the oven, arrange the pecan halves beautifully around the top, and return to the oven for 10 minutes. Serve with the freshly whipped white chocolate cream.

This is a dessert for people who love the best things in life. Two of these are Godiva chocolate and the aroma of a fresh hot soufflé made with Godiva chocolate.

To prepare the flour-butter mixture: In a bowl, with a mixer or by hand, combine the flour and 1 tablespoon of the butter and mix until it forms a ball.

To prepare the soufflé base: In a medium-size pot, warm the milk with ½ teaspoon of the vanilla extract. Once the milk has come to a simmer, mix in the flour-butter mixture. Working quickly with a wire whisk, beat until the flour is dissolved and the mixture begins to thicken. With a rubber spatula, fold over the mixture and continue to cook until it is smooth and shiny. Remove from the heat and pour into an electric mixer bowl. On low speed, add the egg yolks, one at a time, and then add 4 tablespoons of the sugar.

To prepare the soufflé: Once the mixture is cool, transfer it to a large stainless-steel bowl. Mix the remaining vanilla extract, 2½ tablespoons of the cocoa, and the Godiva liqueur into the soufflé base. In another bowl whip the egg whites until they form soft peaks. Gently fold the egg whites into the soufflé base in 2 batches.

To bake the soufflé: Preheat the oven to 375°. Prepare the 6-inch soufflé mold by brushing it with the remaining butter and dusting it with the remaining sugar. Ladle the soufflé base into the prepared dish until it is half full. Drop in the small pieces of Godiva chocolate. Continue to fill the mold to the rim with the soufflé mix. Bake for 30 minutes, until the soufflé has almost doubled in size.

To assemble and serve: Dust with the remaining cocoa powder and serve immediately.

GODIVA CHOCOLATE TRUFFLE SOUFFLÉ

SERVES 4

2   tablespoons all-purpose flour

1½ tablespoons sweet butter

1   cup whole milk

1   teaspoon vanilla extract

3   extra-large eggs, separated

5   tablespoons granulated sugar

3   tablespoons unsweetened cocoa powder

1   tablespoon Godiva liqueur (sold in most liquor stores)

2   ounces Godiva bittersweet chocolate pieces or another good-quality bittersweet chocolate

FALLEN CHOCOLATE SOUFFLÉ ROULADE

SERVES 10

8   ounces chopped semisweet chocolate

6   large eggs, separated

½   cup granulated sugar

1   teaspoon vanilla extract

¼   teaspoon salt

¼   teaspoon cream of tartar

1   cup heavy cream, chilled

2   tablespoons confectioners' sugar

1   tablespoon Grand Marnier

1   pint fresh raspberries, rinsed and dried

I recently prepared this version of soufflé for 900 people feasting at the James Beard Awards gala. That evening I also won the award for Best Chef in 1994—Southeast. It surely was a wonderful night.

To prepare the roulade batter: In a double boiler melt the chocolate. Whip together the egg yolks, sugar, vanilla, and salt. Mix the melted chocolate into the yolks. Whip together the egg whites and cream of tartar. Fold the whites into the chocolate mixture.

To bake the roulade: Preheat the oven to 350°. Line an 11-by-17-inch jelly-roll pan with parchment paper (or grease and dust it with flour). Spread the batter into the pan and bake for 15 minutes, until cooked through.

For the cream filling: In a stainless-steel bowl whip together the chilled heavy cream, confectioners' sugar, and Grand Marnier until stiff peaks form.

To assemble and serve: Place the cooled soufflé sheet on a work surface. Spread it with whipped cream, not quite to the edges. Line one long end with fresh raspberries. Roll the sheet up lengthwise as you would a jelly roll. Slice and serve.

If you loved chocolate pudding when you were a kid, you'll want to serve these very special pots de crème to yourself, your special adult friends, and every fine child you know.

This can be prepared up to a day ahead.

To prepare the cream: Place the chocolate in a large stainless steel-bowl and set it aside. In a medium saucepan heat the cream over a medium flame until bubbles start to form around the edges. Remove the cream from the stove and pour the cream over the chocolate. Allow this mixture to stand for 3 to 5 minutes, then stir until smooth.

To finish the mixture: In a medium bowl, whisk the sugar into the egg yolks. Whisk half of the chocolate mixture into the yolks, then pour the yolk mixture back into the chocolate mixture. Stir in the vanilla extract.

To bake: Preheat the oven to 350°. Divide the chocolate cream evenly into eight 6-ounce ramekins. Place the ramekins in a 2-inch-deep baking pan and add enough water to reach halfway up the sides. Cover the pan with foil. Bake the pots for 45 minutes, until firm.

To serve: Remove the ramekins from the oven and let the pots cool, then refrigerate for a minimum of 2 hours. You can refrigerate them covered for up to 24 hours.

CHOCOLATE POTS DE CRÈME

SERVES 8

8 ounces semisweet chocolate, chopped

3 cups heavy cream

¼ cup granulated sugar

8 egg yolks

2 teaspoons vanilla extract

WHITE CHOCOLATE AND TEA PAVÉ

SERVES 6

2 tablespoons orange pekoe tea

1 cup heavy cream

2 tablespoons sweet butter

14 ounces imported white chocolate

¼ cup granulated sugar

3 large egg yolks

3 tablespoons chantilly cream (loosely whipped heavy cream)

Pavé desserts originated in Paris and are supposed to be reminiscent of the early paved designs of brick streets. Use either a square or triangular mold to set the pavé and serve it in wedges or "bricks."

To infuse the tea: In a small saucepot infuse the tea and heavy cream for 3 minutes on low heat. Remove it from the heat and let cool. Strain the tea infusion, removing the tea leaves. Meanwhile, butter a 4-by-10-by-4-inch mold and line it with waxed paper.

To make the pavé: In a large bowl combine the butter, chocolate, sugar, and infused cream. Place in the top of a double boiler and melt completely over hot water, stirring constantly. Once the chocolate mixture is melted, remove it from the heat and add the egg yolks. Allow the mixture to cool slightly, then gently fold in the chantilly cream. Pour into the prepared mold and chill overnight.

I created this pie for the Florida Derby under the commission of the Florida Derby committee. This is the most important stakes race before the Triple Crown.

To prepare the dough: In an electric mixer combine the butter and sugar on medium speed until smooth. Add the egg and egg yolk separately, beating until each is incorporated. Flavor with the vanilla extract. Add the flour all at once and mix slowly until all the ingredients bind together. Remove from the bowl and refrigerate, covered, for at least 1 hour before use.

To make the filling: In a mixing bowl combine the sugar, flour, salt, and corn syrup. Add the eggs, one by one, then the chopped hazelnuts and the semisweet chocolate.

To bake the pie: Preheat the oven to 325°. Roll out the dough to ¹/₂-inch thickness. Place it into a 9-inch tart pan and gently mold it to the pan. Pour the filling into the shell and bake for 40 minutes. Let the pie cool completely and remove from the tart pan.

To assemble and serve: Arrange the whole hazelnuts around the pie's perimeter. Put the white and dark chocolates in separate mini–pastry bags and squeeze it onto the pie in a double-lattice pattern.

CHEF ALLEN'S DERBY PIE

SERVES 6

FOR THE DOUGH:

¹/₂   cup sweet butter

²/₃   cup granulated sugar

1   large egg, plus 1 egg yolk

1   teaspoon vanilla extract

2¹/₄   cups all-purpose flour

FOR THE FILLING:

1   cup granulated sugar

2   tablespoons all-purpose flour

Pinch salt

³/₄   cup dark corn syrup

3   large eggs

³/₄   cup chopped hazelnuts

8   ounces semisweet chocolate, chopped

FOR THE TOPPING:

¹/₂   cup whole hazelnuts

2   ounces white chocolate, melted

2   ounces dark chocolate, melted

FLOURLESS TIRAMISU TORTE

SERVES 6

3/4 cup sweet butter

1 1/2 cups semisweet chocolate chips

3/4 cup granulated sugar

2 tablespoons finely ground unblanched hazelnuts

5 large eggs, separated

2 tablespoons tiramisu liqueur (or coffee liqueur)

2 tablespoons confectioners' sugar

Being proud of this dessert, I served it to Julia Child one evening at Chef Allen's. Julia asked me abruptly, "What's this business of a flourless cake? Who cares—as long as it tastes great." I was surprised by this response but at the same time happy, because I was watching Julia finish her piece and lick her fork. She was right!

To prepare the chocolate mixture: Melt the butter over hot water in the top of a double boiler. Add the chocolate chips to the melted butter and stir until melted. To the chocolate mixture add 1/2 cup of the sugar and the ground hazelnuts and cool to room temperature.

To make the batter: In a small bowl lightly beat the egg yolks together with the liqueur and fold into the chocolate mixture. In a large mixing bowl whip the egg whites on high speed. When frothy, add the remaining sugar and continue whipping until stiff peaks form. Fold the cooled chocolate mixture into the egg whites with a rubber spatula and gently mix until thoroughly combined.

To bake the torte: Preheat the oven to 300°. Grease a 9-inch cake pan and pour the batter into it. Bake for 1 hour, until a toothpick inserted in the center of the torte comes out clean. Turn the torte out of the pan. When cool, wrap the cake in plastic and refrigerate it overnight. Top with confectioners' sugar and serve at room temperature.

To prepare the dough: In a medium bowl beat together the butter and brown sugar with an electric mixer until light and fluffy. Add the vanilla extract and egg and beat until well incorporated. Next add the flour to the mixture, then blend in the chocolate chips.

To bake: Preheat the oven to 350°. Portion the cookies by dropping tablespoons 3 inches apart onto ungreased cookie sheets. Bake for 8 to 10 minutes. Do not overbake the cookies, remove when light yellow. Let them cool for a few minutes before moving them to a wire rack to cool completely.

WHITE AND DARK CHOCOLATE CHIP COOKIES

MAKES 24 COOKIES

- ½ cup sweet butter, softened
- 1 cup brown sugar, packed
- 1 tablespoon vanilla extract
- 1 large egg
- 1¾ cups all-purpose flour
- ½ cup chopped imported white chocolate chips
- ½ cup chopped imported bittersweet chocolate

MILK CHOCOLATE HAZELNUT BARS

MAKES 30 BARS

1½   cups crushed hazelnuts

½   cup peanut butter

¼   cup peanut oil

1   pound milk chocolate, chopped

3   tablespoons sweet butter

1½   cups crushed Rice Krispies

2   pounds bittersweet chocolate, chopped

To prepare the bars: In a food processor combine the hazelnuts, peanut butter, and oil and puree. Melt the milk chocolate and butter together in a double boiler over hot water. Remove from the heat and combine with the crushed Rice Krispies and the hazelnut puree. Line the bottom of an 8-by-10-by-1¼-inch pan with waxed paper. Spread the mixture evenly over the bottom. Chill for approximately 1 hour until hardened. Remove from the pan and cut into 2-by-1-inch finger-size bars. Place the bars back in the refrigerator.

To prepare the chocolate for dipping: In a large bowl begin to melt the chopped dark chocolate over a double boiler. When half melted, take it off the heat. Finish stirring the chocolate until all the lumps have dissolved. Dip the bars individually in the chocolate and set on a wire rack to dry. Place back in the refrigerator until ready to serve.

To prepare the mango potpie: Place the mango pieces in a bowl. Add the granulated sugar, cinnamon, allspice, and rum and toss the filling together. Roll out the sweet dough to ⅓-inch thickness. Cut 6 circles, each 5 inches in diameter, and place these in a 3-inch non-stick muffin pan. Fill with the mango mixture.

To make the praline topping: Sift the light brown sugar into a bowl. Whip the egg whites and fold them into the sugar. Add the pecans and vanilla. Place the topping on the potpies.

To bake: Preheat the oven to 350°. Bake the potpies for 35 minutes, until the topping is golden brown. Remove from the oven and cool for 5 minutes. Tap out of the pan and serve hot.

MANGO POT PIE WITH PRALINE TOPPING

SERVES 6

2   large mangos, peeled and cut into 2-inch pieces

2   tablespoons granulated sugar

1   teaspoon ground cinnamon

¼   teaspoon ground allspice

2   tablespoons light rum

1   pound sweet pie dough (page 230)

1   cup light brown sugar

2   large egg whites

1   cup chopped pecans

1   teaspoon vanilla extract

MANGO TARTE TATIN

SERVES 6

3   ripe mangos
¼   cup light brown sugar
2   tablespoons sweet butter
2   teaspoons minced fresh ginger
2   tablespoons lime juice
1   sheet frozen puff pastry dough
1   cup Caramel Popcorn (recipe follows)

This caramelized upside-down dessert works well with many firm fruits, the mango's tropical and lush flavors are enhanced by the caramelized brown sugar. For the fun of it, garnish this with Caramel Popcorn.

To prepare the mango: Cut the mango off the pit by slicing the fruit about a third into the center against the pit. Do the same on the other side. After removing the pit, peel the skin off each half with a paring knife, then slice the meat into ¼-inch slices and set it aside. In a 10-inch cake pan combine the brown sugar, butter, ginger, and lime juice. Warm together on a slow burner until the sugar is dissolved. Remove the pan from the heat and line it with the sliced mango, laying the slices next to one another.

To prepare the dough: Remove the puff pastry from the freezer and allow it to soften a little. Cut a circle out of the pastry slightly larger than the cake pan. Poke the pastry with a fork, place it on top of the mango, and tuck in the sides.

To bake and finish: Preheat the oven to 375°. Bake for 10 minutes, until the pastry is brown and the juices bubble up. Remove from the oven and cool for 5 minutes. Invert the tart onto a large plate and replace any fruit that may have stuck to the pan. Cut into servings and garnish with the Caramel Popcorn.

I would suggest that you make a full batch of popcorn so there will be leftovers for you to munch on yourself.

To prepare the caramel sauce: In a large saucepan combine the brown sugar, corn syrup, butter, cream of tartar, and salt. Bring the mixture to a boil and simmer for approximately 5 minutes—to 260° on a candy thermometer.

To coat the popcorn: Preheat the oven to 200°. Remove the caramel sauce from the heat, and stir in the baking soda quickly. Put the popcorn in a stainless-steel bowl and pour the sauce over it, stirring to coat thoroughly. Spread the popcorn out on a cookie sheet and bake for 45 minutes. Mix and turn the popcorn every 15 minutes. Remove from the oven and let cool.

CARAMEL POPCORN

MAKES 2 QUARTS

1 cup light brown sugar

1/4 cup light corn syrup

1/2 cup sweet butter

1/8 teaspoon cream of tartar

1/2 teaspoon sea salt

1/2 teaspoon baking soda

2 quarts freshly popped popcorn

BANANA BONBONS WITH SPICED RUM SAUCE

SERVES 6

FOR THE BONBONS:

- 2 large bananas, diced rough
- 2 teaspoons dark brown sugar
- 1 tablespoon dark rum
- 6 sheets phyllo dough
- 2 tablespoons clarified butter

FOR THE RUM SAUCE:

- 1/2 cup heavy cream
- 1/2 cup half and half
- 1 teaspoon vanilla extract
- 2 tablespoons whole coffee beans
- 1/4 cup granulated sugar
- 3 large egg yolks
- 1 tablespoon unsweetened cocoa powder
- 3 tablespoons spiced dark rum

To prepare the filling: In a bowl combine the bananas, dark brown sugar, and rum.

To make the bonbons: Brush a sheet of phyllo with butter and top with another sheet. Repeat until 3 sheets are stacked. Cut the phyllo in half lengthwise and in thirds crosswise to form 6 squares. Fill and roll each bonbon and twist the ends to close. Repeat this with the other 3 sheets of phyllo.

To bake: Preheat the oven to 375°. Spread the bonbons on a non-stick cookie sheet with plenty of room between them. Bake for 10 minutes, until golden brown.

In a small saucepan warm the cream and half and half with the vanilla and whole coffee beans. In a small bowl whip the sugar and egg yolks together. Ladle some of the warm cream mixture into the yolks to temper them. Then add the yolk mixture to the warm cream. Stirring constantly, cook over medium heat until the mixture is thick enough to coat the back of a spoon. Do not boil! Finally, add the cocoa and spiced rum.

To serve: Remove the rum sauce from the heat, strain it through a fine sieve, and serve warm with the cooled bonbons.

To prepare the filling: Slice the bananas, place in a bowl, and mix with the sugar and lemon juice. In a medium-size sauté pan melt the butter, add the banana mixture, and cook for 3 minutes, until the bananas are softened slightly. Remove the mixture from the heat and cool; then add the almonds, cake crumbs, and cinnamon.

To prepare the dough: Mix the crumbs and cinnamon together. Lay out 1 sheet of phyllo, brush it with melted butter, and sprinkle with some of the crumb mixture. Repeat this procedure 4 more times, layering the phyllo sheets.

To prepare the strudel: Arrange the filling in a band along the end of a phyllo sheet, leaving about 2 inches between the filling and the edge. Roll the strudel up and place it on a waxed paper– or parchment-lined cookie sheet.

To bake and serve: Preheat the oven to 375°. Bake for 35 minutes, until golden brown. Remove from oven and cool for several minutes before slicing.

RED BANANA–ALMOND STRUDEL

SERVES 6

FOR THE FILLING:

6–8	ripe red bananas
1	tablespoon lemon juice
½	cup granulated sugar
1	tablespoon sweet butter
2	tablespoons toasted almonds
3	tablespoons pound cake crumbs
½	teaspoon ground cinnamon

FOR THE DOUGH:

3	tablespoons pound cake crumbs
¾	teaspoon ground cinnamon
5	sheets phyllo dough
3	tablespoons sweet butter, melted

KEY LIME PIE WITH LIME CURD

SERVES 6

FOR THE CRUST:

3	cups graham cracker crumbs
1/3	cup granulated sugar
1	cup ground pecans
1/2	cup sweet butter, melted

FOR THE KEY LIME CURD:

1/2	cup sweet butter
Juice of 6 key limes	
1 1/4	cups granulated sugar
4	large eggs, beaten

Key lime pie has its origins in south Florida. Some Floridians, especially the Conchs who live in the Keys, think it's practically heresy to tamper with the original version. I say that sometimes a little heresy is a good thing.

To make the crust: Preheat the oven to 350°. Mix together the graham cracker crumbs, sugar, and nuts. Add the melted butter. Put the mixture into a pie pan and mold it against the sides and bottom. Bake for 4 minutes. Cool to room temperature, about 25 minutes, then chill in the refrigerator.

To prepare the key lime curd: Heat the butter, key lime juice, and sugar on low in a double boiler and cook gently, stirring occasionally. Whisk in the eggs and continue to cook for 5 minutes, until the mixture is thick enough to coat the back of a spoon. Remove from the heat and transfer to a stainless-steel bowl placed in an ice bath to chill.

To assemble and serve: Fill the crust with the curd and refrigerate for 2 hours before serving.

Desserts don't have to include cream and butter to be delicious. This one is delicate, dreamy, and delightful.

To make the meringues: In a bowl whip the egg whites to a froth and add the cream of tartar. Whip until peaks form and add the superfine sugar little by little. When firm, stiff peaks form, add the confectioners' sugar by carefully sifting it into the mixture.

To cook the meringues: In a large saucepot warm the water and milk together and bring to a simmer. At this point, using a large ice cream scoop, scoop the meringues into the milky water. Cover and simmer for 2 minutes, until firm. Remove the meringues to a pan lined with waxed paper. Place in the freezer. This can be made a day ahead.

To prepare the sauce: In a food processor or blender puree the mango and ginger with the salt. Pass through a fine sieve. Chill the sauce.

To assemble and serve: Clean and slice your choice of the freshest summer fruits and arrange them on a plate with the sauce as a base and the floating island in the center.

FLOATING ISLAND WITH MANGO-GINGER SAUCE AND FRESH SUMMER FRUIT

SERVES 8

4	*large egg whites*
1/8	*teaspoon cream of tartar*
1/2	*cup superfine sugar*
1	*cup confectioners' sugar*
4	*cups water*
1	*cup milk*
1	*large mango*
1/2	*teaspoon minced fresh ginger*

Pinch salt

Summer fruits: assortment of lychees, peaches, blueberries, papaya, raspberries, pineapple, or cherries

PAPAYA-CARROT CAKE

SERVES 6

1	cup sweet butter
2	cups brown sugar
¼	teaspoon salt
½	teaspoon ground cinnamon
¾	teaspoon ground clove
½	teaspoon grated nutmeg
8	large eggs, beaten
2	cups cake flour
1	tablespoon baking powder
½	teaspoon baking soda
1½	cups milk
1	cup grated, medium ripe papaya
1	cup grated carrots
¼	cup finely chopped walnuts
1	teaspoon grated orange zest

So you've had carrot cake before. But here the rich flowery flavor of papaya tangos with the carrot in a dessert that will make your senses dance with pleasure.

To make the batter: Place the butter, sugar, salt, cinnamon, clove, and nutmeg in an electric mixing bowl with the paddle attachment and beat until smooth and creamy. Add the beaten eggs a little at a time. After each addition, beat until the eggs are completely absorbed before adding more. Scrape down the sides of the bowl often. Mix until light and fluffy. In a separate bowl sift the dry ingredients together and add alternately with the milk to the butter-spice mixture, scraping the sides of the bowl constantly. Add the papaya, carrots, chopped walnuts, and orange zest.

To bake: Preheat the oven to 350°. Grease an 8-inch loaf pan. Pour the batter into the pan, and bake for about 1 hour, or until a toothpick inserted into the center of the cake comes out clean. Remove from the pan and cool on a wire rack.

Mamey is a beautiful, lush tropical fruit. Its flesh reminds me of a custard flavored with peach, apricot, and almond. For this recipe, peel the mamey, remove the seed, and puree the flesh. Remove any fibers from the pulp.

To prepare the mamey-cheese mixture: With the paddle attachment to the electric mixer, in a bowl beat the cream cheese until softened and add the sugar. Beat on medium speed until the ingredients are completely incorporated. Add the mamey puree to the cream cheese mixture. In a separate bowl, crack the eggs and gently whip them with a fork. Add the eggs to the mamey-cheese mix in 3 parts, scraping down the bowl each time.

To bake the cheesecake: Preheat the oven to 300°. Line a 10-inch springform pan with waxed paper and coat with butter and then sugar. Wrap the springform pan with aluminum foil to prevent leaking. Pour the cake mixture into the pan and bake in a water bath for 1½ hours. Allow the cake to chill overnight in the refrigerator.

MAMEY CHEESECAKE

SERVES 10

1½ pounds cream cheese, at room temperature

½ pound granulated sugar

1 large mamey fruit, very ripe, pureed (see recipe head)

6 large eggs

BLUEBERRY-STARFRUIT COBBLER

SERVES 8

FOR THE FILLING:

²/₃	cup water
³/₄	cup granulated sugar
1	tablespoon cornstarch
3	cups fresh blueberries
2	large starfruit, sliced
1	teaspoon lemon juice

FOR THE DOUGH TOPPING:

1	cup all-purpose flour
3¹/₂	tablespoons granulated sugar
¹/₈	teaspoon salt
¹/₂	teaspoon ground cinnamon
4	tablespoons cold butter, cut into pieces
¹/₃	cup milk
1	large egg yolk
2	tablespoons heavy cream

To make the filling: Place all but 2 tablespoons of the water and the sugar in a large saucepan and bring to a boil. In a small cup mix the cornstarch with the remaining 2 tablespoons of water. Whisk this into the boiling sugar–water mixture. Add the blueberries, starfruit, and lemon juice, and cook for 1 minute. Remove from the heat and spoon into a 9-inch round buttered baking pan. Set aside while you prepare the topping.

For the cobbler topping: Sift the dry ingredients into a mixing bowl. Add the butter and combine with a wooden spoon until the mixture has a crumbly texture. In a separate bowl combine the milk and egg yolk and add to the dry ingredients, stirring only until combined.

To finish and bake: Preheat the oven to 350°. Spoon the topping with a tablespoon over the fruit mixture in the pan, leaving an uneven surface. Brush this lightly with the heavy cream. Bake for 35 minutes, or until the cobbler is golden brown and the fruit bubbles around the edges. Serve warm.

This semisavory dish derives its sweetness from the natural sugars in the calabaza. The waffles can be served for brunch or as an unusual accompaniment to Cumin-Baked Chicken (page 198).

To make the pumpkin puree: Place the calabaza, water, and salt in a medium saucepot. Bring to a boil and cook for 25 minutes, until tender. Drain the water, puree the calabaza in a blender, and let it cool.

To make the waffle batter: In a large bowl combine the dry ingredients until blended. In a smaller bowl beat the eggs and buttermilk until well mixed; add to the dry ingredients, and next stir in the melted butter and pumpkin puree. The batter is supposed to be lumpy, so don't overmix, which will produce a tough waffle.

To prepare the waffles: The waffle iron should be hot enough to sizzle a drop of water. Pour about ½ cup of batter onto the center of the iron. Lower the lid and cook until the edges are golden brown. Repeat until all the batter is used.

To serve: Combine the cinnamon and brown sugar in a small cup. Dust the waffles with the mixture before serving.

WEST INDIAN PUMPKIN WAFFLES

SERVES 8

FOR THE PUMPKIN PUREE:

1 cup calabaza, peeled and diced small

3 cups water

Pinch salt

FOR THE WAFFLES:

1¾ cups cake flour

1 teaspoon baking powder

½ teaspoon ground cinnamon

½ teaspoon salt

3 large eggs

¾ cup buttermilk

2 tablespoons sweet butter, melted and cooled

FOR THE GARNISH:

½ teaspoon cinnamon

3 tablespoons brown sugar

BAKED GRANNY SMITH APPLES WRAPPED IN PHYLLO COCOA LEAVES

SERVES 6

FOR THE BAKED APPLES:

6   small Granny Smith apples, cored

1   cup honey

4   cinnamon sticks

FOR THE DOUGH:

1   whole package phyllo dough

1   cup sweet butter, melted

½   cup unsweetened cocoa powder

½   cup granulated sugar

To prepare the apples: Preheat the oven to 350°. Place the cored apples in a medium-size baking pan. Pour the honey over the apples and fill the pan about halfway up with hot water. Add the cinnamon sticks to the water. Cover with aluminum foil and bake for 40 minutes, or until the apples are soft. Once the apples are done, drain the water, discard the cinnamon, and allow the apples to cool.

To wrap the apple: Make sure to keep the unused phyllo covered with a damp towel while you are working. Lay out 4 or 5 sheets, brushing each one with the butter, then sprinkling each with cocoa powder and sugar. Layer them on top of each other, then place an apple in the middle of the phyllo layers and wrap the dough around the apple, gathering it on top like a little satchel bag. Repeat this process with each of the apples and the remaining phyllo.

To finish: Place the apples in the refrigerator until ready to use, up to 2 hours in advance. When ready to serve, preheat the oven to 350°, place the apples on a cookie sheet, and bake until golden brown and hot in the center, about 10 minutes.

This is my updated version of that classic American dessert, apple pie and ice cream.

To prepare the pie dough: In a mixing bowl sift together the dry ingredients. Add the shortening and combine with a wooden spoon until crumbly. Add the water and mix until the dough is smooth and blended. Form into a ball, flatten it down, wrap in plastic, and store overnight in the refrigerator before using.

To prepare the streusel topping: In a mixing bowl combine the flour, sugar, and butter, then mix by hand until coarse crumbs form. Add the nuts and work the mix until the nuts are distributed throughout.

To prepare the pie filling: Peel, core, and dice the apples. Melt the butter in a sauté pan, then add the apples and the rest of the ingredients. Sauté the mixture just until the sugar begins to caramelize. The apples should remain firm.

To assemble the apple pie timbale: On a floured surface roll out the pie dough to ⅛-inch thickness. Cut the dough into circles to fit into 3-inch muffin tins, then press the circles into the well-buttered muffin tins, cutting off the excess dough. Fill each dough shell with the apple mixture until slightly mounded at the top. Press the streusel topping over each individual apple timbale.

To bake the timbales: Preheat the oven to 350°. Bake the timbales for 30 minutes, or until the crust is golden brown. To remove from the tin, let cool, then run a paring knife around the perimeter of each timbale to loosen.

Serve warm and top with your favorite ice cream.

APPLE PIE TIMBALE

SERVES 8

FOR THE PIE DOUGH:

2   tablespoons granulated sugar

Pinch salt

2   cups sifted cake flour

1½ cups vegetable shortening

⅔   cup ice cold water

FOR THE STREUSEL TOPPING:

1   cup all-purpose flour

⅔   cup light brown sugar

⅔   cup softened sweet butter

3   tablespoons coarsely chopped pecans

FOR THE APPLE PIE FILLING:

6   Granny Smith apples

2   tablespoons sweet butter

½   cup raisins

½   cup chopped pecans or walnuts

¾   cup granulated sugar

2   teaspoons ground cinnamon

½   teaspoon grated nutmeg

CANDIED LEMON SLICE COOKIES

MAKES 36 COOKIES

FOR THE CANDIED LEMONS:

 3 *lemons, sliced thin, with seeds removed*
 4 *cups granulated sugar*
 3 *cups water*

FOR THE COOKIES:

 1/2 *cup granulated sugar*
 1 *cup sweet butter*
 1/2 *teaspoon grated lemon zest*
 1/2 *teaspoon vanilla extract*
 2 *large eggs*
 3 *cups cake flour, sifted*

The candied lemon melts into the butter cookie for a great sweet and tart dessert.

To prepare the lemons: In a large saucepot of boiling water blanch the sliced lemons and drain them on a wire rack.

To candy the lemons: In another medium-size saucepot combine 2 cups of sugar and 1 1/2 cups of water. Allow the mixture to come to a boil and let it reduce for 10 to 15 minutes. Afterward, drop the lemon slices into this syrup and cook for 10 minutes. Take the saucepot off the heat and let stand overnight. The next day, remove the lemon slices from the syrup and let them drain on a wire rack. Repeat this process again, using the remaining sugar and water. The next day the lemons will be preserved and ready.

To prepare the cookie dough: In a bowl cream together the sugar and butter until the mixture is light. Next, add the lemon zest, vanilla extract, and eggs. Mix to a smooth consistency. Finally, add the sifted flour and mix just until the dough is smooth.

To assemble and bake: Preheat the oven to 375°. Roll out the dough about 1/4 inch thick and cut out 3-inch circles. Place on a waxed paper–lined sheet pan, and top each cookie with a piece of candied lemon. Bake until the edges are golden brown, about 5 minutes. Cool the cookies on racks.

To prepare the dough: In the large bowl of an electric mixer cream the butter, salt, and vanilla extract. Beat in the sugar and then the egg yolk on the lowest speed. Add the flour while scraping the sides of the bowl to blend evenly. Mix only until the dough holds together.

To make the cookies: After the dough is mixed, roll it into balls about 1 inch or less in diameter. Place the cookies 1 inch apart on an ungreased cookie sheet. After shaping, make a small indent with your thumb, dipping it in flour after pressing each cookie. Then fill the thumbprints with the guava jelly.

To bake: Preheat the oven to 325°. Bake the cookies in the center of the oven for approximately 15 minutes, until golden brown. Remove from the oven and cool on a wire rack.

GUAVA THUMBPRINT COOKIES

MAKES ABOUT 36 COOKIES

1   *cup sweet butter*

Pinch salt

1/2   *teaspoon vanilla extract*

1/2   *cup granulated sugar*

1   *large egg yolk*

2³/₄   *cups sifted all-purpose flour*

1   *jar guava jelly (available in the Latin section of your grocery store)*

PINEAPPLE CAKE

SERVES 10

 1   cup softened sweet butter
 1/2 cup granulated sugar
 3/4 cup pure maple syrup
 3   large eggs, separated
 1   teaspoon vanilla extract
 2 1/2 cups cake flour, sifted
 1   tablespoon baking powder
 1/2 teaspoon salt
 1   teaspoon ground cinnamon
 1/3 cup whole milk
 1   cup diced pineapple

To prepare the batter: In a large mixing bowl beat the butter on high speed until it's pale and fluffy, 3 to 4 minutes. Add the sugar and maple syrup, and continue beating until thoroughly mixed. Scrape down the sides of the bowl and add the egg yolks, one at a time, beating thoroughly between each addition. Then add the vanilla extract and beat on medium speed until incorporated.

In a medium bowl combine the dry ingredients then add them to the butter and egg mixture alternately with the milk in 3 stages, beating after each addition. Scrape the sides of the bowl after each addition. Then add the diced pineapple. In another bowl beat the egg whites until stiff but not dry. Stir a third of the beaten whites into the batter to lighten it. Then fold in the remaining whites.

To bake: Preheat the oven to 350°. Grease and lightly flour an 8-inch loaf pan. Line the bottom with greased parchment or waxed paper. Pour the batter into the prepared baking pan. Bake the cake for 50 to 60 minutes, or until a toothpick inserted in the center of the cake comes out clean. Transfer the cake to a wire rack and cool for about 15 minutes. As soon as the pan is cool enough to handle, invert the cake to unmold it onto the wire rack. Let the cake cool completely before removing the paper.

To serve: Using a serrated knife, flatten the top and slice the cake in 2-inch cuts. Lay out the slices overlapping one another on a large platter and serve. Spoon 1 cup of Warm-Ginger Pineapple Salsa over the top, and pass the remaining salsa separately.

ACCOMPANIMENT:
WARM GINGER-PINEAPPLE SALSA

In a large sauté pan warm the butter with the ginger and brown sugar. Let this mixture cook for a minute. Add the cinnamon, vanilla extract, salt, and star anise. Mix well and add the pineapple and macadamia nuts. Sauté together until warmed through. Remove from the heat and serve warm.

WARM GINGER-PINEAPPLE SALSA

MAKES 3 CUPS

3 tablespoons sweet butter

1 teaspoon minced fresh ginger

1/2 cup light brown sugar

1/2 teaspoon ground cinnamon

1/2 teaspoon vanilla extract

Pinch sea salt

1 piece star anise, crushed

1 large pineapple, peeled and diced

1/2 cup toasted macadamia nuts

COCONUT CRÈME BRÛLÉE

SERVES 6

2 cups heavy cream

½ cup canned, unsweetened coconut milk

½ vanilla bean

4 egg yolks

¾ cup granulated sugar

Pinch salt

3 tablespoons light brown sugar

To make the crème: In a medium-size saucepan heat the heavy cream, coconut milk, and vanilla bean over medium heat until it just begins to boil. In a medium-size bowl place the egg yolks, granulated sugar, and the salt. Stir with a slotted spoon until well combined. Once the cream is hot, pour it slowly into the egg mixture, stirring constantly. After all the cream is added, strain the mixture through a fine sieve.

To bake: Preheat the oven to 325°. Pour the crème into six ½-cup brûlée molds and bake in a water bath (a pan that can hold the molds filled with water halfway up the sides) covered with aluminum foil for 45 minutes, or until the custards are set. Remove from the water bath and let cool. Refrigerate for at least 1 hour until ready to serve.

To finish the crème: Preheat the broiler to hot. Sprinkle light brown sugar on top of each mold and place them under the broiler for about 2 minutes. Caramelize the sugar completely so that as it cools, it hardens to a thin glasslike layer. Place on a plate and serve.

To prepare the rice: In a large heavy-gauge saucepan combine the milk and salt. Wash and drain the rice and combine it with the milk. Slowly bring the milk mixture to a boil, stirring occasionally. Then cover, lower the heat, and simmer for 20 minutes, or until the rice is tender.

To prepare the pudding: Add the sugar, cinnamon, vanilla, and pineapple pieces to the rice and continue stirring for several minutes until the sugar is dissolved. Remove from the heat.

To finish and bake: Preheat the oven to 325°. Butter a 2-quart casserole. In a small bowl whisk the egg yolks and slowly add to the rice mixture. Cool completely, then beat the egg whites until stiff and gently fold them into the rice mixture. Spoon the rice into the prepared casserole dish. Bake for 20 to 25 minutes, until the pudding is lightly browned. Remove from the oven and let cool. Serve at room temperature.

PINEAPPLE RICE PUDDING

SERVES 8

1   quart milk

Pinch salt

1/2   cup short-grain arborio rice

1/2   cup granulated sugar

1/2   teaspoon ground cinnamon

1   teaspoon vanilla extract

1   medium pineapple, cored and cut into small dice

4   large eggs, separated

KUMQUAT, NUTMEG, AND ALLSPICE BREAD PUDDING

SERVES 6 TO 8

2   cups thinly sliced kumquats

3   cups bread cubes (preferably challah or brioche)

4   large Bosc pears, cored and sliced thin

4   large eggs

2   cups whole milk

1½ cups light brown sugar

¼   teaspoon salt

¾   teaspoon grated nutmeg

¾   teaspoon ground allspice

To prepare the pudding: In a large bowl combine the kumquats, bread cubes, and sliced pears. In another medium-size bowl combine the eggs, milk, sugar, salt, nutmeg, and allspice. Whisk these ingredients together and pour over the bread-pear mixture. Let this stand for about 10 minutes, so the bread may absorb some of the liquid.

To finish and bake: Preheat the oven to 350°. Butter a large baking dish. Spread the pudding mixture in the dish. Cover with foil and bake in a water bath (a slightly larger pan filled halfway with water) for about an hour. The custard is set when a skewer inserted in the center comes out clean. Remove it from the oven, let it sit out for 10 minutes, and serve warm.

A flan is very similar to a crème caramel. It's baked with a layer of caramel under the custard mixture and is inverted when served.

To prepare the caramel topping: In a saucepan combine ½ cup of the sugar with the lime juice and water. Bring the mixture to a boil about 4 minutes, until it turns a deep caramel color. Pour into an 8-inch round flan mold.

To make the flan: In another saucepot warm the milk and add the ginger and vanilla. Bring the mixture to a simmer and remove from the heat. Whisk the eggs and temper them by adding several ladles of the warm milk. Pour the tempered eggs back into the milk. Carefully pour the mixture into the flan mold over the caramel topping.

To bake the flan: Preheat the oven to 325°. Place the mold into a large shallow roasting pan filled with enough water to come halfway up the sides of the mold. Bake the flan in its water bath for 45 minutes. When the flan is firm, remove it from the oven and let cool.

To assemble and serve: Refrigerate for at least 3 hours. Remove the flan from the mold by turning it over onto a plate. Garnish with the fresh mango slices.

SWEET GINGER FLAN

SERVES 6

2 cups granulated sugar

Juice of 1 lime

¼ cup water

1 quart whole milk

1 tablespoon fresh ginger, peeled and split

½ fresh vanilla bean, split

9 large eggs

1 medium mango, peeled and sliced

PAIN PERDU (FRENCH TOAST)

SERVES 8

1   loaf brioche or challah

1   cup whole milk

2   large eggs

2   tablespoons vanilla extract

1/4 teaspoon ground ginger

1/2 teaspoon ground cinnamon

Pinch sea salt

2   tablespoons sweet butter

3   tablespoons confectioners'
    sugar

To prepare the brioche: Slice the brioche or challah into
3/4 inch-thick slices. In a stainless-steel bowl mix the milk,
eggs, vanilla extract, ginger, cinnamon, and salt. Dip the
brioche slices in this mixture, allowing it to soak for 30
seconds.

To cook the toast: Warm a sauté pan with the butter.
When the butter has melted, add the soaked brioche.
Brown both sides, about 1 minute on each, until slightly
crisp and golden in color.

To serve: Dust the slices with the confectioners' sugar.
Serve this dessert with your choice of either a pint of
Chocolate Espresso Ice or 1/2 cup Orange Balsamic Syrup.

ACCOMPANIMENT:
CHOCOLATE EXPRESSO ICE (PAGE 265)
OR ORANGE BALSAMIC SYRUP (PAGE 168)

Remember where you heard this: grapefruit is too fabulous to be limited to breakfast. Its tart-sweet taste makes for a terrific soufflé that's light, refreshing, and easy to prepare. Romanced, grapefruit can be an evening food.

To prepare the grapefruit: Peel the skin and remove the pith. Cut 18 segments carefully to use as garnish and squeeze the juice from the remaining fruit. Reserve the juice.

To make the egg white mixture: In a small pot combine the sugar with just enough water to moisten it—approximately 1 cup. Bring this to a boil over medium heat and cook to a temperature of 250° on a sugar thermometer (see Note), then remove from the heat. Meanwhile, as the syrup is cooking, whip the egg whites in an electric mixer. The sugar should come to the proper temperature as the egg whites reach soft peaks. At this point, add the hot sugar syrup to the egg whites beating on high speed, carefully, so you don't splash the hot syrup, until it's fully incorporated. Slow the machine down and continue mixing until the whites are cooled. You've now created what's called Italian meringue.

To finish the frozen soufflé: In a saucepan warm the grapefruit juice and vodka together. Dissolve the gelatin in the warm liquid. Fold the gelatin mixture into the whipped cream. Then fold this mixture into the soft Italian meringue. Pour into 6 individual soufflé molds with 2-inch paper collars wrapped around the lip. Freeze for at least 3 hours in your home freezer.

To make the grapefruit garnish: In a saucepot poach the grapefruit segments in the port for 5 minutes, just enough to absorb the color and flavor of the wine. Remove the segments and cool. Serve 3 segments on top of each soufflé for garnish.

NOTE: The hard-ball stage (250° on a sugar thermometer) can also be tested by dipping your finger and thumb into a bowl of ice water. Quickly dip them in the boiling syrup and back to the ice water. The syrup you picked up should form a firm, pliable ball.

FROZEN GRAPEFRUIT SOUFFLÉ

SERVES 6

2   large Florida grapefruits

⅔   cup granulated sugar

4   large egg whites

1   tablespoon vodka

½   packet unflavored gelatin

1   cup heavy cream, whipped to soft peaks

½   cup port wine

KEY LIME–CHOCOLATE NAPOLEONS

SERVES 6

1   pint heavy cream
1   pint half and half
¼   vanilla bean, split
2   cups granulated sugar
9   large egg yolks
4   small key limes, zested and juiced
14 ounces bittersweet chocolate

A sophisticated dance of a dessert that fuses the bright, tart taste of Florida key limes with the deep, rich flavor of bittersweet chocolate. The effect is spectacular but costs a little time and patience. Start the dessert the day before you plan to serve it so that the ice cream can freeze overnight.

To prepare the frozen key lime: In a large saucepan heat the heavy cream and half and half with the vanilla bean. In a bowl whip 1½ cups of sugar and the egg yolks together to the soft-ribbon stage. Warm the egg mixture with some of the warm cream to avoid getting scrambled eggs, then add the eggs to the rest of the cream. Cook the mixture approximately 6 minutes, until it coats the back of a spoon. Remove from the heat, strain, then chill. Next cook the lime juice, zest, and remaining sugar in a saucepan over medium heat for 3 minutes and remove it from the heat. Mix the lime zest syrup into the cream mixture and freeze in an ice cream machine according to the manufacturer's directions. Remove from the machine and freeze in a rectangular mold approximately 3-by-5-by-8 inches.

To prepare the chocolate layers: Melt the chocolate over hot water in a double boiler. When it is smooth, pour it onto a sheet of parchment paper either laid in a sheet pan or on a marble top. After a few minutes the chocolate will solidify again. When it's completely dry, use a sharp knife point to cut chocolate rectangles measuring approximately 3 by 5 inches. Peel the paper back when ready to layer the napoleon.

To assemble and serve: Remove the rectangle of ice cream from the freezer. Using a hot knife, cut 1-inch-thick cuts from the brick. Assemble 2 ice cream layers and 3 chocolate layers stacked up. Freeze until ready to serve.

MANGO PARFAIT

SERVES 6

3   large ripe mangos, peeled and pitted

3   teaspoons lime juice

6   large egg yolks

⅔   cup confectioners' sugar

1½   cups heavy cream, whipped

To prepare the mango: Reserve half a mango for garnish. Puree the remaining mango flesh in a food processor. Strain the puree through a sieve. Add the lime juice and reserve.

To prepare the parfait: In a stainless-steel bowl beat the egg yolks with the confectioners' sugar over a warm water bath until the mixture starts to thicken. Remove from the heat. Fold in the mango puree, then fold in the whipped cream. Pour into 6 tall parfait glasses and freeze for 2 hours. Garnish each serving with a fresh mango slice.

To serve with flair, garnish with whipped cream and candied lemon zest.

In a saucepan combine the sugar and water. Cook this for 10 minutes at a low simmer. Add the hot espresso with the cocoa powder. Stir until the cocoa powder is dissolved, then cool. Add the Kahlúa. Stir until well mixed. Place in an ice cream machine and freeze according to the manufacturer's directions.

CHOCOLATE ESPRESSO ICE

MAKES 1 QUART

1½ cups granulated sugar

1½ cups water

1½ cups hot brewed espresso

½ cup unsweetened cocoa powder

¼ cup Kahlúa liqueur

ICED CAPPUCCINO FLOAT

SERVES 4

¼   cup granulated sugar

2   cups hot brewed espresso

24   large ice cubes

1   cup half and half

½   cup heavy cream, lightly whipped

4   scoops coffee ice cream

2   tablespoons unsweetened cocoa powder

To begin: In a large bowl or container stir the sugar into the espresso. Let cool a few minutes. Fill four tall 16-ounce glass tumblers with ice cubes.

To make the cappuccino: Pour the espresso over the ice cubes, then slowly pour the half and half on top so that it forms a creamy layer above the dark layer of espresso. Top each with 3 tablespoons of lightly whipped cream. Finish with a scoop of coffee ice cream and dust with cocoa powder.

To prepare the café: Melt the chocolate in the hot coffee. Place the egg yolks and sugar in a stainless-steel bowl set on top of a double boiler and beat with a whisk until the mixture is foamy. Then add the chocolate café mixture. Continue to beat over low heat until the custard mixture begins to thicken in about 5 to 6 minutes. Add the rum, remove from heat, and set aside. Beat the egg whites until stiff, then fold them into the café mixture. Pour into tall parfait glasses or extra-large coffee mugs. Chill for 1 hour in the refrigerator.

To prepare the leche: In a small saucepan warm the cream, half and half, vanilla extract, and coffee beans. In a bowl whip the sugar and egg yolks together. Ladle some of the warm cream mixture into the yolks to warm them. Then stir the yolks into the warm cream. Cook over medium heat, stirring constantly, for 3 to 4 minutes, until the mixture is thick enough to coat the back of a spoon. Do not boil! Finally, add the cocoa and spiced rum. Remove the sauce from the heat and strain through a fine sieve. Allow the sauce to cool completely and thicken in an ice water bath.

To finish the parfait: Pour the leche cream on top of the café layer and chill again for 30 minutes in the freezer.

CAFÉ CON LECHE PARFAIT

SERVES 8

FOR THE CAFÉ:

½	cup hot strong black coffee
1¼	cups chopped bittersweet chocolate
8	large eggs, separated
1	cup confectioners' sugar
1	tablespoon dark rum

FOR THE LECHE SAUCE:

½	cup heavy cream
½	cup half and half
1	teaspoon vanilla extract
2	tablespoons whole coffee beans
4	tablespoons granulated sugar
3	large egg yolks
1	tablespoon unsweetened cocoa powder
3	tablespoons Myers's spiced dark rum

FROZEN JAMAICAN BLUE MOUNTAIN SABAYON

SERVES 6

¾ cup granulated sugar

4 large egg yolks

1 tablespoon unflavored gelatin

3 tablespoons strong brewed Jamaica Blue Mountain coffee

1 cup heavy cream, whipped

1 tablespoon whole Jamaica Blue Mountain beans, ground

I think of sabayon as a dessert over which to fall in love with someone, it's so rich, elegant, simple, perfect.

To prepare the syrup: In a small pot combine the sugar with just enough water—approximately 1 cup—to moisten it. Bring this to a boil over medium heat and reduce the liquid by half, approximately 10 minutes.

To prepare the sabayon: In an electric mixer beat the egg yolks until they're pale yellow. Lower the speed and slowly add the hot syrup until completely incorporated. Remove from the mixer. Dissolve the gelatin in the strong brewed coffee and fold this into the yolks. Finally fold in the whipped cream.

To finish the sabayon: Pour the mixture into individual champagne flutes or martini glasses and set to freeze for at least 3 hours. To serve, dust the top of each with freshly ground Jamaica Blue Mountain coffee.

To prepare the fruits: Zest, then juice the oranges. In a saucepan poach the zest for 2 minutes in the Riesling. Remove the zest with a slotted spoon, cool, and reserve for garnish. Reserve the wine for the sorbet. Quarter the kumquats and poach them in a simple syrup of sugar and water for 10 minutes. Strain and cool the syrup. Reserve the kumquats for garnish.

To make the sorbet: Combine the blood orange juice, reserved Riesling, kumquat simple syrup, and orange juice in a sorbet or ice cream machine and freeze according to the manufacturer's directions, 20 to 25 minutes.

To serve: Freeze the sorbet for at least 1 hour in your freezer. Garnish each serving with the blood orange zest and poached kumquat quarters.

BLOOD ORANGE AND KUMQUAT SORBET

MAKES 1½ QUARTS

1	pound blood oranges
½	cup late harvest Riesling wine
10	large kumquats
1	cup granulated sugar
1	cup water
1½	cups orange juice

GRAPEFRUIT SORBET

SERVES 6

Juice of 12 grapefruits

1   cup granulated sugar

1   cup water

1   sprig mint, minced

3   tablespoons vodka

2   pints raspberries

2   tablespoons lime zest

1   starfruit, sliced

A guilt-free indulgence, for those times when your heart lusts after a dessert but your conscience insists it's out of the question.

To prepare the grapefruit sorbet: In a saucepan cook the grapefruit juice, sugar, and water over medium heat until the sugar is dissolved. Add the mint and let cool. Strain and reserve 4 tablespoons of the cooled grapefruit syrup. Add the vodka to the remaining syrup mixture and freeze in an ice cream machine according to the manufacturer's directions.

To prepare the raspberry sauce: In a food processor puree the raspberries and pass them through a china cap–fine mesh sieve.

To prepare the garnish: In a saucepan candy the lime zest in the reserved 4 tablespoons of grapefruit syrup over low heat until no syrup remains.

To assemble and serve: Cover the bottom of 6 chilled plates with the raspberry sauce. Top with a scoop of the sorbet, and garnish with starfruit and the candied lime zest.

PASSOVER

Red Snapper Gefilte Fish

Matzo Club Sandwiches with Grilled Portobello
Mushrooms and Olive Charoseth

Matzo Pasta

Matzo Pasta with Shiitakes, Asparagus,
and Tomato Broth

Red Bean and Dried Fruit Cholent

Sweet Potato and Mango Tzimmes

Tamarind and Ginger–Roasted Game Hen

Rhubarb Crisp

Chocolate Walnut Torte with Macaroon Crust

CHANUKAH

Potato and Red Pepper Pancakes
with Goat Cheese and Applejack

Corn and Black Bean Cakes *served with*
Smoked Salmon Salsa

FOURTH OF JULY

Roast Rack of Shrimp *served with*
Watermelon, Tomato, and Pecan Salsa

THANKSGIVING

Cumin, Garlic, and Lime–Rubbed Turkey *served with*
Old-Fashioned Stuffing and Holiday Cranberry
"Ketchup"

CHAPTER 10

HOLIDAY DISHES

CHRISTMAS
Prime Rib of Veal *served with* Cayenne Spaetzle and
Vegetable Galette

NEW YEAR'S EVE
Mamaliga and Caviar with Quail Eggs
"Sunny Side Up"

olidays bring back memories—they are *supposed* to bring back memories. Holidays mark history, allowing us to take a break, remember where we've been, and think about where we are going. The foods we eat on these occasions are symbolic of historical events and places. In both mind and soul, they punctuate the importance of a departure from daily life.

My strongest memories are of celebrating Passover and Chanukah. During Chanukah, my family lit the candles together, then ate potato latkes fried in oil to commemorate the importance of the small amount of holy oil that burned for eight days. The Passover seder plate actually tells the story of the miracle of Passover, of the Jews being freed from slavery in Egypt. My entire extended family got together for Passover seders. My grandfather conducted the service in Hebrew in those early days; then, when we children could read, we moved on to English. We ate in abundance and one of the things we ate was—and still is—charoseth. At Rosh Hashana, the New Year, we eat honey and apples, which are autumn foods, harvest foods.

The holidays are in tune with the seasons and help bring into focus the different produce, meats, and fish that are available in the marketplace: what we eat at Rosh Hashana, at Thanksgiving, at Christmas, at Easter, are dishes composed of the ingredients traditionally available at those times of year. You feel the Christmas season, with its warmth and promise and heartiness, more intensely when you cook with ingredients available in winter. The holidays of Passover and Easter, coming as they do during spring, bring a different feeling, which is fresh, light, and inspired by the green buds of early crops.

Whether it is Fourth of July, Chanukah, Christmas, Passover, or Easter, holidays are about continuance. People want to have a great time with their families, and it's certainly food—the lamb, the turkey, the ham, the roast beef, the charoseth, the gefilte fish, and the hot dogs—that helps make these family events wonderful.

We nurture each other through the holidays. Through our great-grandparents and grandparents and parents, we pass down to our children the traditions that give us pause for celebration, and we do it with ritual prayers, festivities, and food that is lovingly and joyously prepared.

Red snapper gives a New World twist to this traditional dish. For lovers of heat, this is an excellent vehicle for fresh horseradish.

To make the decorative carrot daisies: Use one carrot to make carrot daisies. With a channel knife cut 5 long channel cuts down the length of the carrot. Slice crosscut in ¼-inch coins. Reserve the ends and uneven cuts to be ground with the snapper.

To prepare the snapper: Have the fishmonger clean, skin, and remove all the bones from the snapper. With a large grinder blade, grind together the snapper, onion, 1 carrot, the parsley, cilantro, Scotch bonnet, and ginger. Place the mixture in a large stainless-steel bowl and add the eggs, matzo meal, and ice water. Mix well. Season with kosher salt and sugar and refrigerate for 30 minutes.

To cook the snapper gefilte fish: In a heavy-sided stockpot bring the fish stock to a simmer. Shape the fish mixture into approximately 25 large, rounded ovals. Add the carrot daisies to the simmering stock and then carefully drop in the fish. Simmer slowly for about 15 minutes. Remove the pot from the heat and let the gefilte fish cool in the stock. Transfer the contents of the pot to a large glass bowl, and cover to refrigerate overnight.

To serve: Arrange the cold gefilte fish on a large platter. Combine in a bowl fresh grated horseradish and the vinegar. Garnish the fish with the horseradish, jellied fish stock, and the carved carrot daisies.

RED SNAPPER GEFILTE FISH

SERVES 12

2   *medium carrots, peeled*

5   *pounds red snapper, cleaned, skinned, and deboned*

1   *medium onion, diced*

3   *tablespoons freshly chopped flat-leaf parsley*

1   *tablespoon freshly chopped cilantro*

½   *teaspoon minced Scotch bonnet*

½   *teaspoon peeled and chopped fresh ginger*

3   *large eggs*

½   *cup matzo meal*

¾   *cup ice water*

4   *tablespoons kosher salt*

1   *teaspoon sugar*

2   *quarts Fish Stock (page 22)*

¼   *head horseradish*

½   *cup white vinegar*

MATZO CLUB SANDWICHES WITH GRILLED PORTOBELLO MUSHROOMS AND OLIVE CHAROSETH

SERVES 4

4 large Portobello mushrooms
1 tablespoon olive oil
1 teaspoon minced garlic
Pinch kosher salt
Pinch coarse ground black
    pepper
1 large avocado
1 large tomato
2 sheets matzo
¼ cup Olive Charoseth
    (recipe follows)

Sometimes even matzo addicts need a break from the traditional. While this isn't a sandwich suitable for brown-bagging, the Matzo Club with Grilled Portobello Mushrooms and Olive Charoseth should surprise and please your guests.

To prepare the vegetables: Remove the stems and clean the Portobello mushrooms, then season them with olive oil, garlic, salt, and pepper. Grill the mushrooms on a medium-hot grill or under the broiler for 3 or 4 minutes, until cooked through. Remove from the heat and let the mushrooms rest for several minutes, then slice them thin, on a bias. Slice the avocado and tomato approximately ¼ inch thick.

To assemble the club sandwich: Carefully crack each matzo into 6 equal squares; we'll use 3 squares for each club. Spread the Olive Charoseth on 2 of the 3 pieces of matzo to be used in each club. Start with a matzo square with charoseth, then layer the sliced mushroom, tomato, and avocado. Top with another matzo square with charoseth, followed by mushroom, tomato, and avocado. Finish with the remaining dry piece of matzo. Prepare each sandwich in this fashion.

Begin by reducing the white wine in a small saucepot until only 4 tablespoons remain. Combine the remaining ingredients in a food processor, add the wine reduction, and process to a smooth paste.

OLIVE CHAROSETH

SERVES 4

1   cup dry white wine

1   cup walnuts

1   medium green apple, peeled and seeded

1/2 cup pitted green olives

3   tablespoons fresh flat-leaf parsley, stems removed

1/8 teaspoon ground cinnamon

1/8 teaspoon cayenne pepper

MATZO PASTA

SERVES 6

2   cups matzo meal

7   large eggs

2   tablespoons sweet butter,
    melted

Pinch kosher salt

Pinch coarse ground black
pepper

2   tablespoons extra-virgin
    olive oil

This is a new addition to an old tradition. I now serve this each year at our Passover seder.

To prepare the matzo meal: Pour the matzo meal into a food processor. Pulse on and off several times, then continue running the processor for 3 or 4 minutes, pulverizing the meal until it is almost as fine as flour.

To make the pasta: Pour the matzo meal into a large stainless-steel bowl. Add the eggs in the center and begin to mix. After 1 minute, add the butter, salt, and pepper. Mix until the dough binds together. Remove from the bowl and knead for 10 minutes. It should be smooth and shiny when done. Cover with a slightly moist towel and let rest for 20 minutes.

To process the pasta: Cut the dough ball into 3 pieces. With a rolling pin, roll out each piece thin enough to go into a hand-cranked pasta machine. Crank the pasta sheet through on the widest opening first (usually #1), then crank it through on the #2 adjustment. Fold this sheet in thirds and begin rolling on #1 again. Follow #1 with #2 and #3. "Knead" the dough once more by folding it in thirds and starting at #1 again. Roll through #2, #3, and #4. I stop on #4 and cut the dough into "linguine" with the crank machine cutting blade.

To cook the pasta: Boil salted water in a very large pot. The key here is not to let the temperature of the water drop too much while cooking the pasta. Put the pasta in the boiling water, then let the water come back to a boil and lower it to a simmer. It should take only 2 or 3 minutes to finish. Serve immediately, tossed in extra-virgin olive oil.

To prepare the vegetables and broth: Warm the olive oil in a medium saucepot. Add the shiitakes and sauté for a minute. Add the asparagus and continue to sauté for another minute. Add the garlic, tomato, and chicken broth and simmer for 3 or 4 minutes.

To finish the pasta: If you're using pasta that has just finished cooking, add it directly into the broth. If you have cooked the pasta in advance, dip it first into boiling salted water. Avoid adding cold pasta to the hot broth—the broth will become very cloudy. Season the pasta with chopped parsley, salt, and pepper. Serve in a large soup bowl.

MATZO PASTA WITH SHIITAKES, ASPARAGUS, AND TOMATO BROTH

SERVES 6

1   teaspoon olive oil

1   cup cleaned and sliced shiitake mushrooms

1   cup peeled, 2-inch asparagus pieces

1   teaspoon chopped garlic

3   tablespoons peeled, seeded, diced tomato

2   cups chicken broth

1/2   pound Matzo Pasta, cooked (page 278)

2   tablespoons chopped fresh flat-leaf parsley

1   tablespoon kosher salt

1   teaspoon coarse ground black pepper

RED BEAN AND DRIED FRUIT CHOLENT

SERVES 6

3   cups red beans

1   cup diced sweet onions

3   tablespoons vegetable oil

½   cup diced carrots

1   tablespoon minced fresh thyme

2   bay leaves

18 large dried figs, quartered

½   cup sun-dried cherries

1   tablespoon kosher salt

1   teaspoon coarse ground black pepper

On Friday nights in Europe, Jews brought their food in cooking vessels to the baker's to be put in the oven overnight, so that they could avoid breaking the prohibition against cooking on the Sabbath and still have hot food the following evening. The dish that resulted from this slow-cooking was called a "cholent." Most often it consisted of beans prepared in a style similar to a cassoulet. Here I've added the richness of dried fruits simmered in chicken stock and thyme to the beans.

To prepare the red beans: Wash the beans under cold running water, then let them soak for 1 hour in enough water to cover them completely. Drain.

To cook the cholent: In a skillet sweat the onions in the vegetable oil until they begin to caramelize. Add to this the drained beans, carrots, thyme, and bay leaves. Add enough water to cover the beans by 3 full inches. Bring to a boil on low heat, then simmer on low heat for 1 hour. At this time add the figs and cherries. Continue to simmer slowly for 45 minutes. Adjust the seasoning with salt and pepper.

Tzimmes is a Yiddish word that means "making a fuss" or "creating excitement about an event." Cooking a tzimmes, on the other hand, requires easygoing, slow cooking over low heat. Use a heavy-sided pot with a cover for this preparation.

In a heavy-sided pot combine all the ingredients and enough cold water to cover them by 2 inches. Cover pot and bring to a very slow simmer. Cook for 1 hour, stirring occasionally. Adjust the seasoning with salt and pepper. Let the tzimmes sit, covered, until ready to serve.

SWEET POTATO AND MANGO TZIMMES

SERVES 6

3 cups peeled 2-inch pieces sweet potato

3 cups peeled 2-inch pieces carrots

1/2 cup diced onion

1/2 cup diced dried mango

2 bay leaves

1/4 teaspoon grated nutmeg

1 tablespoon kosher salt, plus extra to taste

1/2 tablespoon coarse ground black pepper, plus extra to taste

TAMARIND AND GINGER-ROASTED GAME HEN

SERVES 4

5   tablespoons tamarind pulp

4   tablespoons chopped fresh ginger

1   teaspoon ground allspice

½   teaspoon ground cinnamon

1   tablespoon chopped garlic

1   tablespoon kosher salt

¼   cup olive oil

4   medium game hens

1   cup Chicken Stock (page 21)

To marinate the game hens: In a bowl combine all the spices, the garlic, and salt, moisten them with the olive oil. Rub the hens with the mixture and let them rest, covered, in the refrigerator for 1 hour.

To cook the hens: Preheat the oven to 350°. Place the birds breast side up in a rack in a roasting pan. Roast for approximately 20 minutes. Baste the game hens often with a little chicken stock and the pan juices. Turn the birds for 10 more minutes. Finish roasting breast side up for 10 minutes to crisp the top. If you wish, the pan juices can be skimmed, strained, then reduced with the remaining chicken stock in a small saucepot and used for sauce.

ACCOMPANIMENT:
RED BEAN AND DRIED FRUIT CHOLENT (PAGE 280)

Passover is a celebration of age-old traditions, but it is also a welcoming of spring and its full bounty.

To prepare the rhubarb: Peel the rhubarb with a vegetable peeler. Cut the stems into medium dice. Melt 2 tablespoons of the butter on low heat in a large sauté pan and add the rhubarb. After a minute add the sugar and red wine. Cook for only about 3 minutes overall.

To bake the crisp: Preheat the oven to 350°. Butter a baking dish with the remaining butter. Pour the sautéed rhubarb into the baking dish; top with the matzo, raisins, and honey. Bake in the oven for 20 minutes, until the crisp is golden brown. You can serve the crisp directly from the oven or at room temperature.

RHUBARB CRISP

SERVES 6

2	*pounds rhubarb*
4	*tablespoons sweet butter*
½	*cup sugar*
3	*tablespoons sweet red wine*
3	*matzo sheets, broken up*
3	*tablespoons raisins*
3	*tablespoons honey*

CHOCOLATE WALNUT TORTE WITH MACAROON CRUST

SERVES 8

2   cups almond paste

1   cup granulated sugar

10 large egg whites, plus 6 large eggs

1   pound bittersweet chocolate, chopped

½   pound sweet butter

1   cup chopped walnuts

To prepare the crust: Butter a springform torte pan. Combine the almond paste, sugar, and egg whites in a stainless-steel bowl. Using a wooden spoon, combine the ingredients well. Press the crust into the prepared torte pan, spreading it evenly around the bottom and up the sides.

To make the chocolate-walnut filling: Melt the chopped chocolate in a double boiler. Remove from the heat and combine with the butter and whole eggs. Fold in the walnuts.

To finish and bake: Preheat the oven to 350°. Pour the filling into the torte crust. Bake in the lower third of the oven for 35 minutes, until the torte edges are golden brown. Remove from the oven and allow to cool for 20 minutes. Remove the spring mold and cool for another 30 minutes.

This is equally wonderful as a brunch dish or as an accompaniment to roast chicken.

To prepare the red pepper: Coat the red pepper with olive oil and roast it in the oven at 325° until well cooked. Set it aside in a bowl, covered with a towel, for 15 minutes. Then peel, skin, and seed the pepper. Dice evenly in ½-by-½-inch pieces.

To prepare the batter: In a bowl grate the potatoes and onion on an "old-fashioned" hand grater. Mix in the bell pepper, egg, and matzo meal. Season with salt and pepper.

To cook the pancakes: Preheat the oven to 325°. Heat the peanut oil in a sauté pan. Spoon silver-dollar-size dollops of batter into the hot oil. Brown on one side 3 minutes, then turn and brown the other side about 2 minutes. Cook until crisp, then remove from the pan, and drain on paper towels. Place the drained pancakes in an ovenproof baking dish. Cut the goat cheese into ½-inch medallions and place on top of the pancakes. Bake for 5 minutes.

To prepare the apples: In a skillet sauté the apples quickly in the butter and flambé with the applejack for 1 minute. Remove from the heat.

To assemble and serve: Overlap 2 pancakes. Spoon the apples around the pancakes and serve.

POTATO AND RED PEPPER PANCAKES WITH GOAT CHEESE AND APPLEJACK

SERVES 6

1   large red bell pepper

1   tablespoon olive oil

5   medium red Bliss potatoes

½   medium Spanish onion

1   large egg

2   tablespoons matzo meal

Kosher salt and fresh ground black pepper

½   cup peanut oil

6   ounces goat cheese, such as Montrachet

2   medium Granny Smith apples, peeled, cored, and diced fine

1   tablespoon sweet butter

1   ounce applejack brandy

CORN AND BLACK BEAN CAKES

SERVES 6

1   cup all-purpose flour

2   large eggs

2   tablespoons sweet butter, melted

1   teaspoon baking powder

1/2   cup milk

1/2   cup freshly cooked corn kernels

1/2   cup cooked black beans

1   teaspoon sea salt

1   teaspoon coarse ground black pepper

SMOKED SALMON SALSA

SERVES 6 (1 CUP)

1/2   pound smoked salmon, diced fine

1/4   cup finely diced red onion

3   tablespoons chopped fresh cilantro

3   tablespoons chopped fresh flat-leaf parsley

1   tablespoons diced jalapeño

2   tablespoons extra-virgin olive oil

This is a treat I serve for Chanukah, although it's terrific for all holiday entertaining.

To prepare the batter: In a stainless-steel bowl combine the flour, eggs, melted butter, baking powder, and milk. Mix well. Add the corn and black beans. Season the batter with salt and pepper.

To cook the pancakes: Heat a non-stick Teflon-style griddle pan. When it's hot, spoon out enough mixture for a 3-inch cake—you can probably cook 4 at a time. When the batter bubbles slightly and is well browned, turn and brown the other side. It should take no more than 1 minute of cooking overall. Finish the rest of the batter in this manner.

To assemble and serve: Place 2 Corn and Black Bean Cakes in the center of each plate and top with a generous serving of Smoked Salmon Salsa.

ACCOMPANIMENT:
SMOKED SALMON SALSA

To prepare the salsa: In a bowl combine the smoked salmon, red onion, cilantro, parsley, and jalapeño. Toss together carefully, add the olive oil, toss again, and cover. Let this salsa set for 30 minutes before serving.

This is a unique and stunning dish. If you're all thumbs with a needle and thread, use metal skewers bent into semicircles to form the shrimp into racks.

To prepare the shrimp: Leaving the shrimp in their shells, split them down the back but do not open them up. Drizzle with the olive oil and pack with the coarse salt and black pepper combined. Let cure for 1 hour. Rinse the shrimp very well and pat dry.

To prepare the rack: The rack of shrimp is meant to approximate a crown roast of meat with its bones up in the air in a royal circle. To rack the shrimp, use a butcher's needle and thread. Sew 5 shrimp tails together about 1 inch from the end. About an inch further up the back sew another line. Now arrange this in a circle standing up, and tie the 2 ends together to create a standing rack of shrimp. Do the same with the remaining shrimp. You will have four circles of 5 shrimp.

To cook the rack: Preheat the oven to 375°. Roast the racks for 6 to 8 minutes, until the shells are golden-red. Remove from the oven and drizzle with the extra-virgin olive oil. Serve with the Watermelon, Tomato, and Pecan Salsa.

ACCOMPANIMENT:
WATERMELON, TOMATO, AND PECAN SALSA
SEE NEXT PAGE

ROAST RACK OF SHRIMP

SERVES 4

20 uncooked jumbo shrimp, in their shells

2 tablespoons olive oil

2 tablespoons kosher salt

1 tablespoon coarse ground black pepper

2 tablespoons extra-virgin olive oil

WATERMELON, TOMATO, AND PECAN SALSA

SERVES 4 (2 CUPS)

1½   cups seeded and diced watermelon

½   cup peeled, seeded, and diced tomato

1   medium Anaheim chile, seeded and diced

¼   cup toasted and chopped pecans

2   tablespoons snipped fresh chives

2   tablespoons chopped fresh cilantro

½   tablespoon kosher salt

3   tablespoons fresh lime juice

2   tablespoons extra-virgin olive oil

This is a great warm-weather picnic salsa, refreshing and summery. It's important that the 2 key ingredients—the watermelon and the pecans—be the best you can find. Pick a firm, ripe, preferably seedless watermelon—one that smells sweet, with a little give to the flesh. Yellow watermelon, when it's available, gives the salsa an interesting twist. The pecans should be bought fresh, so that the meat is sweet and nutty.

Mix all ingredients together in a large bowl, being careful not to break any of the diced fruits. Chill for 30 minutes.

I love turkey, and Thanksgiving in south Florida has inspired me to come up with a new and subversive way of roasting it. I start 2 days ahead with a rub. On the day before the holiday, I roast the bird and take it off the bone—which means that on Thanksgiving, I'm free to watch the parades, second-call the football games, and sit sanely down with my family and friends to enjoy the turkey and the stuffing.

Figure on about 3½ hours if you have to accomplish this all on Thanksgiving Day—and about 1 pound of turkey meat per person. That way you'll probably have enough left over for turkey sandwiches with Cranberry "Ketchup" the next day.

On Tuesday before Thanksgiving: Wash the bird well inside and out, then dry it. Cut the bird in half, separating the breast from the legs. The bird will actually cook more evenly in 2 pieces. In a bowl combine the seasonings, lime juice, and olive oil. Rub this mixture completely over the inside and outside of the bird. Cover and refrigerate overnight.

On Wednesday (the second day): Bring the bird to room temperature. Preheat the oven to 350°. Use a roasting pan that allows you plenty of room for the 2 bird halves. Put the chopped vegetables in the pan. Place the breast up, and set the leg half "feet up," on top of the vegetables. Pour the water in the bottom of the pan. Brush the turkey with any of the rub mixture that remains from the marinade.

To cook the turkey: If possible, arrange the rack so that the pan with the turkey is in the lower half of the oven. Roast for 1 hour, basting 2 or 3 times. Turn the pan to change the circulation in the oven. Baste the turkey and add more water if necessary. Continue roasting for another

CONTINUED ON NEXT PAGE

CUMIN, GARLIC, AND LIME-RUBBED TURKEY

SERVES 10

1	10-to-12-pound turkey
4	tablespoons ground cumin
2	tablespoons minced garlic
1	teaspoon chopped fresh sage
2	teaspoons ground allspice
1	teaspoon ground ginger
3	tablespoons kosher salt, plus extra, to taste
2	tablespoons coarse ground black pepper, plus extra to taste
½	cup lime juice
¼	cup olive oil
1	cup chopped celery
1	cup chopped carrots
1	cup chopped onions
1	quart water
2½	quarts chicken broth

45 minutes, basting twice more. Reduce the heat to 325° for the final 15 minutes.

To check for doneness: Using a metal skewer, pierce the breast near the wing joints. If the liquid runs clear, the turkey should be ready. If the liquid is rosy or pink, continue to roast for another 15 minutes. Check the leg in the same fashion. If either half is done, remove it and let the other half finish roasting. Remove from the oven and let the bird cool completely in the roasting pan.

To store the turkey: Wrap the turkey halves in plastic wrap and place them in the refrigerator. Skim the grease from the pan and discard it. Save the roasted vegetables and pan drippings for the sauce.

To prepare the turkey on Thanksgiving: Remove all of the meat from the breast and leg bones. Reserve the bones and scraps. Slice the meat and place it in an ovenproof serving platter. Cover until ready to heat later in the day. Heat the meat with a cup of chicken broth at 300° for approximately 20 minutes.

To prepare the sauce: In a large saucepot combine the roast vegetables, pan drippings, and the turkey bones and scraps. Add about 2 quarts of chicken broth and bring to a simmer on medium heat. Let this reduce slowly until there are only about 3 cups left. Strain through a fine sieve and keep warm until ready to serve. Adjust the seasoning with salt and pepper.

To serve: Thanksgiving is a family holiday, so I serve family style—the Old-fashioned Stuffing in a beautiful china serving platter and the Holiday Cranberry "Ketchup" in silver goosenecks.

ACCOMPANIMENTS: OLD-FASHIONED STUFFING AND HOLIDAY CRANBERRY "KETCHUP"

To prepare the stuffing: Preheat the oven to 350°. Warm the olive oil in a large, tall-sided pot. Add the onions and sauté until translucent. Add the celery and carrots. Cook for another minute and add the garlic. Cook until the carrots are soft, 4 to 5 minutes. Add the green apples, chestnuts and syrup, chicken broth, and turkey drippings, then season with the thyme, salt, pepper, and nutmeg. Cook for 5 more minutes, then add the bread croutons and finish with the butter. Stir until well incorporated.

To finish the stuffing: Pour the mixture into an oven-proof pan and bake for 15 minutes.

OLD-FASHIONED STUFFING

MAKES 5 CUPS

- 4 tablespoons olive oil
- 1 cup diced sweet onions
- 1 cup diced celery
- 1 cup diced carrot
- 2 tablespoons chopped garlic
- 1 cup diced green apple
- 1 18-ounce can chestnuts in syrup
- ³/₄ cup chicken broth
- ³/₄ cup turkey drippings
- 1 tablespoon chopped fresh thyme
- 1 tablespoon kosher salt
- 1 tablespoon coarse ground black pepper
- ¹/₂ teaspoon grated nutmeg
- 1¹/₂ cups bread croutons
- 3 tablespoons sweet butter

HOLIDAY CRANBERRY "KETCHUP"

MAKES 1 QUART

1   pound fresh cranberries
3   tablespoons cider vinegar
½   teaspoon chopped fresh ginger
1   teaspoon ground cinnamon
1   tablespoon kosher salt
1   cup sugar
½   cup dry white wine
1   teaspoon ground allspice
1   teaspoon cayenne pepper
1   whole clove

To prepare the cranberry mix: Wash and clean the cranberries. Put them in a food processor fitted with a steel blade. Add the remaining ingredients and pulse together.

To cook the cranberry mix: In a heavy-sided saucepan cook the mixture over a slow heat for 1 hour, until well reduced and thickened. Remove from the heat and strain through a fine sieve (see Note).

To serve: Refrigerate for 24 hours to allow the flavors to mature together. The cranberries will take on a whole new balance of flavor served chilled the next day, so be patient.

NOTE: For long-term storage, pour into small ball jars while still hot. See the manufacturer's directions.

I imagine this as the spectacular centerpiece of a big family holiday meal. Although the dish is actually fairly simple to prepare, it will be a tremendous hit. The veal comes out very tender and is easy to carve either in the kitchen or at the table.

To prepare the rack: The rack of veal is a large piece of meat that you can usually special-order from your favorite butcher. Ask the butcher to trim the rack "French style"—that is, to remove the shoulder blade and flap of meat over the rack as well as trimming down the bones. If the "French style" rack can be tied, it will sit better, but this is not imperative.

To roast the veal: Preheat the oven to 375°. In a small bowl combine the seasonings and olive oil. Cover the rack with this mixture. Put the veal on a roaster rack with the bones down and place in the center of the oven. Roast the meat for 30 minutes then turn the rack over and lower the heat to 350°. After another 20 minutes turn the rack back to its original position. The meat needs only about 15 more minutes to brown well. Remove the veal from the oven and let it rest for 10 minutes in a warm spot over the stove. This resting stage will prevent the juices from running out of the meat, which would result in a tougher, drier roast.

To serve: Place the veal on a large carving board. Slice the meat into 1/2-inch-thick pieces. Give the roasted bones to your favorites at the table. Serve with freshly made Cayenne Spaetzle and the Vegetable Galette.

ACCOMPANIMENTS: CAYENNE SPAETZLE AND
VEGETABLE GALETTE
SEE NEXT PAGE

PRIME RIB OF VEAL

SERVES 10

1	9-pound rack of veal
2	tablespoons minced fresh thyme
1	tablespoon minced fresh rosemary
1	tablespoon crushed garlic
1	tablespoon black peppercorns
1	tablespoon kosher salt
2	tablespoons olive oil

CAYENNE SPAETZLE

SERVES 10

3 cups all-purpose flour

12 eggs

1½ cups milk

2 teaspoons kosher salt

½ teaspoon cayenne pepper

2 tablespoons lemon zest

2 tablespoons olive oil

2 tablespoons snipped fresh chives

To prepare the spaetzle: In a bowl combine the flour and eggs, and mix in the milk, leaving the dough very pasty. Work it with a plastic spatula to develop the elasticity of the paste (like soft taffy). Season it with the salt, cayenne, and lemon zest.

To cook the spaetzle: Use plenty of boiling salted water. To cook the free-form spaetzle, place a colander over the pot of boiling water. Spoon some of the mixture into a colander. Using a plastic spatula, rub the mixture through the holes into the water. As the dough rises to the top, the spaetzle is cooked. Skim the spaetzle off and put it in a pan with the olive oil. Sauté for 1 minute, then add the chives. Serve immediately.

VEGETABLE GALETTE

SERVES 10

2 medium chayote

1 large zucchini

3 medium tomatoes

1 medium eggplant

3 medium onions

1 tablespoon minced fresh thyme

1½ teaspoons minced fresh oregano

1½ teaspoons ground cumin

1 teaspoon kosher salt

½ teaspoon coarse ground black pepper

3 tablespoons olive oil

2 tablespoons extra-virgin olive oil

This is a beautiful and simple accompaniment to the prime rib of veal.

To prepare the vegetables: Preheat the oven to 350°. Slice all the vegetables into about ⅓-inch pieces. In a small bowl combine all the seasonings. Using an earthenware baking dish, alternately layer the vegetables in a colorful pattern in the dish. Season the galette with the herbs and a drizzle of the olive oil.

To bake the galette: Bake the galette of vegetables for 25 minutes, until well caramelized, then remove from the oven. Finish with a drizzle of the extra-virgin olive oil and serve.

Mamaliga, grits, funche, polenta, cornmeal mush; comfort food—each by a different name but all the same. I grew up on mamaliga. Though this is not quite the way my grandmother nor mother would make it. But I know they would be sure not to miss my version.

To prepare the mamaliga: In a medium saucepot warm the chicken stock. Add the cornmeal and stir. Season with salt and pepper. Simmer for 20 to 25 minutes, stirring every few minutes with a wooden spoon. (If you use a precooked polenta or cornmeal, simmer for only about 5 minutes.) Remove from heat and fold in the sour cream, then the chives. Adjust the seasoning with salt and pepper. Spoon into individual serving glasses.

To prepare the "sunny side up" quail eggs: Use a nonstick egg pan. Crack each egg open, taking care not to break the yolk. Cook over medium heat for approximately 1 minute, firming the white yet leaving the yolk soft. Place the egg carefully in the center of the mamaliga.

To finish the caviar: Spoon a small ring of caviar around the edge of the quail egg in each glass.

MAMALIGA AND CAVIAR WITH QUAIL EGGS "SUNNY SIDE UP"

SERVES 4

1½	cups Chicken Stock (page 21)
1	cup cornmeal (medium ground)
1	teaspoon kosher salt
½	teaspoon white pepper
¼	cup sour cream
1	tablespoon chopped fresh chives
4	quail eggs, at room temperature
1	ounce Ossetra caviar

CHAPTER II

PICNICS, OUTDOORS AND IN

Caribbean Antipasto

Grilled Red Snapper Burger *served with*
Mango Ketchup

Yellowfin Tuna Poke with Scotch Bonnet

Charred Blue Mountain Coffee Burgers

Herb-Crusted Tuna with Curried Mayonnaise
on Raisin Pumpernickel

Grilled Vegetable Club Sandwich
with Manchego Cheese

Conch and Garbanzo Bean Chili *served with*
Fried Green Tomatoes

Seven Onion Pie with Aged Goat Cheese

French-Fried Bahamian Lobster with Crisp Cilantro
and Plantinos Maduros

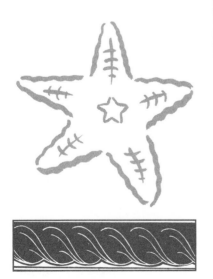

S ometimes the weather is so sublime that it compels us outside. The sun is shining, the palms (or the pines, or oaks, or elms, depending on where you live) are rustling in the breeze, and the ocean (or mountains, or desert, or forest, or garden) forms a backdrop against which you cook, and eat, and enjoy. Some of my best times were spent as a boy scout, cooking steaks out in the woods on wood-flame fires, so I guess you could say I'm a picnic fan from way back. I think most of us are. Outdoors, our senses are more acute, sharpened, so flavors become more pronounced, and food just tastes better. You're not confined, cocooned in a house or office or automobile. Your nose is smelling more natural things, you're listening to birds singing and the crackling of the fire.

Picnic foods should be relatively simple to prepare— no one wants to be a slave to the grill when everyone else is playing volleyball or swimming—and also simple, and joyous, to eat. Since picnics are usually held in casual surroundings, at the beach or park or in one's backyard, I like to serve finger foods, or foods that are as approachable as finger foods.

Sandwiches, of course, are great, the all-American picnic food. I particularly love fish sandwiches—as long as the fish is fresh—using fresh, seasonal fruits and vegetables to add flavor and color, and a good hearty interesting bread. Herb-Crusted Tuna with Curried Mayonnaise on Raisin Pumpernickel Bread and my Grilled Vegetable Club Sandwich with Manchego Cheese are just a couple of the renegade picnic foods you'll find in this section. Most of us expect and want burgers at a picnic, but these don't have to be a home version of the fast food we've grown all too accustomed to eating. Since a picnic represents a change of pace, my perfect picnic demands a change-of-pace burger, such as my Grilled Red Snapper Burger with Mango Ketchup: it's hearty, satisfying, light, and exotic. That beef burger can be transformed when it's coated with ground Jamaica Blue Mountain coffee before it's grilled—only you risk having other picnickers plotting how to join your party, once the fantastic aroma is lifted into the wind.

Some of the finest picnics are spontaneous and held indoors. One of the best in my memory was prepared by Paul Bocuse when he was cooking at a charity event in Palm Beach for the American Red Cross. Michele Richard, the owner of Citrus Restaurant in Los Angeles, Sirio Maccioni from Le Cirque, Paul, Judi, and I were sitting at the pool on the day of the event after we'd finished the prep work. Paul was hungry, but not for hotel food, so he went into the hotel kitchen and prepared a meal for us: cold beef salad, sliced tomatoes with cold vinaigrette, an endive salad, steak frites, cheese, and French bread. So here we were, sitting in the private wine room at the Ritz Carlton in our bathing suits with Paul Bocuse, who has achieved the ultimate in culinary arts, enjoying this simple, marvelous meal with champagne. Paul Bocuse was not preparing haute cuisine but food that creates a good time.

A rainy day or bitter cold is no excuse to sink into the blues. Spread a tablecloth on the floor, or set a table with your best china, and serve some of these wonderfully direct foods that will, I promise, bring sunshine back into your life. Because, like holidays, picnics are a break from the ordinary—and who deserves this break more than you and the people you love?

Anyone who has ever visited Italy, or a fine Italian restaurant in the States, knows that variety—in flavor, texture, sheen, and glisten—is the heart of the antipasto table. My Caribbean antipasto should be the best and freshest combination of local seafood, fruits, and vegetables, either cooked, roasted, grilled, or marinated. Many of the recipes in this book, reduced in quantity, would be perfect here. The antipasto should be served at room temperature or cold, on a huge, colorful glass platter. My favorite components for a Caribbean antipasto to launch a backyard picnic are:

To prepare the jerked calamari: Heat a grill. Clean the calamari. Season the calamari with the jerk mixture (from the Jerk Foie Gras recipe). Grill the calamari over a high heat for about 1 minute, until done. Remove from the heat and let the calamari cool.

To prepare the tangerine barbecued shrimp: Clean the shrimp. Season the shrimp with some tangerine barbecue sauce and grill over high heat for about 3 minutes, until the shrimp firms and turns rosy pink. Remove from the heat and cool.

To serve: Arrange all the antipasto components with an eye for color and texture.

CARIBBEAN ANTIPASTO

SERVES 6

5 pieces calamari

Jerk seasoning (Jerk Foie Gras, page 54)

3 uncooked large shrimp

Tangerine Barbecue Sauce (page 207)

1/2 cup Yellowfin Tuna Poke with Scotch Bonnet (page 302)

1 large avocado, peeled and sliced

1 large mango, peeled and sliced

12 crisp Plantain Chips (page 31)

1/2 cup Green Papaya Slaw (page 203)

1/2 cup Hearts of Palm Ceviche (page 68)

GRILLED RED SNAPPER BURGER

SERVES 4

1 pound fresh red snapper fillets

3 large egg whites

1½ teaspoons kosher salt

¼ teaspoon cayenne pepper

1 tablespoon Thai fish sauce

2 tablespoons chopped scallions

1 teaspoon chopped fresh dill

¼ cup fresh bread crumbs

2 tablespoons olive oil

1 loaf French bread, quartered

1 cup spinach, cleaned and dried

A New World burger for those who have—and haven't—given up red meat.

To prepare the snapper burger: Chop the red snapper by hand or with a steel blade in a food processor. Place the chopped snapper into a large stainless-steel bowl. Add the egg whites, salt, cayenne, fish sauce, scallions, and dill. Mix together well. Add enough bread crumbs to bind all together. Form into 4 burgers ½ inch thick and chill for about 30 minutes in the refrigerator.

To grill the burgers: Heat a grill or broiler until very hot. Drizzle a little olive oil over the burgers just before grilling. Grill over high heat for about 1½ minutes on each side, being careful not to overcook the fish.

To assemble and serve: Serve the burgers immediately on the French bread with the spinach leaves and a tablespoon of Mango Ketchup on each.

ACCOMPANIMENT:
MANGO KETCHUP

This is one of my favorite condiments. I make it in large batches because it keeps so well refrigerated, even though it never stays too long. I use it on fish, seafood, chicken, and roasted vegetables.

To prepare the mangos: Peel and pit the mangos. Puree the pulp in a food processor fitted with a stainless-steel blade. Add the remaining ingredients and pulse together.

To make the ketchup: In a heavy-sided saucepan cook the mixture over a low heat for 1 hour, until well reduced and thickened. Remove from the heat and cool. Strain through a fine sieve. Let set refrigerated for 24 hours. Now it is ready for use.

MANGO KETCHUP

MAKES 2 QUARTS

5   medium mangos

3   tablespoons vinegar

1   tablespoon chopped fresh ginger

Dash ground cinnamon

1   teaspoon kosher salt

1/2   cup granulated sugar

1/2   cup white wine

1/2   teaspoon ground allspice

1/2   teaspoon cayenne pepper

1   whole clove

YELLOWFIN TUNA POKE WITH SCOTCH BONNET

SERVES 6

1   pound fresh, raw yellowfin
    tuna

3/4 cup finely cut scallions

3   tablespoons soy sauce

1/2 teaspoon minced Scotch
    bonnet

3   tablespoons sesame oil

2   tablespoons chopped fresh
    cilantro

1   tablespoon minced fresh
    ginger

1   large ripe mango

When I was visiting Hawaii I realized that many of the local fish and tropical fruits were almost identical to south Florida's. While Hawaii's cuisine is influenced by what's eaten in the Pacific Islands and Japan—known as the Pacific Rim—I think this recipe for poke (raw, marinated fish) works equally well whether Pacific or Caribbean inspired. As with all raw fish dishes, the tuna must be perfectly fresh for this recipe to be successful.

To prepare the tuna: Cut the tuna into small chunks approximately 1/2 inch by 1/2 inch. Place in a large glass bowl.

To prepare the poke: Season the tuna with 1/2 cup of the scallions, the soy sauce, Scotch bonnet, sesame oil, cilantro, and ginger. Cover and marinate for 1 hour.

To serve the poke: Clean and dice the mango the same size as the fish. Place the poke in the center of a large wooden bowl. Surround with the mango and garnish with the remaining scallions.

Little did I know, when a local magazine asked me to prepare a meal for a couple shopping at a local market using the ingredients in their shopping basket and their home, that I'd wind up with a couple who were moving the next day—and had practically emptied their cupboards and refrigerator. What I had to work with was the ground sirloin they'd just purchased and the Blue Mountain coffee beans they'd bought on a recent visit to Jamaica. Inspiration was born of necessity—but you'll love the aroma of the coffee, peppercorns, and garlic roasting together.

To prepare the coffee coating: Using a coffee mill, grind the coffee beans and whole peppercorns together roughly.

To prepare the burgers: Season the ground sirloin with half the garlic and the coarse salt. Form the beef into oblong-shaped hamburgers. Combine the remainder of the garlic with 2 tablespoons of the olive oil and rub this mixture into the burgers. Roll the burgers in the ground coffee beans and peppercorns.

To cook the burgers: Drizzle the remainder of the olive oil on the burgers and sear in a hot cast-iron pan or barbecue grill.

CHARRED BLUE MOUNTAIN COFFEE BURGERS

SERVES 6

2   scoops Jamaica Blue Mountain coffee beans

10   whole black peppercorns

2   pounds ground top sirloin

3   tablespoons chopped garlic

2   tablespoons coarse salt

4   tablespoons olive oil

HERB-CRUSTED TUNA WITH CURRIED MAYONNAISE ON RAISIN PUMPERNICKEL

SERVES 6

- 4 8-ounce tuna steaks, cut 1 inch thick
- 1 tablespoon chopped fresh chervil
- 1 tablespoon chopped fresh chives
- 1 tablespoon chopped fresh tarragon
- 1 teaspoon finely chopped garlic
- 1 cup olive oil
- 3 egg yolks
- 1 tablespoon Dijon mustard
- 1 tablespoon curry powder
- 1 teaspoon ground turmeric
- 2 tablespoons white vinegar

Kosher salt and fresh-ground black pepper

- 1 loaf raisin pumpernickel bread
- 1/2 head romaine lettuce, cleaned and julienned

This satisfying sandwich transforms my childhood delight—as a kid I loved raisin-pumpernickel bread—into an adult experience. The tuna must be served medium-rare. If you're afraid of overcooking it, place the fish in the freezer for 20 minutes before you sear it.

To marinate the tuna: Trim the tuna clean of any blood marks. In a bowl combine the chervil, chives, tarragon, and garlic. Moisten the mixture with 2 tablespoons of the olive oil. Place the tuna in a ceramic dish and cover with the chervil-garlic mixture. Marinate at room temperature for 30 minutes or cover and refrigerate overnight.

To make the curry mayonnaise: Using the steel blade of a food processor, pulse together the egg yolks, mustard, curry, and turmeric. Add the vinegar. Next add the remaining olive oil in a slow steady stream with the processor running. Season with salt and pepper to taste. Set aside until ready to serve, or refrigerate tightly covered for up to a week.

To cook the tuna: Heat a heavy-sided, preferably cast-iron, pan on the stovetop for 5 minutes, until almost gray hot. Sear the tuna for 45 seconds on the first side and 30 seconds more on the other. The tuna is served medium-rare—don't overcook the fish. Remove from the pan and let cool. Slice the tuna steaks across the grain on a bias.

To assemble and serve: Serve the tuna between 2 slices of raisin pumpernickel with the romaine lettuce and a smear of curried mayonnaise.

Manchego cheese is one of a variety of sheep's milk cheeses produced in Spain. Its flavor runs from very mild to very sharp, its texture from a soft Brie style to one that's aged to a dry crumbly firmness similar to Parmesan. Here I use a sharp, firm Manchego.

To prepare the vegetables: Slice each of the vegetables about ¼ inch thick. Drizzle them with the olive oil and season with the oregano, turmeric, pepper, and salt.

To grill the vegetables: Preheat the grill. Over hot coals grill each of the seasoned vegetables, cooking them for barely a minute on each side. Set aside.

To assemble the club sandwich: Slice the French bread lengthwise into three slices. Brush each slice with Manzanilla Olive Tapenade. Layer the mushrooms, onion, tomato, and poblano chilies on the bottom piece. Place the middle bread slice on top of this and layer with the red peppers, tomatillos, eggplant, and chayote. Finish with the Manchego cheese and top with the last slice of bread.

To finish: Return the sandwich to a slow grill and brown both sides. Cut into 2-inch pieces for finger food.

GRILLED VEGETABLE CLUB SANDWICH WITH MANCHEGO CHEESE

SERVES 6

2   medium chayotes

3   medium tomatillos

1   large Spanish onion

1   large tomato

2   large red bell peppers

3   large poblano chilies

2   large portobello mushrooms

1   large eggplant

5   tablespoons olive oil

1   tablespoon minced fresh oregano

1   teaspoon ground turmeric

1   teaspoon coarse ground black pepper

1   teaspoon kosher salt

1   large loaf French bread

½   cup Manzanilla Olive Tapenade (page 155)

¼   pound sharp Manchego cheese (sheep cheese), sliced thin

CONCH AND GARBANZO BEAN CHILI

SERVES 8

2   pounds conch, tenderized (see Glossary)

4   tablespoons olive oil

³/₄   cup dry white wine

1   medium onion, diced

2   tablespoons minced garlic

1   medium red bell pepper, diced

4   small tomatillos, diced

¹/₂   cup tomato paste

3   tablespoons chili powder

1   tablespoon ground cumin

¹/₂   medium Scotch bonnet, chopped

2   cups cooked garbanzo beans

1   medium lime

1   tablespoon kosher salt

1   teaspoon coarse ground black pepper

Next time you're in the mood for chili, try this easy-to-prepare New World version with conch and garbanzo beans. Served on a Sunday afternoon of football watching, it might even make everyone forget the score.

To prepare the conch: Clean and dice the conch. In a medium saucepot cook the conch with 2 tablespoons of the olive oil until the meat just turns white, 3 or 4 minutes. Add the white wine. Remove the conch from the heat.

To cook the chili: In another saucepot, heat the remaining olive oil, then add the onion and cook until translucent. Add the garlic, the conch, red pepper, and tomatillos. Mix well. Sauté for 2 minutes. Add the tomato paste, chili powder, cumin, and Scotch bonnet. Mix well. Add the garbanzo beans and continue to cook for 10 minutes. Season well with a squeeze of lime and salt and pepper.

To serve the chili: Place 2 pieces of Fried Green Tomatoes on the bottom of each bowl. Ladle the hot chili over the tomatoes, and serve with toasted French bread and good beer.

ACCOMPANIMENT:
FRIED GREEN TOMATOES

Tart green tomatoes pan-fried with a crust of cornmeal add great texture to many dishes.

To prepare the tomatoes: Cut the tomatoes into ³/₄-inch-thick slices. Season with salt and pepper. Dredge the tomato slices in the cornmeal.

To fry the tomatoes: Warm the peanut oil in a heavy-bottomed skillet; the pan should be about ½ inch deep with oil. When the oil is hot, pan-fry the tomato slices, browning them well on both sides. Drain the finished slices on paper towels.

FRIED GREEN TOMATOES

SERVES 8

3 large green tomatoes

1 tablespoon kosher salt

½ tablespoon fresh ground black pepper

1 cup cornmeal

1½ cups peanut oil, for frying

SEVEN ONION PIE WITH AGED GOAT CHEESE

SERVES 8

FOR THE ONION PIE FILLING:

1/4 cup sweet butter

2   medium leeks, diced

5   medium purple shallots, chopped

2   teaspoons minced garlic

3   medium red onions, julienned

3   medium sweet onions, julienned

1   teaspoon chopped fresh thyme

1   teaspoon kosher salt

1   teaspoon fresh ground black pepper

3   tablespoons late harvest Riesling wine

3   tablespoons snipped fresh scallions

3   tablespoons snipped fresh chives

1/2 cup grated dry aged goat cheese

This serves well either hot or at room temperature, so it's wonderful for a picnic or Sunday brunch. The late-harvest Riesling sweetens and enriches the onions and binds their flavor with the goat cheese. Although I prefer to make my own pie dough, you can use a ready-bought pie shell prebaked for half the time specified on the package.

P.S.: The seven onions are red onion, sweet onion, green onion (scallion), chive, leek, shallot, and garlic.

To prepare the seven onion pie filling: In a heavy sauté pan warm the butter, then sauté the leeks, shallots, and garlic. Add the red onions, sweet onions, and thyme. Slowly sauté, caramelizing the onions. Season with salt and pepper, then add the Riesling. Continue cooking slowly for 5 minutes. Add the scallions and chives. Cook for 1 minute more and remove from the heat.

To prepare the savory piecrust: Preheat the oven to 350°. Sift the flour onto the work area, then add the butter and rub together to form a crumbly mixture. Make a well in the center. Add the egg, pepper, salt, and water. Knead just enough so that the dough clings together. Quickly form the dough into a ball. Cover and let rest in the refrigerator for 1 hour. Flour the work surface. Roll out the dough larger than the pan. Roll the dough up onto the rolling pin and unroll it into the pan. Trim the edges. Bake for 12 to 15 minutes, just until the crust firms but before it starts to color.

To assemble, bake, and serve: Place the filling in the prebaked savory crust. Push the onion mixture tightly into place. Then top with the grated goat cheese. Bake the tart in the 350° oven for 15 minutes, until golden brown. Remove from the oven and let rest for 5 minutes. To serve, cut into pie-shaped wedges.

FOR THE SAVORY CRUST:

   2   *cups all-purpose flour*

   ½   *cup cold sweet butter, cut into small pieces*

   1   *large egg*

Pinch fresh ground black pepper

   ¼   *teaspoon sea salt*

4 to 6 tablespoons cold water

FRENCH-FRIED BAHAMIAN LOBSTER WITH CRISP CILANTRO AND PLANTINOS MADUROS

SERVES 6

6   large spiny lobster tails

1   teaspoon chopped fresh thyme

1   teaspoon chopped garlic

1   tablespoon Dijon mustard

2   tablespoons dry white wine

1/4 teaspoon cayenne pepper

1/2 teaspoon kosher salt

1/2 cup chestnut flour

1   bunch cilantro

2   quarts peanut oil, for deep frying

3   ripe black-skinned plantains

One of the great informal American feasts is fried seafood. This New World version uses chestnut flour, which has a nutty flavor and produces a light and nearly greaseless crust. The 3 pounds of shrimp or scallops can be substituted for the lobster in this recipe.

To prepare the lobster: Split the lobster tails and remove the meat from the shells. In a pan marinate the meat with the thyme, garlic, Dijon mustard, white wine, cayenne, and salt for 20 minutes. Dredge the tails in chestnut flour and deep-fry in 375° peanut oil until golden brown, 5 to 6 minutes. Drain onto paper towels or newspaper.

To prepare the garnish: Deep-fry the bunch of cilantro in 400° oil. It will crisp almost immediately. Drain well. Peel and cut the ripe plantains into 3-inch pieces. Deep-fry these for about 2 minutes, until soft and caramelized.

To serve: Place the crisp cilantro in the center of the plate with the plantains for garnish. Arrange the French-fried lobster around the cilantro.